THE SECOND DOCTOR SOURCEBOOK

LINE DEVELOPER: Gareth Ryder-Hanrahan

WRITING: Walt Ciechanowski

EDITING: Dominic McDowall

COVER: Paul Bourne

GRAPHIC DESIGN AND LAYOUT: Paul Bourne

CREATIVE DIRECTOR: Dominic McDowall

ART DIRECTOR: Jon Hodgson

SPECIAL THANKS: Georgie Britton and the BBC Team for all their help. Dedicated to Zoe.

"My Second Is An Instrument Of The Past"

The Second Doctor Sourcebook is published by Cubicle 7 Entertainment Ltd (UK reg. no.6036414).
Find out more about us and our games at www.cubicle7.co.uk

Printed in the USA

CONTENTS

INTRODUCTION

'I've been renewed have I? That's it, I've been renewed! It's part of the TARDIS. Without it I couldn't survive.'

Everything changed.

When Ben and Polly first met the Doctor, he was a crotchety old man in Edwardian clothes who owned a machine capable of travelling through time and space. While he claimed to be an alien, there was nothing to suggest that he was anything more than a wise old man. They had become used to travelling in time, but the Doctor had never removed them from Earth.

During his latest adventure the Doctor seemed a bit more tired than usual and, after foiling the Cybermen's plans, he made a hasty retreat to his TARDIS. Ben and Polly followed behind and walked in just as an exhausted Doctor collapsed to the floor. As the two companions watched incredulously, the old man began to transform into someone else as the Ship took them to their first alien world...

Welcome to **The Second Doctor Sourcebook**. Here you'll find a wealth of information on the Second Doctor and his adventures, to help you recreate this era or to add vintage spice to your current **Doctor Who: Adventures in Time and Space** campaign.

HOW TO USE THIS BOOK

This book is designed to be a primer on capturing the feel of the Second Doctor's era and incorporating it into your adventures. **Chapter One: The Second Doctor and Companions** provides information on the Doctor's second incarnation and his companions. **Chapter Two: Tools of the Trade** offers advice for creating characters for this era, as well as new traits and gadgets. **Chapter Three: Enemies** looks at the various opponents that the Doctor faced between his regeneration and his trial and **Chapter Four: Designing Second Doctor Adventures** offers advice on crafting your own Second Doctor adventures as well as alternative ways to use the material in this book. **Chapters Five** to **Eleven** describe the Second Doctor's adventures. Each adventure has the following sections:

- **Synopsis:** Where did the TARDIS materialise? Who did the Doctor meet? And what horrible fates awaited the travellers there? This section summarises the key events of the adventure as experienced by the Second Doctor and his companions.

- **Running this Adventure:** Next, we discuss how to run the adventure. We get into the nuts and bolts of plotting and gamemastering, how to adapt the adventure to different Doctors or different groups of player characters, and how to use bits and pieces of the adventure in your own games.

- **Characters, Monsters & Gadgets:** If there are important non-player characters, interesting monsters, or shiny new gadgets in the adventure, you'll find them here. Sometimes, we'll give you full statistics for a character. At other times, when their Attributes and Skills are obvious or irrelevant, we'll just list their key Traits.

- **Further Adventures:** So, what happens after the Doctor leaves? (Or what happened before he arrived?) These further adventure seeds give ideas on spinoffs, sequels and alternate histories that expand on the Doctor's initial adventures.

There are lots of ways to use these adventures. You can use our suggestions for Further Adventures, or build your own adventures using the material provided. In fact, if your players aren't familiar with these classic stories, then you can substitute your player characters for the Second Doctor and his companions and 'rerun' the adventures. Maybe your player characters will take other paths and make different decisions!

CHAPTER ONE:
THE SECOND DOCTOR AND COMPANIONS

"I am not a student of human nature. I am a professor of a far wider academy of which human nature is merely a part."

WHO IS THE DOCTOR?

The Doctor in his first incarnation was an irascible old man that often wandered into trouble out of sheer curiosity. It often fell to his companions to be the true heroes, urging the Doctor to take action rather than just slip away in the TARDIS and let history take its course. He understood the implications of temporal interference and avoided conflict whenever possible. It is telling that, in his last adventure, the First Doctor's plan was to do nothing and let events unfold naturally, as he already knew that the Cybermen would not succeed.

To Ben and Polly's horror, the exhausted Doctor collapsed in his TARDIS and underwent a startling transformation. In place of the stern, authoritarian, distinguished schoolmaster was a short, rumpled man with a mop of hair and fingers too thick to wear the First Doctor's ring. His ill-fitting clothes made him look more like a tramp than the Edwardian gentleman of his previous self.

While Polly was quicker to accept the new Doctor as the same man, the regenerated Time Lord did little to help. He referred to the First Doctor in the third person and had no recollection of some recent events.

While the Doctor certainly has difficult regenerations in his future, this one seems the worst. While this could be chalked up to being the first regeneration, another likely reason is the fact that his previous incarnation's body had worn out. It had been deteriorating for years (perhaps decades or even centuries) and so there was more for the regenerative process to handle. The 'renewed' Doctor helps his mental regenerative process along by reading his 500 year diary. By the end of his 14 hour regenerative cycle (and the defeat of the Daleks) the Doctor seems fully recovered.

Unlike his previous incarnation, the Second Doctor preferred a more active role in investigating and fighting evil. Even before his first regeneration was complete, he impersonated a murdered Earth Examiner on Vulcan to discover the truth behind the crime. The appearance of the Daleks only steeled his resolve. He carried this crusading spirit throughout his adventures, often refusing to slip away in the TARDIS even when convenient to do so. Indeed, at his own trial the Doctor defended his active efforts to do what was right as the proper thing to do.

In short, the Second Doctor is a hero.

PLAYING THE SECOND DOCTOR

The Second Doctor is best described as a paradox. He dresses like a sort of intergalactic tramp, yet is charming and witty. He panics and shows fear when trouble arrives, yet he bravely deals with it. He sometimes recklessly springs into action, yet always seems to understand what's going on and how to deal with it long before anyone else. His demeanour sometimes frustrates his Companions, yet they trust him implicitly. He is like a beloved and crazy uncle who sometimes gets them into trouble as the price for sharing adventures with him.

In contrast to his previous incarnation, the Second Doctor has a clownish, dishevelled appearance. His trousers are far too wide for his frame and his coat is short and rumpled. Even his tie is off-centre. In addition, the Second Doctor shows an affinity for hats and enjoys playing the recorder, often as a aid to concentration. As time goes on the Second Doctor loses his hat and recorder and his trousers fit better, but he still maintains an unkempt appearance.

Due to his appearance the Second Doctor is often underestimated, a fact that he uses to his fullest advantage. Even when discovered to be not whom he seems, the Second Doctor uses his charm to convince others to aid him, generally by folding his hands and looking up like a child caught with his hand in the cookie jar. It's possible that the Second Doctor uses this pose in tandem with his hypnotic powers as people ready to throttle him a moment before suddenly give him the benefit of the doubt.

The Second Doctor also shows a penchant for disguises, often adopting an accent to match. During his travels he has impersonated an Earth Examiner, a German aristocrat, a kitchen maid, a British soldier, a gypsy entertainer, a civil servant, and even a would-be world dictator (he is aided in this last disguise by having an uncanny resemblance to said dictator). The Second Doctor uses such disguises to further his investigations and to pull both his companions and himself out of danger.

The Second Doctor also acts as a father figure to his companions, so it is perhaps no surprise that all three companions that he invited to join him were teenagers (he 'inherited' Ben and Polly from his previous incarnation). He genuinely enjoys teaching them new things and is quite pleased when his companions take to their lessons well.

In spite of all this, however, the Second Doctor also has a dark side and can be quite ruthless in pursuit of his goals. He doesn't just stop the Ice Warrior invasion of Earth; he causes the entire fleet to plunge into the sun. He solves a logical problem on Telos in order to find the Cybermen and endangers an Earth expedition even though he suspects some of its members to be unscrupulous. He manipulates Jamie into running the gauntlet for the Daleks to further his plan to stop them. In many cases he seems quite pleased with himself and often leaves once the danger is over before he can be held accountable for the collateral damage.

His 'ruthless' actions can perhaps be explained by his almost precognitive ability to determine what needs to be done. Not only does he have centuries of experience with many races, but the Doctor can also recognise certain traits in an alien or even an entire race that warrants decisive action. When the Second Doctor chuckles after sending a battle fleet into the sun or throwing a ticking bomb into a departing spaceship he's not amused at what he's done, he's overjoyed that he's prevented something much worse from happening.

Like his previous incarnation, the Second Doctor has little control over his TARDIS and can't steer it. The Doctor vehemently denies this and often looks for some other reason why they've strayed off-course. This generally doesn't fool his companions, especially Jamie, who constantly needles the Doctor over his inability to properly pilot the TARDIS. In spite of his insistence that he can steer the TARDIS, the Second Doctor never risks using it during an adventure. In addition, the TARDIS is much more prone to malfunctions and breakdowns with the Second Doctor than with any other incarnation.

DOCTOR WHO?

One way to capture the feel of the Second Doctor's era is to ask the player of the Doctor not to refer to the Time Lords, Gallifrey, the High Council, two hearts, or anything else related to his home culture. It's probably inappropriate to have other renegade Time Lords cross paths with the Doctor prior to his adventure with the War Lord, but if you do such encounters should be handled with care.

You should also impress upon the player that the TARDIS is to be used to get the characters to their destination and to take them away from it after the adventure is over. The TARDIS is little used during adventures by the Doctor and should not become a crutch for the players. In order to cut down on the temptation, however, you may still want the TARDIS to arrive in a relatively inaccessible location.

THE SECOND DOCTOR

STORY POINTS **8**

ATTRIBUTES

4 AWARENESS OOOO
3 COORDINATION OOO
7 INGENUITY OOOOOOO
4 PRESENCE OOOO
6 RESOLVE OOOOOO
2 STRENGTH OO

SKILLS

1 ATHLETICS
5 CONVINCE
2 CRAFT
0 FIGHTING
4 KNOWLEDGE
0 MARKSMAN
1 MEDICINE
5 SCIENCE
5 SUBTERFUGE
1 SURVIVAL
4 TECHNOLOGY
2 TRANSPORT

BIODATA

PERSONAL GOAL
To Fight Evil

PERSONALITY
Excitable, clownish, and impulsive, the Doctor sometimes gets himself into trouble as much as he gets himself out of it. His outward behaviour belies a keen intellect, and the Doctor often works out what's going on long before he lets anyone else know about it. The Doctor cares deeply for his companions and is a tireless crusader against evil.

BACKGROUND
The Doctor is on the run from his own race and is never in control of where the TARDIS is going (in spite of numerous arguments to the contrary). He resents the Time Lords' policy of non-interference and takes a stand against evil whenever he encounters it. The Doctor treats his companions as his family as they explore the universe together.

DISTINCTIVE FEATURES
Clownish
Unimposing
Playing the recorder helps him think

TRAITS

Adversary (major) (The Doctor picks up a few adversaries during his travels, including the Cybermen, the Daleks, and the Great Intelligence), **Boffin, Brave, Charming, Code of Conduct** (The Doctor abhors violence, will not use a gun, and will always protect the innocent and the helpless. He still may resort to terminal means to eliminate a tenacious foe (such as sending an Ice Warrior fleet into the sun). Should the Doctor break his code then he may lose some or all of his story points), **Eccentric, Feel the Turn of the Universe, Hypnosis (minor), Impulsive, Indomitable, Insatiable Curiosity, Obsession, Psychic, Random Regenerator, Resourceful Pockets, Run for Your Life!, Technically Adept, Time Lord (Experienced), Time Traveller (All TLs), Vortex.**

STUFF

TARDIS Key
Sonic Screwdriver Mk 1 (see page 24)
Recorder
500 Year Diary (see page 23)
Handkerchief

Faulty TARDIS: While the Doctor is perfectly capable of flying a TARDIS at this point in his life the TARDIS is effectively un-steerable. He cannot pilot it with any degree of accuracy and thus cannot use the TARDIS during an adventure without it effectively taking him away from the adventure. As a result once the Doctor has involved himself in an adventure he won't return to the TARDIS until he has ended the threat.

Time Lord 10

THE DOCTOR'S COMPANIONS

Unlike his previous incarnation, the Second Doctor genuinely enjoys having people aboard the TARDIS for company. He adopts a mentoring attitude, helped by the fact that his new companions are either technologically primitive or young and inexperienced.

Still, he allows them to make their own decisions regarding whether to stay with him; the Second Doctor won't persuade them either way (although in Victoria's case he elects to remain a day in case she changed her mind).

BEN JACKSON

Ben was a sailor serving aboard the *HMS Teazer* before being caught up in the Doctor's adventures. He was slow to accept the new Doctor as being the same person he'd come to know, but came round to the idea by the end of their adventure with the Daleks. He stayed with the Doctor until, by coincidence, the TARDIS arrived at Gatwick airport on the same day that he and Polly had left in the TARDIS. They both took the opportunity to return to their native time, and the Doctor believes that the two of them will remain together. He also hints that Ben will become an Admiral.

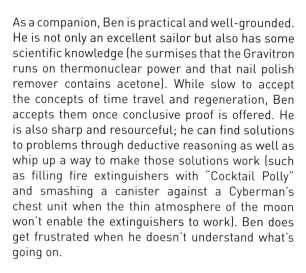

As a companion, Ben is practical and well-grounded. He is not only an excellent sailor but also has some scientific knowledge (he surmises that the Gravitron runs on thermonuclear power and that nail polish remover contains acetone). While slow to accept the concepts of time travel and regeneration, Ben accepts them once conclusive proof is offered. He is also sharp and resourceful; he can find solutions to problems through deductive reasoning as well as whip up a way to make those solutions work (such as filling fire extinguishers with "Cocktail Polly" and smashing a canister against a Cyberman's chest unit when the thin atmosphere of the moon won't enable the extinguishers to work). Ben does get frustrated when he doesn't understand what's going on.

As a man of action, however, Ben's impulsiveness sometimes lands him in trouble. He leaps out of hiding to Polly's defence during a rebel meeting on Vulcan and is quickly subdued by overwhelming odds.

His ripping up of the work contracts on a slave ship in 1746 nearly gets him drowned. Perhaps surprisingly, he is the only companion that succumbs to the Macra's hypnosis, although this can be explained as the Macra feeding his suspicions about people hiding things from him.

Ben has a good relationship with the Doctor, Polly and, later, Jamie. In particular he has a fondness for Polly, calling her "Duchess" due to the differences in their respective upbringings.

Ben is one of the Second Doctor's more experienced companions, which is reflected in his slightly higher attribute scores. Ben is considered to have nautical areas of expertise where appropriate. He's also depicted as something of a renaissance man, in various episodes he's a brawler, an engineer, an investigator, and even a scientist. In all cases he's a quick thinker and generally offers practical solutions to problems.

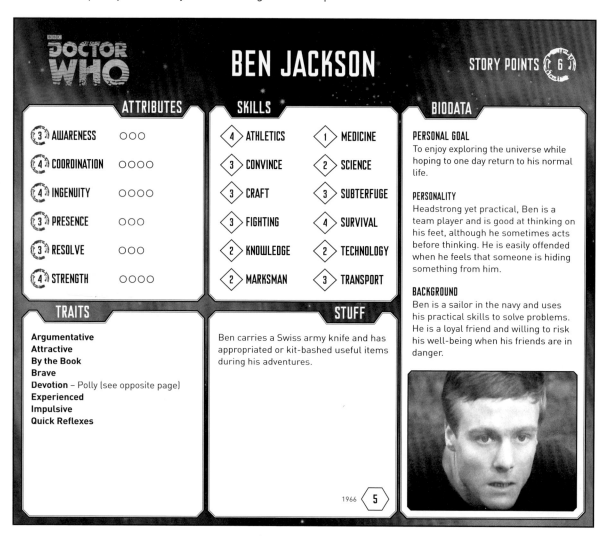

BBC DOCTOR WHO

BEN JACKSON

STORY POINTS 6

ATTRIBUTES

- 3 AWARENESS ○○○
- 4 COORDINATION ○○○○
- 4 INGENUITY ○○○○
- 3 PRESENCE ○○○
- 3 RESOLVE ○○○
- 4 STRENGTH ○○○○

SKILLS

- 4 ATHLETICS
- 3 CONVINCE
- 3 CRAFT
- 3 FIGHTING
- 2 KNOWLEDGE
- 2 MARKSMAN
- 1 MEDICINE
- 2 SCIENCE
- 3 SUBTERFUGE
- 4 SURVIVAL
- 2 TECHNOLOGY
- 3 TRANSPORT

BIODATA

PERSONAL GOAL
To enjoy exploring the universe while hoping to one day return to his normal life.

PERSONALITY
Headstrong yet practical, Ben is a team player and is good at thinking on his feet, although he sometimes acts before thinking. He is easily offended when he feels that someone is hiding something from him.

BACKGROUND
Ben is a sailor in the navy and uses his practical skills to solve problems. He is a loyal friend and willing to risk his well-being when his friends are in danger.

TRAITS

Argumentative
Attractive
By the Book
Brave
Devotion – Polly (see opposite page)
Experienced
Impulsive
Quick Reflexes

STUFF

Ben carries a Swiss army knife and has appropriated or kit-bashed useful items during his adventures.

1966 5

POLLY WRIGHT

Polly began her travels through time and space with the First Doctor (*see The First Doctor Sourcebook*). Unlike Ben, she immediately concluded that the Second Doctor and the First must be the same man, in spite of the new Doctor referring to the old in the third person. Her faith was rewarded as the new Doctor proved himself against his hated enemies, the Daleks.

Polly took a liking to young Jamie and asked the Doctor to let him join them on their travels. She demonstrates her resourcefulness when they face the Cybermen on the moon, concocting a chemical mixture (playfully dubbed "Cocktail Polly" by Ben) that destroys their chest units.When they return to Earth on the same day they had left, she elects to stay behind with Ben and promises the Doctor that she will look after him.

Polly is a flirtatious, independent young woman that can be bravely fighting Cybermen one minute and screaming at the sight of a rat the next. She gets along well with the Doctor, Jamie, and especially Ben, whom she gently teases.

Like Ben, Polly is one of the Second Doctor's more experienced companions.

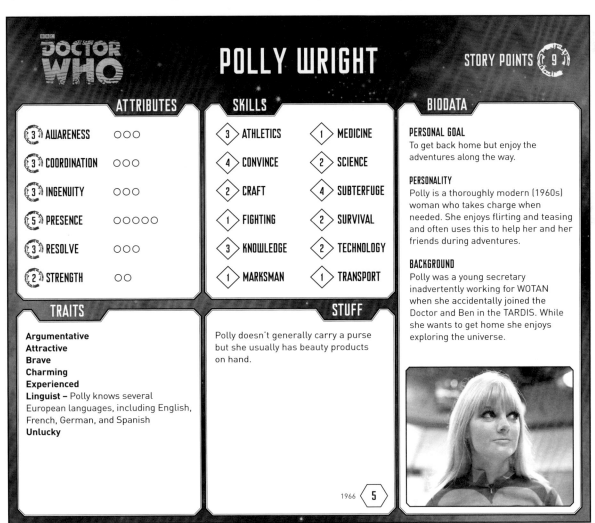

DOCTOR WHO

POLLY WRIGHT

STORY POINTS 9

ATTRIBUTES

3	AWARENESS	○○○
3	COORDINATION	○○○
3	INGENUITY	○○○
5	PRESENCE	○○○○○
3	RESOLVE	○○○
2	STRENGTH	○○

SKILLS

3	ATHLETICS		1	MEDICINE
4	CONVINCE		2	SCIENCE
2	CRAFT		4	SUBTERFUGE
1	FIGHTING		2	SURVIVAL
3	KNOWLEDGE		2	TECHNOLOGY
1	MARKSMAN		1	TRANSPORT

BIODATA

PERSONAL GOAL
To get back home but enjoy the adventures along the way.

PERSONALITY
Polly is a thoroughly modern (1960s) woman who takes charge when needed. She enjoys flirting and teasing and often uses this to help her and her friends during adventures.

BACKGROUND
Polly was a young secretary inadvertently working for WOTAN when she accidentally joined the Doctor and Ben in the TARDIS. While she wants to get home she enjoys exploring the universe.

TRAITS

Argumentative
Attractive
Brave
Charming
Experienced
Linguist – Polly knows several European languages, including English, French, German, and Spanish
Unlucky

STUFF

Polly doesn't generally carry a purse but she usually has beauty products on hand.

1966 5

JAMIE MCCRIMMON

Scottish piper James Robert McCrimmon was the longest-serving of the Second Doctor's companions, joining him on his second adventure and remaining with him until the Time Lords forced him to go home.

Jamie was born in the Scottish Highlands and served the Laird Colin McLaren during the Jacobite Rebellion, fleeing with him after the Battle of Culloden in 1746. He was captured by English soldiers, along with the strangely attired Ben Jackson and the mysterious Doctor von Wehr. He was almost sold into slavery when the Doctor and his companions rescued him and the rest of the Highlanders slated for work in the West Indies. Jamie offered to take the Doctor, Ben, and Polly back to their ship and was invited to join them. The young Highlander soon found himself in an underwater civilisation, a base on the moon, an alien colony, and a modern airport. He remained with the Doctor as Ben and Polly left, staying on to explore new wonders with Victoria and, later, Zoe. He is a loyal friend to the Doctor, although there have been times when he has questioned the Doctor's motives.

Jamie is surprisingly well-grounded for someone from a relatively primitive time period, often equating strange technologies to things he understands or pretending to understand something beyond his comprehension with a dismissive response. As a rebel, Jamie is good in a fight and an expert with the dirk he keeps in his sock.

Jamie enjoys travelling with the Doctor so much that he only left because he was forced to by the Time Lords. He was returned to the time he left with only his knowledge of that first adventure with the Doctor.

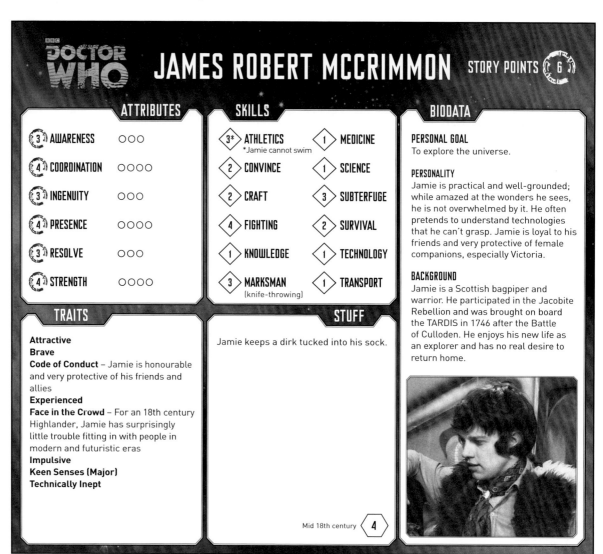

BBC DOCTOR WHO

JAMES ROBERT MCCRIMMON
STORY POINTS 6

ATTRIBUTES

- 3 AWARENESS ○○○
- 4 COORDINATION ○○○○
- 3 INGENUITY ○○○
- 4 PRESENCE ○○○○
- 3 RESOLVE ○○○
- 4 STRENGTH ○○○○

SKILLS

- 3* ATHLETICS *Jamie cannot swim
- 2 CONVINCE
- 2 CRAFT
- 4 FIGHTING
- 1 KNOWLEDGE
- 3 MARKSMAN (knife-throwing)
- 1 MEDICINE
- 1 SCIENCE
- 3 SUBTERFUGE
- 2 SURVIVAL
- 1 TECHNOLOGY
- 1 TRANSPORT

BIODATA

PERSONAL GOAL
To explore the universe.

PERSONALITY
Jamie is practical and well-grounded; while amazed at the wonders he sees, he is not overwhelmed by it. He often pretends to understand technologies that he can't grasp. Jamie is loyal to his friends and very protective of female companions, especially Victoria.

BACKGROUND
Jamie is a Scottish bagpiper and warrior. He participated in the Jacobite Rebellion and was brought on board the TARDIS in 1746 after the Battle of Culloden. He enjoys his new life as an explorer and has no real desire to return home.

TRAITS

Attractive
Brave
Code of Conduct – Jamie is honourable and very protective of his friends and allies
Experienced
Face in the Crowd – For an 18th century Highlander, Jamie has surprisingly little trouble fitting in with people in modern and futuristic eras
Impulsive
Keen Senses (Major)
Technically Inept

STUFF

Jamie keeps a dirk tucked into his sock.

Mid 18th century 4

VICTORIA WATERFIELD

Victoria Waterfield is a young woman from the Victorian era whose father, Edward Waterfield, conducted time travel experiments with Theodore Maxtible. Unfortunately those experiments attracted the attention of the Daleks, who held Victoria hostage while laying a trap for the Doctor. She is later removed to Skaro and joins the Doctor and Jamie aboard the TARDIS after her father was killed.

Victoria is a study in contradictions. On one hand, she exemplifies the stereotypical Victorian lady. She initially balks at wearing a leg-baring skirt and generally screams at the first sign of trouble. On the other hand, she is very independent, upset at being left behind and is a good judge of character.

These two sides of Victoria struggle over whether she should stay with the Doctor. In her heart she doesn't want to, as she only joined as a victim of circumstance. Still, she demurred to the Doctor as a surrogate guardian until she finally decides to remain behind. Interestingly she chooses to remain on Earth a full century after she'd left, joining a stable family who will look after her.

Victoria is curious and sensible, but a bit timid. She feels a kinship with Jamie because they are both close in age; both are generally just as bewildered when faced with advanced technology. Unlike Jamie, however, Victoria doesn't adapt easily and lacks a thirst for adventure. She feels a bit trapped in the TARDIS.

Her enthusiasm eventually wanes to the point where she decides to remain on Earth, even though it is over a century later than her home time.

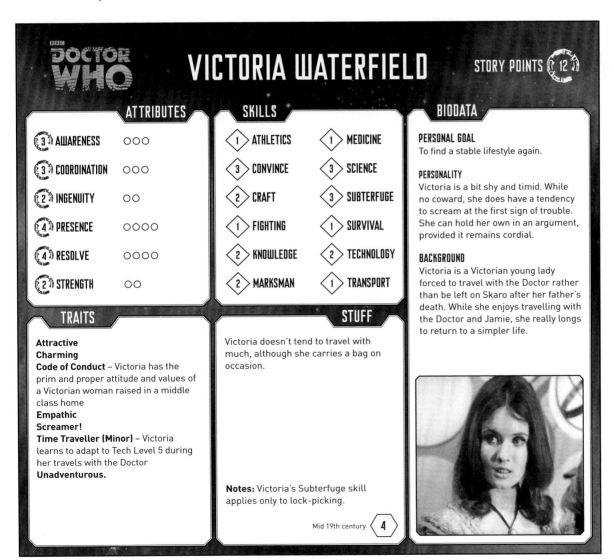

VICTORIA WATERFIELD

STORY POINTS 12

ATTRIBUTES

- 3 AWARENESS ○○○
- 3 COORDINATION ○○○
- 2 INGENUITY ○○
- 4 PRESENCE ○○○○
- 4 RESOLVE ○○○○
- 2 STRENGTH ○○

SKILLS

- 1 ATHLETICS
- 3 CONVINCE
- 2 CRAFT
- 1 FIGHTING
- 2 KNOWLEDGE
- 2 MARKSMAN
- 1 MEDICINE
- 3 SCIENCE
- 3 SUBTERFUGE
- 1 SURVIVAL
- 2 TECHNOLOGY
- 1 TRANSPORT

BIODATA

PERSONAL GOAL
To find a stable lifestyle again.

PERSONALITY
Victoria is a bit shy and timid. While no coward, she does have a tendency to scream at the first sign of trouble. She can hold her own in an argument, provided it remains cordial.

BACKGROUND
Victoria is a Victorian young lady forced to travel with the Doctor rather than be left on Skaro after her father's death. While she enjoys travelling with the Doctor and Jamie, she really longs to return to a simpler life.

TRAITS

Attractive
Charming
Code of Conduct – Victoria has the prim and proper attitude and values of a Victorian woman raised in a middle class home
Empathic
Screamer!
Time Traveller (Minor) – Victoria learns to adapt to Tech Level 5 during her travels with the Doctor
Unadventurous.

STUFF

Victoria doesn't tend to travel with much, although she carries a bag on occasion.

Notes: Victoria's Subterfuge skill applies only to lock-picking.

Mid 19th century 4

ZOE HERIOT

Zoe Heriot was raised in the 21stcentury. She was given extensive and advanced logical training, honing a photographic memory and the ability to make lightning-fast calculations. She becomes an astrophysicist at a young age and is assigned to Space Station W3 (which orbits the sun between Mercury and Venus). While not emotionless, her logical training made it easier for her to accept the inevitable, a trait that irked her co-workers.

After an attempt by the Cybermen to take over her station, Zoe decides to travel with the Doctor and stows away after being told not to come with them. She is highly intelligent and considers herself to be smarter than the Doctor (whether he truly believes this as well is a matter of pride). Like the Doctor, Zoe is considered a 'high brain' by the Krotons and she is able to cause a receptionist computer to break down at International Electromatics. She uses her fast calculating ability on multiple occasions, including saving the Earth by instantly calculating courses for missiles to destroy an invading Cybermen fleet.

For all of her scientific knowledge, Zoe is not very good at history. This is exemplified in her first meeting with Jamie by her failing to identify a Scottish kilt (Scots apparently stop wearing them at some point in the 21st century, obviously a ripple in the Time War). She also fails to recognise the Cybermen when they invade the Wheel in spite of their two previous attempts to conquer Earth in 1968 and 1986 (not counting the Cybermen remaining in the London sewers through 1985 or their small-scale invasion in 1988).

In all other respects, Zoe is an average teenager and enjoys travelling with the Doctor. She remains with him until the Time Lords put him on trial, after which she is returned to the Space Wheel just after she'd left, with no memories of the Doctor and Jamie except for their help in stopping the Cybermen.

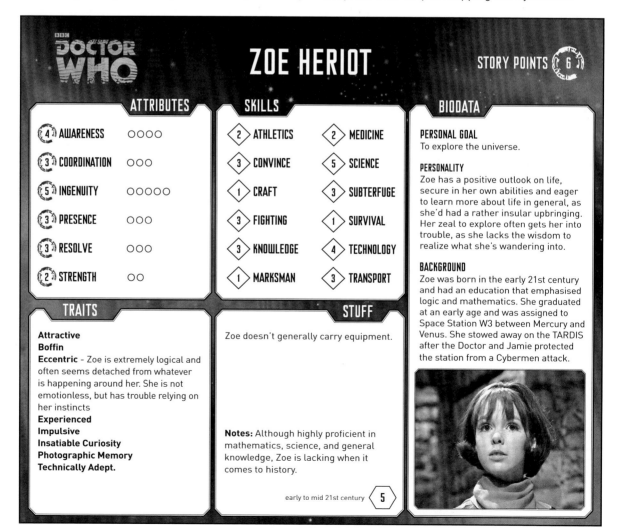

 THE SECOND DOCTOR'S TARDIS

The Second Doctor continued to fly the same battered Type 40 TARDIS as his predecessor. During his tenure, the TARDIS suffered more injuries and indignities – struck by a Cyberman missile, buried in lava with blown fluid links, engulfed in Yeti webs – but came through more or less intact. (Well, it was blown to pieces once, but got better.)

Without access to supplies and spare parts from Gallifrey, the Doctor learned to maintain his Ship using scavenged parts and the expertise of others, such as Professor Travers.

The TARDIS continued to have problems with its mercury fluid links and chameleon circuit, and remained as unpredictable and stubborn as ever. Unlike his previous incarnation, however, the Second Doctor seemed to accept his fate as a cosmic hobo, and rarely tried to drag the TARDIS to a specific destination.

The main console, control room and overall internal configuration remained largely unchanged during this period. A power room containing equipment related to the ship's power source adjoined the console room at least some of the time.

THE SECOND DOCTOR'S TARDIS

AWARENESS	3	PRESENCE	3
COORDINATION	3	RESOLVE	4
INGENUITY	4	STRENGTH	3

SKILLS
Knowledge 8, Medicine 2, Science (Temporal Physics) 6, Survival 1, Technology 4, Transport 3

TRAITS
Clairvoyance (Major), Face in the Crowd, Feel the Turn of the Universe, Psychic, Resourceful Pockets, Telepathy, Vortex, Argumentative, Impulsive, Restriction (Tricky Controls, 6 Pilots), System Fault (Unsteerable, Chameleon Circuit)

GADGET TRAITS: Scan(x3), Transmit, Forcefield (Major)

ARMOUR: 30

SPEED: 12

STORY POINTS: 17

CHAPTER TWO:
TOOLS OF THE TRADE

"It's the TARDIS. It's my home – at least it has been for a considerable number of years."

NEW CHARACTERS

One of the easiest ways to play adventures in the era of the Second Doctor is to use the characters described in chapter one, but this certainly isn't the only way. Your players may wish to use a different incarnation of the Doctor (especially if there is already an ongoing campaign) and their companions, or they may wish to create new characters.

In addition, the Doctor's universe is a dangerous place that has bred the most terrible things, which might spell doom for a character, and your players might need to create a replacement. While everything you need is in the core box set, this section offers guidance on the types of characters best suited for adventures inspired by the Second Doctor's travels.

NEW COMPANIONS

The Second Doctor's companions tend to fall into two types. Ben and Jamie are strong military men of their respective time periods and are often called upon to utilise their physical prowess. They also come from lower class backgrounds. Polly, Victoria, and Zoe are pretty young women that came from comfortable lives. The obvious gender split in these roles is a sign of the times, and should not be enforced!

There is also another major difference between the companions that the Second Doctor inherited from the First and those whom he allowed to accompany him on his own terms. Ben and Polly are self-reliant young adults that often come up with their own solutions to problems. Jamie, Victoria, and Zoe are, on the other hand, impressionable teenagers. They see the Doctor as a surrogate father figure and rely on him for explanations. They also have a tendency to get into trouble when they wander off on their own.

While a player is free to create any companion, he or she should keep these things in mind if she is trying to create a companion in the mould of the Second Doctor's. A new companion is likely teenaged and inexperienced, although their reasons for jumping aboard may vary. Jamie and Victoria joined because it was dangerous for them to remain, while Zoe stowed away. In every case, the Second Doctor ensures as best as he is able that the potential new companion has an opportunity to turn him down.

NEW TIME LORD

Just because you're using the **Second Doctor Sourcebook** doesn't mean that the players have to use the Second Doctor. They may wish to play a different incarnation of the Doctor or may even wish to create their own Time Lord. In these cases, adventures designed for the Second Doctor may need some tweaking, as new Time Lords have different motivations and, in some cases, more reliable TARDISes.

If a player wishes to use the First Doctor then little adjustment is necessary, although you may wish to ensure that simply leaving via TARDIS is not an option if the player wishes to portray the crotchety version of the first incarnation. On the other hand, the later Doctors have more control over their TARDISes destinations and can short-circuit some adventures in this manner. Finally, a player that wants to play an Earth-bound Third Doctor may find himself brought to the adventure by the Time Lords.

If the player wishes to play a new Time Lord then he'll have to decide whether his Time Lord has been sanctioned or is considered a renegade. A sanctioned Time Lord may be able to request aid, while a renegade is constantly watching their back. Assuming that the new Time Lord isn't a vigorous crusader against evil, you'll have to adjust the adventure to pique his interest in seeing it through.

You'll also have to decide whether to make an original Time Lord's TARDIS more reliable than that of the Second Doctor. One way to give a Time Lord more control while maintaining the integrity of the Second Doctor's adventures is to allow the Time Lord the ability to plot general trips, but making them unable to be precise. Thus, while a Time Lord might be able to set a course for the late Roman Republic, they wouldn't have command of exactly when they landed and would certainly be unable to steer the TARDIS during an adventure set there.

OTHER GROUPS

Perhaps the most difficult group to run Second Doctor adventures for is the group without a Time Lord. Unless the group has access to a time travel capsule, they'll be stuck in a single period. Luckily, this still provides you with plenty of inspiration, as

the Doctor not only had plenty of adventures in the late 20th century, but most of his future adventures took place in the same century (although it seems to be a very different 21st century than our own is shaping up to be).

If your campaign is set within a single time period, then the best way to get into the spirit of the Second Doctor's era is to become familiar with the adventures that fit the period in which you are playing (and if you plan to run those adventures, you may want to change dates to put them closer together).

Time Agents

If the characters are members of the Time Agency then they can also easily get involved in Second Doctor-style adventures, especially if they believe that to not do so would disrupt the timeline.

Modern Day Investigators

Modern Day Investigators can either be independent investigators, like Sarah Jane Smith, or a more military group like UNIT or Torchwood. In keeping with the spirit of the Second Doctor's adventures, 'modern' investigations would take place in the late 1960s. You can take inspiration from *The Underwater Menace*, *The Faceless Ones*, *The Web of Fear*, *The Fury from the Deep*, and *The Invasion*.

Some of these adventures, such as **Fury from the Deep**, will need a bit of date massaging to fit in the late 1960s. **Evil of the Daleks** is a special case, as the Daleks have a personal reason for baiting the Second Doctor. This can be easily transferred to any scientific genius on a modern investigative team. Alternatively, you could use the early 21st century as your base, utilising some of the suggestions offered in the relevant adventures in Chapters Six, Eight and Nine.

Space Opera

Given the number of futuristic stories that take place after the year 2000 but prior to the Dalek Invasion, you can have your group play Earth Examiners or Space Patrol agents having adventures very similar to the ones that the Doctor has. You can even adapt the six adventures that take place during this era, massaging the dates a bit so you can run them more or less concurrently.

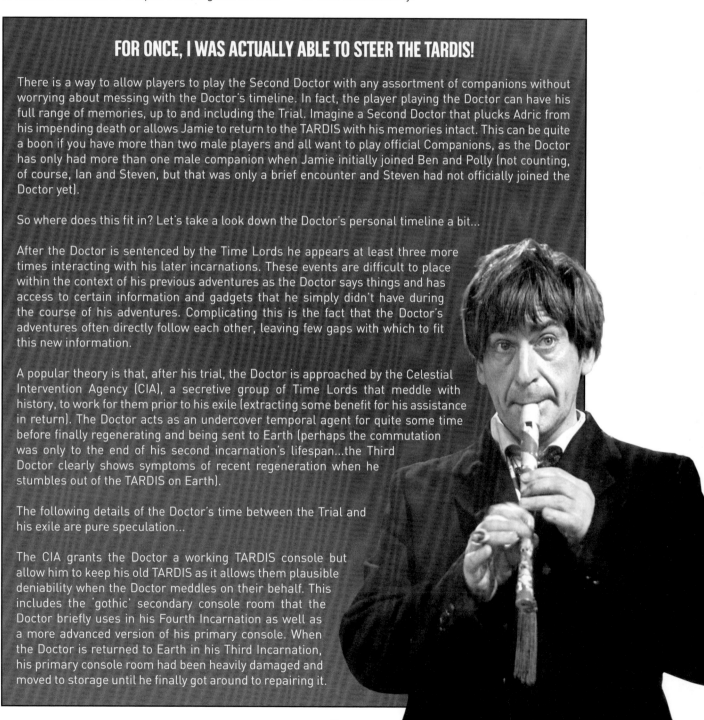

FOR ONCE, I WAS ACTUALLY ABLE TO STEER THE TARDIS!

There is a way to allow players to play the Second Doctor with any assortment of companions without worrying about messing with the Doctor's timeline. In fact, the player playing the Doctor can have his full range of memories, up to and including the Trial. Imagine a Second Doctor that plucks Adric from his impending death or allows Jamie to return to the TARDIS with his memories intact. This can be quite a boon if you have more than two male players and all want to play official Companions, as the Doctor has only had more than one male companion when Jamie initially joined Ben and Polly (not counting, of course, Ian and Steven, but that was only a brief encounter and Steven had not officially joined the Doctor yet).

So where does this fit in? Let's take a look down the Doctor's personal timeline a bit...

After the Doctor is sentenced by the Time Lords he appears at least three more times interacting with his later incarnations. These events are difficult to place within the context of his previous adventures as the Doctor says things and has access to certain information and gadgets that he simply didn't have during the course of his adventures. Complicating this is the fact that the Doctor's adventures often directly follow each other, leaving few gaps with which to fit this new information.

A popular theory is that, after his trial, the Doctor is approached by the Celestial Intervention Agency (CIA), a secretive group of Time Lords that meddle with history, to work for them prior to his exile (extracting some benefit for his assistance in return). The Doctor acts as an undercover temporal agent for quite some time before finally regenerating and being sent to Earth (perhaps the commutation was only to the end of his second incarnation's lifespan...the Third Doctor clearly shows symptoms of recent regeneration when he stumbles out of the TARDIS on Earth).

The following details of the Doctor's time between the Trial and his exile are pure speculation...

The CIA grants the Doctor a working TARDIS console but allow him to keep his old TARDIS as it allows them plausible deniability when the Doctor meddles on their behalf. This includes the 'gothic' secondary console room that the Doctor briefly uses in his Fourth Incarnation as well as a more advanced version of his primary console. When the Doctor is returned to Earth in his Third Incarnation, his primary console room had been heavily damaged and moved to storage until he finally got around to repairing it.

With his directional circuits fixed the Doctor can actually steer his TARDIS. As a test run he visits the Brigadier and has the ability to not only pin-point the location, but also to steer the TARDIS back a day. He is also given a Stattenheim Remote Control in order to summon the TARDIS whenever he needs it. The CIA can still override the TARDIS, stranding the Doctor until he completes his current mission.

When the Time Lords want to bring the first three incarnations of the Doctor together to combat Omega, the Second Doctor provides them with coordinates in which to retrieve the First Doctor on condition that they do not bring him to trial or otherwise disrupt the timestream.

While acting as an agent the Doctor requests that old Companions accompany him. The CIA allows this, and the Doctor travels with Jamie and Victoria. While Jamie is an obvious choice, Victoria's seems a bit odd. Perhaps she found it difficult acclimatising to a new century and the Doctor offers to aid her in return for her service. Jamie is recruited at some point after the Doctor is brought to the Death Zone.

Once the Doctor regenerates, the Time Lord's wipe his memory of working for the CIA so that the Doctor believes his exile took place immediately after his trial. Thus he has no memory of owning a Stattenheim remote or using the backup control room.

RUNNING POST-TRIAL SECOND DOCTOR ADVENTURES

In order to run a post-Trial adventure you can have one player play the Second Doctor while the other players play Companions from any period in the Doctor's life, including his future. For full creative freedom, ensure that the Companion is plucked after his or her last appearance in the Doctor's timeline. You can also allow the players to make original Companions as well. With this set-up, there is no safety from continuity. We don't know what happens to Turlough after he leaves the Doctor for Trion, so it's possible that he meets the wrong end of a Dalek exterminator while working with the Second Doctor. The player involved would simply replace him with a new Companion.

Nor is the Doctor safe from permanent harm. If he manages to get injured enough to force a regeneration, then the CIA intervenes, wipes his memory, sends his Companions back to their home times, and exiles the Third Doctor to Earth as per his sentence.

NEW TRAITS

The following new traits were used in designing characters for the **Second Doctor Campaign Pack** and are available for general use. Some of these traits can also be found in the **Time Traveller's Companion** and the Eleventh Doctor Edition of **Doctor Who: Adventures in Time and Space** and are repeated here for convenience.

BIOCHEMICAL GENIUS (MAJOR, GOOD)

The character is a dab hand with chemistry and biology and has a natural 'feel' for the way the two combine.

Effects: The character gains Areas of Expertise for the Science Skill in Biology and Chemistry and may create biological or chemical 'Gadgets' using the Jiggery-Pokery rules, using the Science Skill instead of Technology for all relevant rolls.

DEVOTION (MINOR, GOOD)

The Character has deep and intense feelings for another character. This can inspire them to great heights of accomplishment or force them to act impulsively when the object of their devotion is threatened.

Effect: Once per adventure, when an action is directly related to protecting the well-being of the object of the character's devotion or impressing them, the character may gain a single temporary Story Point which can only be used on that action.

EPICUREAN TASTES (MINOR, GOOD)

The character appreciates the finer things in life, like good food, good drink, fashionable clothing and fine art.

Effect: The character gains a +2 bonus on any roll to judge the quality of luxury items. They also gain a +2 bonus to any roll to impress others with their sense of taste, assuming the targets are actually impressed by such things.

HEALER (MINOR, GOOD)

This character can make medical miracles happen no matter what resources are available to him.

Effect: +2 bonus on Medicine rolls when trying to heal someone.

LINGUIST (MINOR, GOOD)

Some people have the knack for learning new languages. This is considered a minor trait because the TARDIS generally compensates for lack of linguistic skills.

Effect: Select three languages in which the Character is proficient (other than their native tongue). At the Gamemaster's discretion, a Character can also instantly know an additional language during an adventure by spending a Story Point and having a rational reason for knowing the language. For example, Polly knows French, German and Spanish. When the TARDIS lands on a 17th century Dutch East Indies vessel, Polly can spend a Story Point to "have learned Dutch before" as well. However, she could not plausibly know the Martian tongue the first time she meets an Ice Warrior.

NOTE: Most characters are assumed to know their native language and familiar with at least one other, so this trait isn't necessary for a character to be considered bilingual.

MENACING (MINOR, GOOD)

Some characters appear charming but their words are tinged with a hint of menace. They influence others through quiet threats rather than outright Intimidation.

Effect: +2 bonus on attempts to get people to do what you want. Characters you have menaced also get a +2 to resist attempts by others to act against you.

MILITARY RANK (MINOR/MAJOR/SPECIAL GOOD)

The character holds a high rank in some military force, be it Army, Navy, Air Force or UNIT. The character has authority over any lower ranking member of their service and can give orders that will typically be followed. They also have access to military resources commensurate with their rank. They have an obligation to their service and failure to uphold that obligation can lead to severe consequences.

Effects: The Minor version of this Trait starts the character as a non-commissioned officer of a rank equivalent to an Army Sergeant. This gives them command over a squad of troops and all the requisite equipment that comes with that squad, including specialist equipment for specific Military Operations Specialties (like demolition equipment for an engineering unit) and limited use of transport vehicles.

The Major Version of this Trait starts the character as an officer of a rank equivalent to an Army Lieutenant. This gives them command over a squad of troops and all the requisite equipment and vehicles that comes with that squad.

The Special Version of this Trait costs 6 Character Points, and reduces the character's Story Point

Total by 1, but starts the character as an officer of a rank equivalent to a Brigadier General. This gives them command over a Brigade of troops and all the requisite equipment and vehicles that comes with that Brigade, including the ability to call in artillery and air support and take command of local law enforcement agencies. It also provides the Friends (Government and Military) Trait to represent the officer's political and military connections.

The ranks given above are starting ranks and it is possible to raise them through promotion during active service, but taking ranks outside of that level of Trait (to move from Colonel to Brigadier General for example) requires the normal expenditure of character points (and a Story Point in the case of the Special version) as well.

RANDOM REGENERATOR (MAJOR BAD)

The Time Lord has no control over their body during Regeneration, and they're pretty much stuck with whatever they get.

Effects: Regardless of how well the Time Lord does on their Regeneration Roll, they can never achieve more than a regular Success.

SLOW (MINOR/MAJOR BAD)

A lot of the Doctor's adversaries are incredibly dangerous but thankfully many of them move slowly. Cybermen are walking tanks able to withstand gunfire and damage but the Doctor is quick to avoid them as they lumber from one place to the next with a slow marching stomp. This trait can also be used for characters that are physically impaired from moving properly.

Effect: Slow is a Minor or a Major Bad Trait which means that the character is slower than average. As a Minor Bad Trait, the character's effective Speed is halved (round down), so a Coordination of 4 means that the character has a Speed of 2 in a chase. The character's Speed has a minimum of 1, though particularly slow creatures can sometimes have Speeds that are slower (down to 0.5, etc).

Such slow speeds, however, require additional calculations on behalf of the Gamemaster and may be ignored. As a Major Bad Trait, the character's Speed is effectively zero. The character does not move or, if it does, it moves so slowly that it is regarded as stationary in a chase situation.

TIME LORD ENGINEER (MAJOR GOOD, PREREQUISITE: TECHNICALLY ADEPT)

Some Time Lords eschew the more theoretical and philosophical sciences and concentrate, instead, on the more practical application of technology. Obsessed with honing their technical skills, these inveterate tinkerers typically find themselves working to maintain Gallifrey's vast infrastructure or working in a TARDIS repair bay after they graduate from the Academy.

Effects: This Trait doubles the effect of the Technically Adept Trait, giving a +4 to all uses of the Technology Skill.

UNCREATIVE (MINOR/MAJOR/SPECIAL BAD)

The character lacks the creative spark to 'think outside the box' and think of creative ways to approach a situation. The character doesn't handle new situations well and relies on past experiences or wisdom to approach problems.

Effect: Uncreative is a bad trait that makes it difficult for characters to try new solutions. As a minor trait, the character takes a -2 penalty on any roll that the Gamemaster decides requires creativity. As a major trait, the character takes a -4 penalty. As a special trait, the character is so coldly logical and unimaginative that it is simply impossible for her to perform any action that requires creative thought. The special trait is generally not for player characters. You cannot have both the Uncreative trait and the Boffin trait.

WANTED RENEGADE (SPECIAL BAD)

The Time Lord is an outlaw, on the run from Gallifrey and the Time Lords. While the High Council's official policy is 'good riddance to bad rubbish' when it comes to upstarts and revolutionaries, there are secret organizations, like the CIA, whose task it is to hound the more dangerous criminals to the ends of time.

Effects: The Time Lord committed, or is accused of committing, a heinous crime and is actively hunted by his former people. The Time Lord may regain 6 Story Points by having the Gamemaster introduce an agent or agents from the CIA into the adventure. These agents will attempt to disrupt the Time Lord's plans and try to capture them or bring them to justice, assuming that they are interfering in the natural course of events no matter what the truth of the matter really is. This Trait costs 1 Story Point.

⚙ NEW GADGETS

The following new gadgets appear during the Second Doctor adventures. Some of these are designed for a single adventure but may be used in subsequent adventures with the Gamemaster's permission.

BIGGER ON THE INSIDE
(MINOR/MAJOR/SPECIAL GADGET TRAIT)

This Trait can be applied to any object with an interior space or holding area, like a bag, backpack or vehicle interior. In effect, the interior of the item is a pocket dimension of greater size than is possible for the actual volume of the object, allowing one to store vastly larger items inside, assuming they can fit through the opening.

Effect: As a Minor Trait the item has an interior roughly 10 times its apparent volume. As a Major Trait, the object holds roughly 30 times its apparent volume. Weight is still a factor in both cases, so even if you can fit a hundred gold bars into your 'magic bag' you still have to be able to lift it. As a Special Trait, the item has 30 times capacity and its weight is negligible. This counts as two Major Traits.

NOTE: All TARDISes are assumed to have the Special version of this Trait by design, but their interior space is infinite and the exterior is as weightless as the operator chooses.

500 YEAR DIARY

The Doctor has travelled extensively throughout time and space and has left himself many notes on those journeys. When his own memory fails him the Doctor can use the 500 Year Diary to jog his memory about someone or something he's encountered before.

Traits: This gives a Hint once per adventure, as if the owner had spent a Story Point to gain a hint.
Cost: 1 Story Point

RECORDER

The Doctor's recorder helps him think when he plays it; in game terms, he gets a +2 bonus to any Ingenuity-based roll if he has time to play and think for a while first. He can also use the recorder to avoids answering awkward questions – if he loses a Social Conflict that would normally force him to talk, he can just play the recorder instead.

Cost: 1 Story Point

SONIC SCREWDRIVER MARK 1

This is the Doctor's original sonic screwdriver which, in addition to its Traits, can also turn a screw.

Traits: Open/Close, Restriction (Cannot open Deadlock Seals, Tricky Controls), Scan, Transmit, Weld.
Cost: 2 Story Points

THE SONIC SCREWDRIVER CAN DO WHAT?

The Sonic Screwdriver is seen to burn through brick and metal in "the Dominators." Astute Gamemasters that read this section will notice that this ability is not listed within the Mark 1 Sonic Screwdriver's capabilities. The reason for this is that not only does it greatly increase the utility of the gadget, but it also wasn't used by the Doctor for this purpose when it would've been helpful in other adventures.

If you want to add this capability to the sonic screwdriver, then increase the story points to 4 and give it the Delete trait.

STATTENHEIM REMOTE CONTROL

A Stattenheim Remote Control is keyed to a specific TARDIS and allows the holder to summon the TARDIS from anywhere in time and space.

Traits: Transmit
Cost: 1 Story Point

TARDIS CHEST

The TARDIS contains a chest that often provides the Doctor with something that he'll need in his current adventure. As the Doctor has yet to go on the adventure he often won't know why he needs the item, only that it's interesting and he should keep it for now. The nature of the object taken often provides a clue as to what the Doctor is about to face.

Traits: Resourceful Pockets, Restriction: No input (the character can't ask for the resourceful item; she merely takes what the TARDIS (i.e. the Gamemaster) offers.
Cost: 2 Story Points

NOTE: The TARDIS Chest is a regular repository, so the character can keep retrievable objects in there as well; this gadget's trait only emulates the odd thing the character may pull out and stuff into her pocket without thinking too much about it.

TIME VECTOR GENERATOR

The Time Vector Generator is a rod that, when removed, disengages the real world interface of the TARDIS and leaves only the shell of the last exterior appearance. Any Characters inside the TARDIS are dumped inside the shell. The Time Vector Generator is also capable of unleashing deadly bolts of energy (4/L/L) as well as providing a power source for other devices.

Cost: 2 Story Points

CHAPTER THREE:
ENEMIES

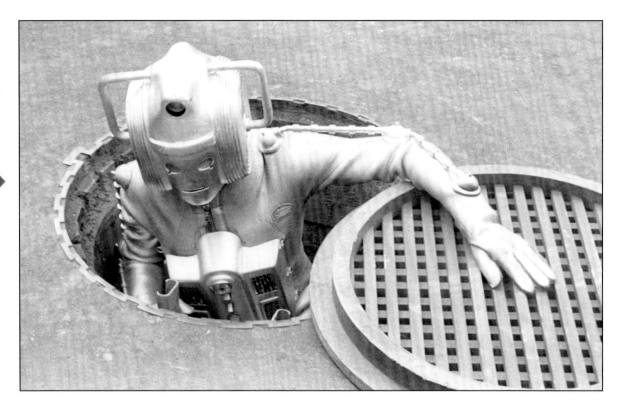

"There are some corners of the universe which have bred the most terrible things, things which act against everything which we believe in. They must be fought."

The Doctor faces many adversaries during his second incarnation. He sees the end of the Daleks and the further development of the Cybermen as well as new species such as the Dominators, the Ice Warriors, and the Yeti (actually robot minions of the Great Intelligence). The Doctor is truly fearful of encountering such adversaries, but he never lets his fear get in the way of defeating them.

This chapter takes a look at some of the major and recurring enemies that the Second Doctor faced.

◎ CYBERMEN

While the Cybermen's home planet of Mondas was destroyed in the First Doctor's final adventure, it was by no means the end of the Cybermen. Unlike the Mondasians, however, the Cybermen that the Second Doctor faced are even more robotic, encased in full metal bodysuits and helmets. These Cybermen speak with electronically synthesized voices and lack personal names. The Second Doctor gains an insight into the evolution of the Cybermen – he meets three distinctly different variants during his four encounters with them.

Chronologically speaking, the Second Doctor first met the Cybermen in 1968. These Cybermen, led by a Cyber Coordinator (an early version of the Cyber Planner, had been working with International Electromatics founder Tobias Vaughn for five years, providing him with technology while preparing the vanguard of the Cybermen invasion. They were stopped due to the combined efforts of the Second Doctor and the newly-formed UNIT (a small force of Cybermen were stranded in the sewers and later dealt with by the Sixth Doctor). These Cybermen referred to a previous encounter with the Doctor on "Planet 14," which may be the origin of the invasion force.

In the mid-21st century the Cybermen attack Space Station W3, in orbit between Mercury and Venus, as part of another plan to conquer Earth. The Second Doctor foiled this scheme with help from new companion Zoe (who, due to the nature of time travel, already helped defeat the 1968 invasion). It is here that they encountered Cybermats, as well as a new model of Cybermen directed by an upgraded Cyber Planner.

The Second Doctor next clashed with the Cybermen in 2070 when they attempted to take over the Gravitron on the moon. Once again the Cybermen wanted to conquer Earth. They had decided that they lacked the numbers and resources for a frontal attack, so planned to use the weather-making device to cause an apocalypse and weaken the planet's resistance to their invasion.. It is unknown where these Cybermen came from, although they were of the same model found later on Telos, seemingly less advanced than the ones from Planet 14.

The Second Doctor's latest encounter with the Cybermen (again, chronologically speaking) took place on Telos, a barren world that the Cybermen invaded in order to use the underground refrigerated cities of the native Cryons. The remnant of their once-great army was entombed there until suitable candidates would pass a number of tests to become the leaders of a new Cybermen army. In the late 24th century an archaeological expedition from Earth visited Telos, financed by the Brotherhood of Logicians. The Brotherhood had a secret agenda, to join forces with the Cybermen, but they soon learned that the Cybermen make poor allies.

On this final occasion, the Second Doctor met the Cyber-Controller. The Cyber-Controller was aware of the Doctor's involvement with the destruction of Mondas and the Cybermen invasion of the Moonbase (but not, apparently, of his participation in foiling the 1968 invasion or the attack on the Wheel). In the end, the Doctor resealed the Cybermen in the Tomb. The Cyber-Controller, whom the Doctor believed destroyed, survived to rebuild his race.

The Cybermen that faced the Doctor in his Second incarnation came in three basic models, labelled 2-4 (1 being the version that invaded Earth in 1986). While each model shares the same general characteristics, there are stylistic differences as well as variation in the weapons they carried. It is unknown whether these Cybermen models were susceptible to gold like later models.

Model 2: The Doctor encountered the Model 2 Cybermen on the Moon in 2070 and in their tomb on Telos. This model was a streamlined version of Model 1, with a full bodysuit and a helmet (with only two 'handlebars' as opposed to the Model 1's three). It was far less bulky, with a much smaller chest unit and tubes running down the side of the arms and legs. Curiously, it only had two fingers and a thumb on each hand. The Model 2 spoke with an electronic voice, carried a stun weapon built into its wrist and had a hand laser sheathed beneath its chest unit.

Model 3: The Model 3 Cybermen threatened Space Station W3 in the mid-21st century. These Cybermen were more streamlined than the Model 2 and eyeholes with 'teardrops' in their helmets. Rather than a handheld laser pistol, Model 3 Cybermen had a laser built directly into their chest units. Their voice, while still electronic, sounded deeper and more human-like.

Model 4: This Cybermen's most distinguishing feature was the distinctive 'headphone' design of the handlebars that covered each side of the helmet. These Cybermen tended to use flame rifles (though more like a submachine gun in size) when on patrol.

Regardless of model, Cybermen also had access to heavier weapons and bio-weapons. One such bio-weapon, Neurotrope X, was used to poison humans and make them susceptible to hypnotic control. Humans controlled in this way behaved much like zombies.

WHY ARE EARLIER CYBERMEN MORE ADVANCED THAN LATER CYBERMEN?

To keep things simple, we've named the Cyberman models in the order that the Second Doctor encountered them. You could argue that the Model 4 Cyberman is actually the first model, as it appears chronologically earlier, or that the Model 2 and Model 3 should switch designations, as the Model 3 Cybermen invade Space Station W3 decades before the Model 2 Cybermen invade the Moonbase (and are the same model found on Telos centuries later).

However, with temporal disturbances, rewriting of history, and the Time War, it's certainly possible that history has been rewritten more than once, leading to stagnation or acceleration of Cybermen designs. Given that the Cybermen later capture a time travel machine, it's possible that several designs and upgrades were shared between various groups of Cybermen. Also, later Cybermen appear to have evolved from the Model 4, and the Model 3 shares characteristics of both the Model 2 and the Model 4.

MODEL 2 CYBERMAN

AWARENESS	2	PRESENCE	3
COORDINATION	3	RESOLVE	2
INGENUITY	4	STRENGTH	7

SKILLS
Athletics 4, Convince 2, Craft 2, Fighting 2, Knowledge 1, Marksman 3, Medicine 3, Science 2, Subterfuge 2, Survival 3, Technology 4, Transport 2

TRAITS
Armour (Minor): The Cybermen's metallic armour reduces damage by 5.

Cyborg: The Cybermen were once human, but have everything apart from their major internal organs replaced with machinery.

Environmental (Minor): Cybermen can survive in the vacuum of space.

Fear Factor (3): Cybermen are pretty scary and gain a +6 to rolls to actively scare someone.

Natural Weapon – Hand Laser: Model 2 Cybermen have a small, hand-held laser pistol that is normally sheathed beneath their chest unit - 4/L/L.

Natural Weapon – Stun Weapon: Built into the Cyberman's wrist, stun weapons can knock a humanoid unconscious at short range – S/S/S.

Networked (Major): Cybermen in a particular unit are in communication with others of that unit.

Slow: Due to their heavy cybernetic bodies, Cybermen are slow. They only have a Speed of 1 in chases.

Special Trait (Override): A Cyberman can use the energy from his stun weapon to override a computer or electronic system's security and control it. This trait is only present in Cybermen Model 3.

Technically Adept

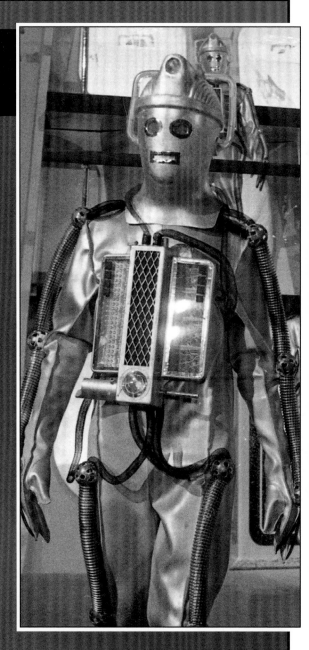

Weakness (Major): The Cybermen's chest unit is particularly vulnerable to clogging or dissolving with chemical mixtures (e.g. 'Cocktail Polly') and liquid plastic (it is unknown whether these early chest units are also vulnerable to gold dust). Cybermen are also vulnerable to radiation.

TECH LEVEL: 6   STORY POINTS: 3-6

DOCTOR
WHO

MODEL 3 CYBERMAN

AWARENESS	2	PRESENCE	3
COORDINATION	3	RESOLVE	2
INGENUITY	4	STRENGTH	7

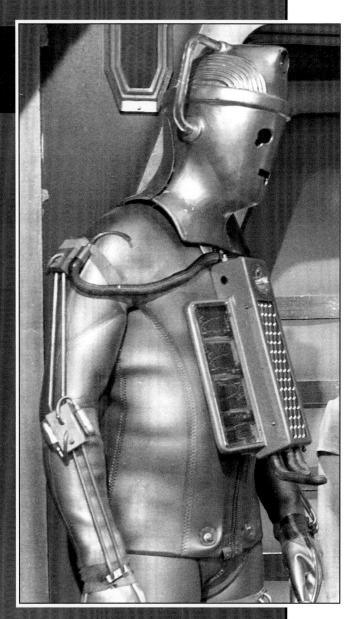

SKILLS
Athletics 4, Convince 2, Craft 2, Fighting 2, Knowledge 1, Marksman 3, Medicine 3, Science 2, Subterfuge 2, Survival 3, Technology 4, Transport 2

TRAITS
Armour (Minor): The Cybermen's metallic armour reduces damage by 5.

Cyborg: The Cybermen were once human, but have everything apart from their major internal organs replaced with machinery.

Environmental (Minor): Cybermen can survive in the vacuum of space.

Fear Factor (3): Cybermen are pretty scary and gain a +6 to rolls to actively scare someone.

Natural Weapon – Chest Laser: Model 3 Cybermen have a laser weapon directly into their chest units - 4/L/L.

Natural Weapon – Hypnosis (Major): Model 3 Cybermen can hypnotise people at short range. They can also use this power to communicate orders to other Cybermen or controlled humans.

Natural Weapon – Stun Weapon: Built into the Cyberman's wrist, stun weapons can knock a humanoid unconscious at short range – S/S/S.

Networked (Major): Cybermen in a particular unit are in communication with others of that unit.

Slow: Due to their heavy cybernetic bodies, Cybermen are slow. They only have a Speed of 1 in chases.

Special Trait (Override): A Cyberman can use the energy from his stun weapon to override a computer or electronic system's security and control it. This trait is only present in Cybermen Model 3.

Technically Adept

Weakness (Major): The Cybermen's chest unit is particularly vulnerable to clogging or dissolving with chemical mixtures (e.g. 'Cocktail Polly') and liquid plastic (it is unknown whether these early chest units are also vulnerable to gold dust). Cybermen are also vulnerable to radiation.

TECH LEVEL: 5   STORY POINTS: 3-6

MODEL 4 CYBERMAN

AWARENESS	2	PRESENCE	3
COORDINATION	3	RESOLVE	2
INGENUITY	4	STRENGTH	7

SKILLS
Athletics 4, Convince 2, Craft 2, Fighting 2, Knowledge 1, Marksman 3, Medicine 3, Science 2, Subterfuge 2, Survival 3, Technology 4, Transport 2

TRAITS
Armour (Minor): The Cybermen's metallic armour reduces damage by 5.

Cyborg: The Cybermen were once human, but have everything apart from their major internal organs replaced with machinery.

Environmental (Minor): Cybermen can survive in the vacuum of space.

Fear Factor (3): Cybermen are pretty scary and gain a +6 to rolls to actively scare someone.

Natural Weapon – Chest Laser: Model 4 Cybermen have a laser weapon directly into their chest units. - 4/L/L

Natural Weapon – Flame Rifle: The Model 4 Cybermen invasion force carried flame rifles during the Doctor's last encounter with the Cybermen. These had a longer range than their laser weapons – 4/L/L

Natural Weapon – Stun Weapon: Built into the Cyberman's wrist, stun weapons can knock a humanoid unconscious at short range – S/S/S.

Networked (Major): Cybermen in a particular unit are in communication with others of that unit.

Slow: Due to their heavy cybernetic bodies, Cybermen are slow. They only have a Speed of 1 in chases.

Special Trait (Override): A Cyberman can use the energy from his stun weapon to override a computer or electronic system's security and control it. This trait is only present in Cybermen Model 4.

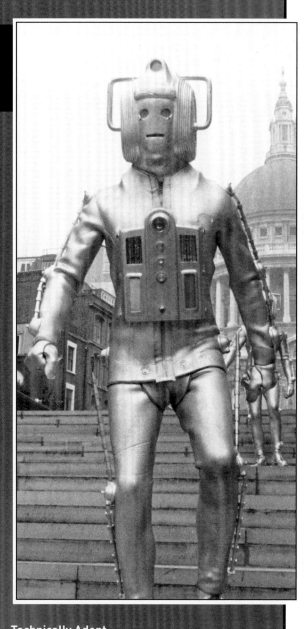

Technically Adept

Weakness (Major): The Cybermen's chest unit is particularly vulnerable to clogging or dissolving with chemical mixtures (e.g. 'Cocktail Polly') and liquid plastic (it is unknown whether these early chest units are also vulnerable to gold dust). Cybermen are also vulnerable to radiation.

TECH LEVEL: 6   STORY POINTS: 3-6

CYBERMATS

The Cybermen occasionally employ small cybernetic organisms known as a Cybermats. A Cybermat is a metallic creature that resembles a squat metallic insect and comes in at least two sizes; a smaller one that can fit in the palm of one's hand and a larger one about the size of a small cat. Cybermats can crawl through small openings and make excellent sentries, assassins, saboteurs, and advance units. A Cybermat can track human brainwaves and emit an electrical discharge from its eyes. A Cybermat can also bite; injecting a potent poison or powerful corrosive. A strong burst of electricity can scramble their brains, stunning or even killing them.

CYBERMAT

AWARENESS	4	PRESENCE	1
COORDINATION	4	RESOLVE	5
INGENUITY	2	STRENGTH	5

SKILLS
Athletics 5, Fighting 2, Marksman 4, Subterfuge 5, Survival 2, Technology 3, Transport 3

TRAITS
Alien Appearance: Cybermats look like large metallic bugs. They can be built in various sizes, although the smaller ones aren't as well armed.

Alien Senses: A Cybermat has a number of senses, including infrared and ultraviolet vision. It also has the ability to home in on human brainwaves.

Armour (Minor): The Cybermats' metallic armour reduces damage by 5. Cybermats are particularly susceptible to electric charges; their armour does not count against an electric charge.

Clinging: The Cybermat can climb even smooth surfaces without difficulty.

Cyborg: While it looks like a small robot, a Cybermat is a partially-organic creature like the Cybermen themselves.

Enslaved: The Cybermats are the servants of the Cybermen.

Jumping: A Cybermat's advanced hydraulics enable it to leap 5-6 feet in the air, perfect for landing on a humanoid's back or shoulder.

Natural Weapon (Bite): A Cybermat can bite an opponent, although its damage is reduced depending on size. Larger Cybermats tend to do 2/5/7 damage while smaller Cybermats tend to do 1/3/4 damage. The bite often contains a corrosive or poison that ranges from damaging circuits to causing Stun (S/S/S) damage to causing Lethal (4/L/L) damage or to transmitting an artificial disease.

Natural Weapon (Electric Discharge): Larger Cybermats have the ability to discharge electricity at close range, delivering either Stun (S/S/S) or Lethal (4/L/L) damage.

Weakness (Major): Cybermats have the same major weaknesses as their masters, such as solvents, liquid plastic, and radiation. A solvent is more difficult to administer to a Cybermat as it has to go through the mouth. They are also susceptible to electric charges (see Armour entry).

STORY POINTS: 1-2

Note: A Cybermat's Strength is for pushing or pulling only. Similarly, a Cybermat only does as programmed; its Technology and Transport skills are only for seeking out the proper wiring or circuitry to corrode and destroy equipment or gadgets.

CYBER-CONTROLLER

The Cyber-Controller is the leader of the Cybermen on Telos. He is chosen for his intelligence and houses his large brain in a great helmet. Unlike other Cybermen, the Cyber-Controller does not require a chest unit; his larger size (the Cyber-Controller towers over the other Cybermen) likely enables him to have everything he needs built-in. The Cyber-Controller has more redundant internal systems than the average Cyberman, allowing him to take more damage before falling. While the Cyber-Controller first seen by the Doctor was a variation on the Model 2 Cyberman, they are upgraded to the latest available model.

CYBER-CONTROLLER

AWARENESS	3	PRESENCE	4
COORDINATION	3	RESOLVE	5
INGENUITY	6	STRENGTH	8

SKILLS
Athletics 6, Convince 4, Craft 3, Fighting 5, Knowledge 5, Marksman 3, Medicine 4, Science 5, Subterfuge 2, Survival 3, Technology 5, Transport 4

TRAITS
Armour (Minor): The Cyber-Controller's metallic armour reduces damage by 5.

Cyborg: The Cyber-Controller was once human, but has everything apart from his major internal organs replaced with machinery.

Fast Healing (Major): The Cyber-Controller's redundant systems quickly repair damage done.

Fear Factor (3): While physically larger than other Cybermen, the Cyber-Controller's intimidating figure is mitigated somewhat by his lack of weaponry.

Natural Weapon – Hypnosis: The Cyber-Controller can hypnotise people at short range. He can also use this power to communicate orders to Cybermen or controlled humans.

Natural Weapon – Stun Weapon: Built into the Cyber-Controller's wrist, stun weapons can knock a humanoid unconscious at short range – S/S/S.

Technically Adept

Weakness (major): Without a chest unit, the Cyber-Controller is immune to most Cybermen weaknesses except radiation.

STORY POINTS: 10-12

Note: The Cyber-Controller lacks a chest unit, probably because the conditions beneath the surface of Telos don't require one or the Cyber-Controller's body is still largely organic. As he is upgraded with a chest unit the next time the Doctor meets him, one can presume that the repairs he needed required him to add a chest unit.

PARTIAL CYBERMEN

The conversion process from man to Cyberman is long and arduous, but like the Cybermen's own ancestors it's possible to function after being only partly converted. In the Ice Tombs of Telos Toberman is given a bionic arm and brainwashed, but otherwise he is still human. Tobias Vaughn undergoes a more complete conversion, leaving only his head, brain, and other internal organs intact. In Vaughn's case he seems to have been given a realistic-looking body as well, as he lacks the outer armour and chest unit of a Cyberman (yet his body is still invulnerable to bullets). He is also more independent than standard partial Cybermen. It is clear in both instances that the Cybermen wish to complete the process rather than leave the human in a partially-converted form.

CYBER PLANNER

The Cyber Planner (or sometimes called the Cyber Coordinator) is a human-sized machine that functions as an immobile Cybermen Controller. It is constructed of metal and transparent tubing surrounding a central braincase. Whether the Cyber Planner is a cyborg or robot is unknown, although its susceptibility to emotional impulses suggests that it has an organic brain.

Unlike a Cybermen Controller, the Cyber Planner has enhanced information-gathering sensors as part of its design, enabling it to discover and process information quickly and allow it to settle on a course of action with the highest probability of success.

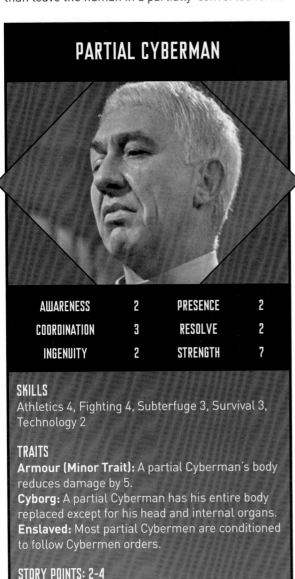

PARTIAL CYBERMAN

AWARENESS	2	PRESENCE	2
COORDINATION	3	RESOLVE	2
INGENUITY	2	STRENGTH	7

SKILLS
Athletics 4, Fighting 4, Subterfuge 3, Survival 3, Technology 2

TRAITS
Armour (Minor Trait): A partial Cyberman's body reduces damage by 5.
Cyborg: A partial Cyberman has his entire body replaced except for his head and internal organs.
Enslaved: Most partial Cybermen are conditioned to follow Cybermen orders.

STORY POINTS: 2-4

CYBER PLANNER

AWARENESS	3	PRESENCE	3
COORDINATION	3	RESOLVE	3
INGENUITY	6	STRENGTH	-

SKILLS
Convince 4, Knowledge 5, Marksman 3, Technology 5

TRAITS
Alien Appearance: The Cyber Planner looks like a computer.
Armour (Major): Most of the Cyber Planner's body is hardened, reducing damage inflicted on it by 10.
Cyborg
Fast Healing (major): The Cyber Planner's redundant systems quickly repair damage done.
Natural Weapon – Hypnosis: The Cyber Planner can hypnotise people at short range. He can also use this power to communicate orders to Cybermen or controlled humans.
Natural Weapon – Stun Weapon: Built into the Cyber Planner's wrist, stun weapons can knock a humanoid unconscious at short range – S/S/S.
Slow (Major): The Cyber Planner cannot move.

STORY POINTS: 6-8

⊙ DALEKS

The Second Doctor encountered the Daleks twice. In their first encounter, the Daleks were in a state of hibernation on the planet Vulcan. While these Daleks resembled the free-moving Daleks they appeared to need an external source of static electricity like the Daleks in the Doctor's first encounter with them on Skaro. As a Dalek is found near the TARDIS in the wilderness, however, it's likely that they only needed the external source until they had fully recharged.

The Daleks were at their craftiest on Vulcan. There they pretended to be eager servants of the colonists while playing factions against each other. Their ultimate aim was to steal enough power to run their factory and build a new Dalek army.

Later, the Doctor encountered them in a scheme that spanned three time zones. Frustrated at their continual defeats at the hands of the 'inferior' human race, the Daleks wanted to isolate the human factor. Rather than incorporate the human factor into themselves, however, the Daleks aimed to replace the human factor with the Dalek factor in humans. The Doctor succeeded in infusing a large number of Daleks with the human factor and a civil war erupted on Skaro between the modified Daleks and the unaltered Daleks.

The Doctor believed that this civil war would end with the extermination of the Dalek race (a belief which is later shattered when the Time Lords recruited him to stop the creation of the Daleks).

BLACK DALEK

The Black Dalek is somewhat misnamed, as it is a standard-coloured Dalek with a black dome. Black Daleks are the Imperial Guard and protect the Emperor Dalek from outside threats. Absent this distinction, Black Daleks are no stronger or weaker than a standard Dalek.

While the Doctor has seen Black Daleks of various paint schemes in leadership positions in his earlier and later incarnations, he only rarely encounters these elite guards.

HUMANISED DALEK

Humanised Daleks are those infused with the Human Factor, which seems to override Davros' genetic coding and enables Daleks to feel and think like humans (or, perhaps more appropriately, original Kaleds). Physically they are still Daleks and require a casing to move about and interact comfortably with others.

DALEK

This entry can be used for Black Daleks and Humanized Daleks as well.

AWARENESS	3	PRESENCE	4
COORDINATION	2	RESOLVE	4
INGENUITY	4	STRENGTH	7*

SKILLS
Convince 4, Fighting 4, Marksman 3, Medicine 3, Science 8, Subterfuge 3, Survival 4, Technology 8

TRAITS
Armour (Major Trait): The Dalekanium casing reduces damage by 10. This does reduce the Dalek's Coordination to 2 (already accommodated in the Attributes).

Cyborg

Environmental: Daleks are able to survive in the vacuum of space or underwater.

Fear Factor (3): Once you realise how deadly the Daleks are, they are terrifying, getting a +6 to rolls when actively scaring someone.

Flight: Daleks are able to fly. When hovering their Speed is effectively 1, when in open skies or space they have a Speed of 6. Note that Daleks rarely fly during the Second Doctor's adventures so this trait costs a story point to use.

Natural Weapon – Exterminator: The legendary Dalek weapon usually kills with a single shot – 4/L/L.

Technically Adept: Daleks are brilliant at using and adapting technology.

TECH LEVEL: 8   STORY POINTS: 5-8

*The Dalek mutant inside has different attributes when removed from the Dalekanium casing. Of course, movement outside of the armour is incredibly limited (Speed 1) and they do not usually survive very long. If the mutant is exposed at any time, damage inflicted to the Dalek may bypass the armour.

AWARENESS	3	PRESENCE	3
COORDINATION	3	RESOLVE	4
INGENUITY	4	STRENGTH	5

EMPEROR DALEK

The Emperor Dalek is a large (between two to three times the height of a regular Dalek), immobile Dalek that speaks with a booming, echoing voice. The casing of the Emperor Dalek is conical and contains no weapons or appendages; instead, it is hooked up to a large computer system through various tubes. Safe within his throne room in the Dalek City on Skaro, it doesn't occur to the Emperor Dalek that he might need to defend himself; he believes that his Black Dalek guard are sufficient. While the Seventh Doctor discovers that Davros becomes the Emperor, whether the Emperor Dalek that the Second Doctor meets is actually Davros is unknown. In any case, it's possible that this Emperor Dalek, like Davros, may have a mobile casing in reserve and perhaps uses this to escape destruction in the Dalek Civil War.

EMPEROR DALEK

AWARENESS	5	PRESENCE	8
COORDINATION	1	RESOLVE	5
INGENUITY	7	STRENGTH	10*

SKILLS
Convince 4, Knowledge 10, Science 8, Technology 8, Survival 4

TRAITS
Armour (Major Trait): The Dalekanium casing reduces damage by 15. This reduces the Emperor Dalek's Coordination by 3 (already reflected in the attributes).

Cyborg

Environmental: The Emperor Dalek's casing provides the standard Dalek immunities to environmental conditions. As the casing is attached to various cables, however, the Emperor Dalek has weak points that can be exploited until the Emperor Dalek disengages the cables and seals his shell.

Fear Factor (5): The Emperor Dalek commands respect and awe when met in his throne room. This initially gives him a +10 to scare characters, but this may be mitigated by the Dalek Emperor's inability to actually carry out any threats without the aid of other Daleks (dropping the Fear Factor to 1 after the initial encounter).

Scan: The Emperor Dalek is directly connected to the central computer system of the entire Dalek City. He literally knows all knowledge that the Daleks have accumulated.

Technically Adept: The Emperor Dalek, like all Daleks, is brilliant at using and adapting technology from other cultures.

TECH LEVEL: 9   STORY POINTS: 9

*The Dalek mutant inside has different attributes when removed from the Dalekanium casing. Of course, movement outside of the armour is incredibly limited (Speed 1) and they do not usually survive very long. If the mutant is exposed at any time, damage inflicted to the Dalek may bypass the armour.

AWARENESS	5	PRESENCE	7
COORDINATION	3	RESOLVE	5
INGENUITY	7	STRENGTH	5

◎ GREAT INTELLIGENCE

The Great Intelligence is a powerful being of mental energy that is trapped in another plane of existence. It desperately wants to attain physical form and needs living servants to achieve that goal. It is unknown what the Great Intelligence's true form is like beyond the sludgy foam seen emanating from a pyramid focus.

The Great Intelligence's prison is something of a mystery. It might be a true astral plane, able to be visited only by those that can send their minds into the plane, or it may actually be the space-time vortex. The fact that the Great Intelligence is able to manifest a web around the TARDIS while it is in the space-time vortex lends credence to the latter idea.

The Great Intelligence has a relatively straight forward method of operation. It waits until someone can get close enough to the barrier between the physical world and its own (astral projection is a good method) and it then possesses that person. The possessed person then starts construction on the pyramids needed to bring it into the physical world as well as create robots to ward off snooping investigators. The Great Intelligence needs to create two pyramids to enable it to manifest. If one of the pyramids is destroyed, the other is destroyed as well and the Great Intelligence has to start over elsewhere.

The Great Intelligence, true to its name, has great mental powers and is able to hypnotize people in its presence. It can also possess others, speaking through them with the voice of its initial possessed victim (this is likely a mental projection, as it doesn't modify the second victim's vocal chords). The Great Intelligence also appears to have a regenerative effect on his victim; he enabled one victim, already aged, to live for another 200 years. Unfortunately, such a long-lived victim tends to die from the strain and exhaustion after the Great Intelligence leaves him.

ROBOTIC SERVANTS

Once the Great Intelligence establishes control over a sentient humanoid, it gathers material to construct robotic servants. Such servants are designed to adequately perform physical tasks as well as act as a deterrent, so imposing forms are generally chosen. The Great Intelligence is also limited by the technologies available to it. While the Great Intelligence can certainly improve upon the local technology to suit its interest, such efforts are time-consuming and emotionally draining.

GREAT INTELLIGENCE

AWARENESS	3	PRESENCE	4
COORDINATION	0	RESOLVE	5
INGENUITY	7	STRENGTH	0

SKILLS
Convince 4, Craft 3, Knowledge 4, Science 4, Subterfuge 5, Technology 6

TRAITS
Alien

Boffin: The Great Intelligence is adept at creating items impossible to conceive of using the current technology of the period. It is capable of jiggery-pokery.

Fear Factor (2): People are uncomfortable when nearing the presence of the Great Intelligence and it gets a +4 to rolls to make someone avoid approaching it.

Hypnosis (Special): The Great Intelligence is so adept at hypnotizing others that it effectively possesses them as well as its initial victim. It can perform the lesser forms of hypnosis as well.

Immortal (Major): The Great Intelligence is an extra-dimensional creature of pure mental energy. It doesn't age nor does it seem able to be killed., although the Doctor claims that he could have drained it.

Photographic Memory: As a being of psychic energy the Great Intelligence may instantly recall anything it has experienced.

Psychic: The Great Intelligence gains a +4 bonus to see into the minds of others and resisting mind reading or psychic possession.

Psychic Training: The Great Intelligence is adept at thwarting psychic attacks against it and gains a +2 modifier on Resolve rolls when trying to resist psychic attack or deception.

Technically Adept: The Great Intelligence gets a +2 on Technology rolls to adapt local technology for its own use.

Telekinesis: The Great Intelligence has the power to move things with its mind. It has a strength equal to its Resolve.

Telepathy: The Great Intelligence can speak into the minds of others. The voice manifested is usually that of its host, even if it is 'speaking' through another hypnotised victim.

Time Traveller: The Great Intelligence can adapt and manipulate the local technology for its own ends.

TECH LEVEL: 8   STORY POINTS: 12

The Great Intelligence uses the mind of the servant it has contacted to suggest an appropriately imposing form for its robotic servants. For less advanced cultures, these tend to be fearsome creatures of myth and legend, so that would-be investigators will be frightened by their appearance and realize that they can't negotiate with them.

After taking control of a Tibetan lama in 1935, the Great Intelligence constructed robotic servants in the form of Yeti, as this was an imposing mythological creature that struck fear in the local population. The Great Intelligence reserved its energy in a future plot by streamlining its old design, creating a new army of smaller Yeti that plagued the London Underground with web guns.

The core of every robotic servant is a small sphere that is capable of independent action. When activated, these spheres find the closest available robotic servant and interface with it, providing power for the creature. The Great Intelligence works through the spheres, often using visual aids (such as a map and figurines) to ease its mental strain when issuing commands.

It appears that robotic servants are constructed in such a way that, if the Great Intelligence exerts its will, they can modify their physical appearance somewhat. At least one of the Tibetan Yeti instantly transforms into the slimmer 'Mark II' Yeti after the control sphere re-establishes contact with the Great Intelligence.

Mark I Yeti
The Mark I Yeti is a tall, wide-hipped shaggy humanoid. While based on the legend of the Yeti, the robotic yeti is actually quite different from the genuine article.

Mark II Yeti
Mark II Yetis are a bit taller and certainly slimmer than the previous model, with large glowing eyes and bigger claws. Mark II Yeti carry web guns.

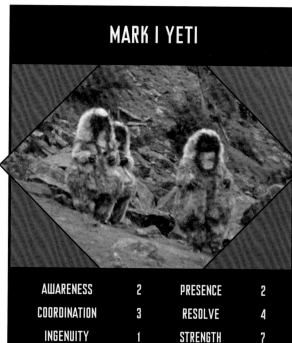

MARK I YETI

AWARENESS	2	PRESENCE	2
COORDINATION	3	RESOLVE	4
INGENUITY	1	STRENGTH	7

SKILLS
Athletics 4, Fighting 4

TRAITS
Alien Appearance: Yetis are designed to look like large shaggy humanoids.
Alien Senses: Yetis can see in the dark.
Armour (Major): The Yeti is a robot with an armoured body beneath its fur that can stop bullets. It offers 8 points of protection and reduces the Yeti's Coordination by one. The reduction is already reflected in the Attribute number.
Enslaved: The Yetis are under the control of the Great Intelligence and can't act on their own. When not given orders, a Yeti simply stands still.
Fear Factor (3): Yetis are pretty scary and gain a +6 to rolls to actively scare someone.
Natural Weapon (Claws): A Yeti has sharp claws that do 4/9/13 damage when attacking foes.
Robot

STORY POINTS: 3-4

MARK II YETI

AWARENESS	2	PRESENCE	2
COORDINATION	4	RESOLVE	4
INGENUITY	1	STRENGTH	6

SKILLS
Athletics 4, Fighting 4, Marksman 3

TRAITS
Alien Appearance: Yeti are designed to look like large shaggy humanoids with glowing eyes.
Alien Senses: Yeti can see in the dark.
Armour (Major): The Yeti is a robot with an armoured body beneath its fur that can stop bullets. It offers 8 points of protection and reduces the Yeti's Coordination by one. The reduction is already reflected in the Attribute number.
Enslaved: The Yeti are under the control of the Great Intelligence and can't act on their own. When not given orders, a Yeti simply stands still.
Fear Factor (3): Yetis are pretty scary and gain a +6 to rolls to actively scare someone.
Natural Weapon (Claws): A Yeti has sharp claws that do 4/8/12 damage when attacking foes.
Robot

WEAPONS: Web Gun - The Yeti carries a web gun that can shoot webs of lethal energy. (4/L/L)

STORY POINTS: 3-4

YETI COMMAND UNIT
This handheld device allows the user to issue commands to a control sphere programmed to accept them.

Traits: Possess (Yeti with reconfigured control sphere)
Cost: 3 Story points

YETI CONTROL SPHERE
This device is the heart of a robot Yeti. Without it, the Yeti can't move. The control spheres are programmed to seek out the nearest Yeti and pop inside.

Traits: Scan (look for Yeti)
Cost: 1 Story Point

YETI CONTROL UNIT
This handheld device allows the user to shut down Yeti control spheres at short range. It does not allow the wearer to control the sphere.

Traits: This device effectively acts as a stunning effect (S/S/S) on nearby Yetis.
Cost: 1 Story Point

TALK ABOUT AN ACHILLES' HEEL...

In spite of their ferocity, both types of Yeti have a remarkably easily exploitable weakness; their control spheres can be removed simply by lifting a flap and pulling them out. Given that the Yeti have a tendency to stand immobile until ordered to do something, all you need to do is observe from the shadows, wait until a Yeti stops moving, sneak up to it, and pop out the control sphere. While this doesn't always work (sometimes the Yeti is simply on guard duty), it works often enough that players will try it.

This weakness seems a bit odd when you take into consideration that a Mark I Yeti morphed into a Mark II. If the Yetis are capable of this, then why not 'morph' an opening for the sphere and seal it up once the control sphere is inside? One possible answer is that the control sphere needs to be relatively exposed in order to receive orders from the Great Intelligence.

Gamemasters should decide if this weakness works as-is or if the control spheres are protected but easily accessed by Characters with appropriate equipment. For example, perhaps the sonic screwdriver can pop the hatch open or a boffin can use a little jiggery-pokery to create a method of extraction. Perhaps a time agent with a vortex manipulator can take a Yeti through time, severing its connection to the Great Intelligence and causing its control sphere to explode (which risks damage to the time agent and the vortex manipulator as well).

ICE WARRIORS

The Ice Warriors (or, more properly, Martians) come from the fourth planet in the solar system. They are an ancient race whose civilisation developed when Mars was still a wet, snowy world. While a martial race, Ice Warrior civilisation was once considered honourable and noble. Unfortunately, they never explored much outside the solar system and when Mars started to die the Ice Warriors suddenly had nowhere to go.

At least one militaristic faction of Ice Warriors decided to make a new home on Earth in the 21st century. A vanguard took control of the Travel Mat relay on the moon and used it to send Martian spores to Earth. These spores would transform the Earth's atmosphere into something more suitable for Martians while exterminating the human population. Thanks to the Second Doctor's intervention, the spore seeds were destroyed and the Ice Warrior invasion fleet was sent into the gravitational pull of the sun.

Several centuries into the future, an Ice Warrior ship and crew are excavated during an attempt to hold back a new Ice Age. Unfortunately, this group of militaristic Ice Warriors believe that the humans are out to destroy them and won't listen to reason. Further complicating matters is the fact that Mars is now a dead world. As the Ice Warriors plan to dismantle a device that the humans need to hold back the glacial advance threatening all of Earth, the Second Doctor ensures that they are destroyed and the world saved.

While 'Ice Warrior' is not the Martians' proper designation, it's worth noting that only soldiers have been encountered. In spite of their appearance the Ice Warriors are cyborgs, incorporating technology into their armoured carapaces. The Second Doctor has encountered two types of Ice Warrior. Rank-and-file Ice Warriors wear large, bulky armour suits while officers wear slimmer carapaces. Both types have sonic weapons built into their forearms. All Ice Warriors have difficulty in Earth-like environments which makes them move slowly and speak in harsh whispers. They do not have such difficulties in Martian-like environments, although their voices still have a natural rasp.

ICE LORDS

Ice Lords are higher ranking Ice Warriors. They tend to have slimmer armour and a different-shaped helmet. One such Ice Lord is Slaar, whose rank is never mentioned but he obviously commands the Ice Warriors on the moon. Another Ice Lord is the Grand Marshall, who wears a more ornate version of the Ice Lord helmet.

ICE WARRIOR

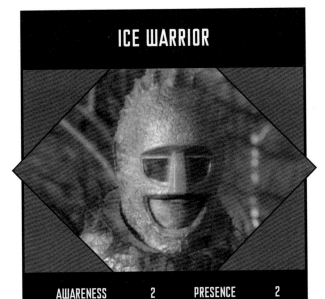

AWARENESS	2	PRESENCE	2
COORDINATION	1	RESOLVE	3
INGENUITY	2	STRENGTH	5

SKILLS
Fighting 4, Marksman 3, Survival 3

TRAITS
Alien
Alien Appearance: Ice Warriors appear to be reptilian humanoids.
Armour (Major): Ice Warriors wear a bio-armour that resembles a carapace or shell. This armour reduces damage taken by 10. It also slows their coordination; in their native atmosphere an Ice Warrior has his Coordination lowered by 1. In Earth-like atmospheres his Coordination is lowered by 2 (the attribute score already takes an Earth-like atmosphere into account).
Cyborg
Natural Weapon (Sonic Gun): Ice Warriors have a sonic gun attached to their forearms. These seem to be fired by mental command and are thus part of the armor. – 4/L/L
Slow (Minor): An Ice Warrior's speed is halved in Earth-like environments.
Weakness (Major): An Ice Warrior prefers cold weather and can't stand intense heat. An Ice Warrior gets a -2 to all actions when the temperature rises to 32°C and takes 4 levels of attribute damage as the temperature gets closer to 100°C.

TECH LEVEL: 6   STORY POINTS: 3-4

ICE LORD

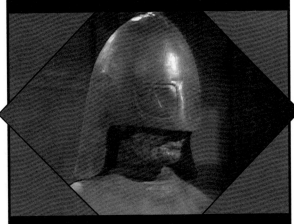

AWARENESS	2	PRESENCE	4
COORDINATION	2	RESOLVE	3
INGENUITY	3	STRENGTH	4

SKILLS
Convince 4, Fighting 2, Knowledge 3, Marksman 3, Survival 3

TRAITS
Alien
Alien Appearance: Looks like a reptilian human.
Armour (Minor): Ice Lords wear a slimmer version of Ice Warrior bio-armour. This armour reduces damage taken by 5. Wearing the armour in Earth-like atmospheres lowers his Coordination by 1 (the attribute score already takes an Earth-like atmosphere into account).
Cyborg
Menacing: An Ice Lord gets a +2 bonus on attempts to get people to do what he wants. Characters he has menaced also get a +2 to resist attempts by others to act against him.
Natural Weapon (Sonic Gun): Ice Lords have a sonic gun attached to their forearms. These seem to be fired by mental command and are thus part of the armour. – 4/L/L
Slow (Minor): An Ice Lord's speed is halved in Earth-like environments.
Weakness (Major): Ice Lords prefers the cold and can't stand intense heat. An Ice Lord gets a -2 to all actions when the temperature rises to 32°C and takes 4 levels of attribute damage as the temperature rises to 100°C.

TECH LEVEL: 6   STORY POINTS: 6-8

CHAPTER FOUR:
DESIGNING SECOND DOCTOR ADVENTURES

'Our lives are different from anybody else's. That's the exciting thing. Nobody in the universe can do what we're doing!'

Chapter 7 of the **Gamemaster's Guide** offers general advice on running adventures. This chapter focuses on the adventures of the Second Doctor and how you can create and run adventures that evoke the spirit of his era.

One advantage that a Gamemaster has when running games set in this era is that it's less likely that players will know a lot about the adventures of the Second Doctor. This means that you can probably play through most of the Second Doctor's adventures and not have to worry too much about spoilers. Information and advice on running the Second Doctor's adventures as your own are given in the following chapters. Of course, you'll want to design original adventures eventually, so let's look at some of the features of the Second Doctor's adventures.

ADVENTURE LENGTH AND PACING

The Second Doctor's adventures were often lengthy, developing over a period of time and through a number of stages of investigation. Here are some points to consider when designing your own Second Doctor adventures:

- **Plot adventures as multi-parters** – give your plot room to breathe, with numerous twists and turns. Red herrings, chases, captures and escapes can all be used to keep a longer adventure action-packed and engaging.

- **Keep the true villain concealed for a session or two** – menace the players with the effects of the villain's plans before they can identify the cause. Maintain the mystery, and make them investigate! For example, the time travellers may be menaced by space pirates in the first two sessions, only for it to be revealed at the end of session three that the space pirates are working for the Dominators.

THE LOST ADVENTURES

Usually when planning to run a *Doctor Who: Adventures in Time and Space* campaign based on a particular Doctor, the best preparation you can do is to sit down and watch a few of that Doctor's adventures. With the Second Doctor, however, most of his early adventures (and the penultimate adventure) are missing. None of his adventures with Ben and Polly nor his two encounters with the Daleks can be seen in full (the odd episode exists, but there are no full stories).

Fear not, however. The audio recordings of the missing adventures are available as well as novelizations. The BBC website contains photo-novels too!

- **Making friends** – focus some of the first session of an adventure on interaction between the players and non-player characters. The more they get to know these characters, the more they will care what happens to them over the course of the adventure.

- **Cliff-hanger endings** – leave your players excited about the next session. Cliff-hangers are also used at the end of a Second Doctor adventure to whet the appetite for the following adventure. It can be difficult to plot cliff-hangers for an adventure because the Players often go in directions that the Gamemaster hasn't considered, or work out the plot quicker than anticipated. It's a good idea to think of a number of potential cliff-hanger situations and tailor one of those to the current situation as you get to the end of your game session.

CAMPAIGN ARCS OR LACK THEREOF

Unlike the Doctor's more recent adventures, those of his second incarnation tended to be standalone adventures; there are no greater story arcs that offer hints at an epic finale (although ironically the Second Doctor ends his adventures with perhaps the most epic of all endings).

This isn't to say that there aren't some things revisited during the Second Doctor's adventures. The Second Doctor gives us details of his life throughout his adventures; he starts as a different person, later gives his age in centuries, and finally reveals that he is a Time Lord. Professor Travers provides a link to three adventures (and the Great Intelligence links two of those) and the final of these leads to the

creation of UNIT. If you'd like to add campaign arcs to your adventures then the **Gamemaster's Guide** provides good advice on doing so.

SECOND DOCTOR THEMES

There are a number of elements that are common to several Second Doctor adventures. This section addresses some themes that you may wish to incorporate into your own Second Doctor adventures. While you certainly wouldn't want to cram everything here into each adventure, using one or two of these elements in a single adventure should help you capture the feel of a Second Doctor adventure.

EVIL MUST BE FOUGHT

The Second Doctor is a moral crusader against evil, so it is easy to get the Second Doctor involved – just present a situation that needs solving. When using characters other than the (Second) Doctor and companions, make sure that they have a strong moral imperative to fight evil if you wish to include this theme.

ABSENT CHARACTERS

One real-world concern with multiple-session adventures is dealing with absent players. If a player can't make it to a particular session that their character would be involved in, it can be a problem.

Fortunately, the Second Doctor's adventures provide plenty of examples for dealing with this issue. They could be incapacitated (due to injury or illness), captured or controlled by the enemy. They could be separated from the rest of the group until the next session. Or they could fall victim to mind control, where the character is controlled by the Gamemaster because he's been taken over by an evil personality.

There are a few things to keep in mind when using this technique. First, the absent character should have a critical scene when he returns that offers the party a clue or other information to help the adventure along. This will aid the player in reintegrating into the adventure after missing a session's worth of material. Second, if the absent player suffers any negative impact from actions that took place in their absence, they should be granted a few story points.

CHAPTER FOUR: DESIGNING SECOND DOCTOR ADVENTURES

While evil comes in many forms, the most common type of evil in Second Doctor adventures is the Monster of the Week. While some monsters have potentially sympathetic back stories (arguably the Chameleons, the Cybermen, and the Ice Warriors are simply dying races concerned with survival), they are generally portrayed as galactic thugs. Their back stories exist to provide motivation for the assault.

For example, the crew of the Moonbase in 2070 can't believe that they are being attacked by Cybermen as all of the Cybermen were destroyed (presumably when Mondas exploded), yet they reappear with a sleeker redesign and more powerful than ever. These new Cybermen never mention where they've come from nor does the Doctor inquire about it. Within the context of the adventure, it doesn't matter. The Cybermen have come to threaten the Earth and the Doctor needs to stop them.

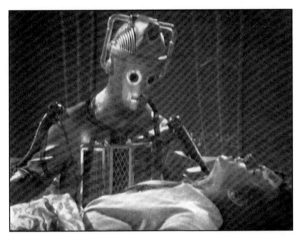

What all this means is that you don't have to get wrapped up in explanations to have a cracking adventure in the mould of the Second Doctor's era. Just pick an interesting monster (or design your own), drop it into one of the adventure archetypes outlined below, and challenge your group to defeat it.

UNRELIABLE TARDIS

The TARDIS is un-steerable by the Second Doctor and frequently breaks down. The Doctor can't rely on using it for short jumps (which is why he pilots an experimental rocket when the Ice Warriors take over the Moonbase, rather than hop in the TARDIS and go to the moon) so the TARDIS is effectively not a gadget except as a laboratory or storage cabinet.

If your players are using a future Doctor, another Time Lord, or an alternative group, then you'll need to ensure that the characters don't have access to a time-space capsule during an adventure. The reason may be mechanical (perhaps Time Rings use up too much power to jump around within an adventure) or imposed (you spend story points to prevent the characters from using it or, even better, grant them story points for staying true to the spirit!).

A WORLD GOVERNMENT

The mid to late 20th century saw the rise of international power blocs. The largest of these was the United Nations. Europe was divided between NATO and the Warsaw Pact and some European nations began working toward a common market and, eventually, a common currency. It seemed logical that, as time marched onward and the Cold War thawed, a true world government might emerge from the United Nations.

Corporations and governments often work together in Second Doctor futuristic stories. The Euro Sea Gas Corporation has an ambassador from the Netherlands as well as the authority to call a Royal Air Force strike on its own rigs. Salamander has his own company in the early 21st century that can predict and control the weather.

By Salamander's time in the early 21st century the United Nations has been superseded by the stronger World Zones Organisation (probably an evolution of the Eurozone applied globally). The world is divided into zones that are drawn along regional lines. For the rest of the 21st century the WZO evolves into a true world government, although national identities remain in place. So too would seem the idea of zones, as many international crews that the Doctor encounters seem primarily comprised of Western Europeans. This new world government reverts to the United Nations moniker for a while before being referred to as simply Earth Government in the decades prior to the Dalek invasion.

WHERE ARE THE SUPERPOWERS IN THE FUTURE?

While one might expect American, Chinese, Indian, and Russian representation, international teams in the future of the Second Doctor are mostly represented by (Western) Europeans.

Using the World Zones Organisation as a blueprint, it's possible that future projects are organised along regional lines. For example, the Space Wheel could be primarily staffed from the European Zone, while others are staffed by the North American Zone, the East Asian Zone, the Mediterranean Zone, the Southern African Zone, etc. There is occasional cross-pollination, but with a united government treating each zone equally there's less incentive to move.

Alternatively, it's probable that the powerful nations of today simply aren't as powerful in the future. In the mid-1980s Japan was seen as an economic giant, only to have its economy collapse in the 1990s. No one would have foreseen the collapse of the Soviet Union either (St. Petersburg is called Leningrad on the Travel Mat network). Given that America, China, and Russia have veto powers in the United Nations, there would need to be a dramatic political and economic shift for any of them to lose that power to a united world government.

ARMS CONTROL

A recurring theme for Second Doctor adventures in the future is the lack of weaponry. Key installations are often left unguarded without a security officer in sight. Even when weapons are introduced, they tend to have little effect on the enemy. In contrast to the victims, the enemy is usually well-armed and a lethal show of force is often enough to prompt surrender.

The Moonbase is a good example. By 2070, humans are well aware of aliens, if only because of the Cybermen invasion of 1986 (to say nothing of the earlier Cybermen invasions, the Yeti in the London sewers, or the string of alien invasions in the 1970s). Yet the Gravitron, which is sitting out on the Moon and is so sensitive that even a few minutes of misuse could cause massive catastrophes on Earth, is unprotected. Worse, the attacking Cybermen are worried about reinforcements from Earth, meaning that Earth weaponry at that time is capable of harming Cybermen.

However, just because there is a scarcity of conventional weapons it doesn't mean that the characters can't take direct action – it's just that they will have to use their ingenuity to cobble together something useful from the materials at hand. Realising that a venting system, gravity control, or solar power relay can be used as a weapon is perfectly in keeping with the Second Doctor era. Generally speaking, if a violent solution is necessary, then the means to that end should be within the Characters' grasp, often just under their noses.

When scripting Second Doctor adventures you'll want to take this into account, especially since your players will likely go looking for them. Even sensitive installations don't have weapons hanging on the walls and if security is armed, then they're likely going to be used against the Characters at some point. A good **Doctor Who: Adventures in Time and Space** adventure requires the Characters to use their wits, not have them running through corridors like space marines gunning down every Dominator in sight.

OVERPOPULATION AND RESOURCE MANAGEMENT

One easy way to design a futuristic adventure is to involve the theme of overpopulation. During the 1960s there was a growing awareness of the dangers of world overpopulation (culminating with the 1971 publication of **The Population Bomb** by Paul Ehrlich) and many of the Doctor's near future adventures touched on it. Various methods are employed, from alternative food sources to weather manipulation to instant travel to artificial food. Simply select a method to control overpopulation and an agency to run it, then create an enemy that either wants to control or disrupt the method chosen.

RECURRING LOCATIONS

The Doctor returns to two places in particular during his travels. He visits the Moonbase several times over the course of the 21st century (notably in *The Moonbase* and *Seeds of Death*, and both adventures tie in with the themes of ecological collapse and humanity's 'teething trouble' in the 21st century). He also visits the 1960s multiple times, and repeatedly encounters first Professor Travers (*The Abominable Snowman*, *The Web of Fear* and, to a lesser extent, *The Invasion*) and later the Brigadier and UNIT. Repeated visits to the same place or group of people give a nice sense of stability and continuity to a game – and give a baseline to compare against truly weird adventures, like *The Mind Robber.*

NATURE'S RAGE

Another recurring theme in the Second Doctor's adventures is the wrath of nature, which is often tied to the solutions of overpopulation and resource management. Mankind has so enforced its will on nature that nature rebels, often with catastrophic effects, for example the new Ice Age brought about by the destruction of all plant life on Earth. This provides a great challenge to player characters in avoiding the catastrophe while solving the adventure. Ironically it is usually the continued application of technology, or humanity continuing to assert its dominance, which saves the day.

TRICKY SPACE TRAVEL

Space travel is a dangerous business during the times and places visited by the Second Doctor in the course of his adventures. Space ships (or rockets) have to plot exact courses or risk being caught in the gravitational pull of the sun, resulting in a slow but inevitable death. Space ships are generally short on provisions as well and even a minor detour from the anticipated schedule risks running out of food. Worse, most space ships lack failsafe mechanisms or other means of staying on course if a beacon transmitter is disabled or changed.

Quite a few of the Second Doctor's adventures involve a rocket (or even entire battle fleets) being lost to the sun because of a false signal or other means of misdirection. Sometimes it's the badly needed cavalry that gets flung into the sun, at other times it's the enemy's invasion force. When designing a futuristic adventure you'll certainly want to consider adding the threat of a roasting death if a space ship misses its mark and hurtles toward its doom.

Space flight is considered so inefficient and dangerous that humans forsake space ships and space exploration in the latter part of the 21st century altogether once T-Mat technology is installed. When the Ice Warriors take over the T-Mat lunar station the Doctor and his allies are forced to cobble together an experimental rocket that was being built in a retired engineer's spare time. After the threat is over there is a debate over rebuilding rockets, one in which rockets ultimately win and humanity spreads to the edge of the solar system and beyond.

ELECTRONIC SCIENCE FICTION

There seems to be a theme in futuristic Second Doctor adventures that any advanced technology manifests itself as electronic or mechanical in nature. As an example, while the Great Intelligence is a being of pure astral energy, the Yetis and control spheres are mechanical and electronic devices. Other forms of advanced technology, such as psychic power or bio-technology, are either absent or, as in the case of the Krotons, indistinguishable (while they are crystalline entities, both the Krotons and the Dynatrope have a mechanical appearance). This approach means that the Doctor, or any other bright scientist, can deduce a futuristic device's inner workings and modify it with existing technology. While this is a characteristic of the Boffin trait, non-Boffin characters can often recognise advanced technology because it uses familiar, if slightly more advanced, components.

SCIENCE WIZARDS

Another staple of the Second Doctor's adventures is the concept of scientists and technicians as generalists, rather than specialists in a particular field. For example, while Professor Eldred is a rocket scientist, he'd been offered a high position within the T-Mat network. Similarly, the Doctor thinks that Professor Travers, and later Professor Watkins, would be able to fix some parts of his TARDIS.

While areas of expertise are optional in **Doctor Who: Adventures in Time and Space**, you should be careful to avoid having every scientist that the characters meet be capable of solving all scientific problems. That's the player characters' job! Related to the scientific wizard is scientific wizardry, also known as jiggery-pokery. Science can perform feats that seem magical and are often the solution to many adventures. Examples include Cocktail Polly, the Human Factor, and the Cerebration Mentor.

TRUST THE COMPUTER

Characters in the Second Doctor's 21st century and beyond seem to place a high value and trust in computers and logic. In addition to running virtually all systems and piloting all vehicles (a situation not all that much different from our own early 21st century), computers tend to make many decisions for their operators and leaders (or at least dissuade them from taking certain actions). It can even be argued that the World Computer rules the Earth during the New Ice Age.

This almost-worship of computers leads to new teaching techniques and philosophies that place logic above all else. Zoe is an early example of a woman whose been given intensive logical training, as she appears to be little more than a humanoid computer to her older co-workers. This logical

philosophy never quite finds mass acceptance as the Brotherhood of Logicians a few centuries later is still considered a small and distinct group (and, due to their frustration, the Brotherhood futilely turns to the Cybermen for help).

MIND CONTROL

A few of the Doctor's adventures involve brainwashed characters. In most of these cases, the mind control is a symbol of authority versus individualism, with joining authority leading to very bad consequences. The Cybermen brainwash humans to use the Gravitron to destroy the Earth as well as invade the Space Wheel, the Macra enslave a human colony to feed themselves, and the Seaweed Creature controls humans to spread its influence over the world.

Mind control is an effective technique, as it makes everyone a suspect. Interestingly, most forms of mind control in the Second Doctor's adventures tend to mute a victim's personality, making them appear somewhat more stiff and prone to speak in monotone. This surprisingly tends to go unnoticed until the mind-controlled victim actually does something suspicious. A notable exception is the Dalek mind control device, which fails to function properly (likely due to shortcomings in their knowledge of the humanity).

THE MEGALOMANIAC

Several of the Second Doctor's most memorable adversaries are the megalomaniacs, villains with the goal of enforcing their will on a world (inspired, no doubt, by the villains of a certain British secret agent). Megalomaniacs typically have a position of influence and forge alliances of convenience. The megalomaniac will turn on his allies as soon as he no longer needs them. Megalomaniacs often have an air of manifest destiny about them and are quick to anger when challenged.

⊙ ADVENTURE STRUCTURE

Most of the Second Doctor's adventures follow one of five structures: the base under siege, the historical, the alien invasion, insatiable curiosity, or hooked. Of these, the base under siege is the most common, while the pure historical was only used once. Using one of these structures will aid you in crafting a Second Doctor adventure.

THE BASE UNDER SIEGE

Many of the Second Doctor's adventures involve a base under siege. The characters arrive at a relatively isolated location and help the locals fight off an attack from hostile aliens. The following elements are keys to designing a good base under siege adventure.

First, the base of operations needs to be relatively isolated. This could be an underwater research station, a moon base, a remote monastery, or a space vessel. The base's staff members are forced to confront the threat if they are to survive. The base typically has a claustrophobic feel with a relatively small staff.

Second, there must be a threat that can overcome the defences of the base. This threat is usually a small alien taskforce that needs to secure the base as part of a greater plan. Taking the base is the lynchpin of the aliens' plan and overcoming the threat virtually assures that the greater plan is defeated as well.

Third, the base's staff should be unable to defeat the threat on their own. There are many reasons for this but two of the most common are that the aliens are in a stronger position or they are working with a mole within the base (usually it's a combination of both). The mole usually aids in disabling the base's defences. If the base is large enough then the aliens might start taking it section-by-section, pushing the characters back until they have nowhere left to run.

Fourth, the characters are sealed within the base. The Doctor often willingly seals himself in rather than flee in the TARDIS, but at other times it's because the Doctor and Companions are physically separated from the TARDIS and can't reach it until the threat is neutralized. In many cases the Doctor and Companions are initially confined as they tend to show up unannounced as the trouble begins.

Fifth, there should be a mystery involved. The aliens rarely show up and make their presence known, as the base defences generally need to be weakened before they begin their assault. Instead, they use clandestine tactics that keep the characters guessing as to their true identity. It is the characters' investigation of this mystery that forces the aliens to reveal themselves.

Sixth, while the aliens should be immune to conventional assaults (unless you're running a UNIT campaign) the means to defeat them must be available within the base. The actions of the aliens themselves might tip the characters off as to their weakness.

As the Doctor's adventures prove, the base under siege scenario can be re-run several times just by altering a few elements. Simply pick a place, add a threat, come up with a motive and you're good to go.

THE HISTORICAL

While the Second Doctor only had one purely historical Earth adventure (i.e. no alien involvement), this adventure reflected aspects of him that were rarely seen. The Doctor adopted a number of aliases in attempts to save his companions and ensure that history remained on course. The following steps can help to create an historical adventure along the same lines.

First, choose a historical era where there is an ongoing conflict, as it gives the natives a reason to suspect and accuse the characters of working for the other side. Civil wars are a good choice, as neighbours could support different sides, heightening the paranoia.

Second, put the characters in a situation that they need to resolve before they can leave. In the Doctor's case, it is the capture of Ben, Jamie, and himself during the Second Jacobite Rebellion. Another good plot to use is the need to fix history, especially if the change is caused by the presence of the characters themselves.

Third, ensure that the characters understand that they cannot change history and need to limit their impact. Disguises, cover stories, or other clever notions can throw off suspicion from natives that might use the character's knowledge of the future for twisted ends.

Fourth, allow the characters to foil a local plot. In the process of rescuing Ben and Jamie, the Doctor and Polly foil a slave trader's plan to ship Scotsmen to the West Indies. This should not affect the time stream and give the players some satisfaction that their efforts weren't in vain.

Canny players might ignore such a subplot, as history will take care of it. In this case, you could have the Doctor (or other lead character) remind his friends that sometimes their actions matter (as the Fourth Doctor did with Sarah while fighting Sutekh) and use his Feel the Turn of the Universe trait to inform them that they do need to fix something before leaving.

If you are using the Second Doctor, ensure that his player has plenty of opportunities to disguise himself

and adopt foreign accents. He's been known to adopt the guise of a German Doctor, an old woman, an English soldier, and an Atlantean street musician (although his adoption of shaded spectacles is a bit surprising in that instance).

A variant of the historical is the alien historical, in which an alien element is introduced. This is most prominently seen during the Doctor's adventure with the Yeti in Tibet. Characters are generally more free to act in such adventures, as their goal is to prevent the aliens from disrupting history rather than changing it themselves.

THE ALIEN INVASION

This category is similar to the base under siege but less claustrophobic. The aliens' goals may vary; while the Daleks invaded England in 1866, they did not want to conquer the Earth but simply lay a trap for the Second Doctor. The Chameleons come to Earth to kidnap 50,000 young people to assume their identities. The Cybermen...well the Cybermen actually do want to invade and conquer Earth. The Krotons are a special case, as they've already invaded and enslaved the local population.

For an invasion, first you need an alien. Recurring aliens are good choices as the characters already have a reason to defeat them. Original aliens are also good choices if you want to give your players a dilemma over whether the new aliens are friends or foes.

Second, you need a plan. What do the aliens want and how do they plan to get it? During the Second Doctor's adventures the aliens were rarely on the verge of a full-scale invasion; like the base under siege they planned to use clandestine methods to achieve their goals. The Cybermen use subterfuge to conquer Earth because they aren't strong enough to take it by force. The Dominators simply want to blow Dulkis up for fuel.

Third, you need stakes. What happens if the aliens win? Are large numbers of people affected? Could a world be destroyed?

Fourth, you need a resolution. Do the characters need to battle the aliens directly or is there another way to defeat them? Many aliens have weaknesses that can be exploited or can be tricked into destroying themselves. Unless you're running a UNIT campaign, the answer shouldn't be to go in with guns blazing.

INSATIABLE CURIOSITY

Occasionally the TARDIS deposits the Second Doctor and his companions into an interesting situation and the Doctor refuses to leave until he fixes the problem. He doesn't need to get involved, but he does simply because it's the right thing to do, whether to inform Gatwick airport authorities about alien involvement, to discover why a plague is affecting the crew of the Moonbase, or to determine why the Krotons are helping and killing the Gonds.

This is sometimes thought of as a lazy hook because you're throwing the characters into the adventure's path and hope they bite. Some players may resent this approach, particularly if their characters aren't normally the type to bite, so take your players and characters into account when using it.

For the Doctor, alien involvement is usually a key element in attracting his attention. Alien in this case includes any person or creature not of the culture that they are affecting. This includes the Macra controlling a human colony (technically the humans are the aliens) and the Seaweed Creature from the depths of the sea. Aliens generally notice when the status quo is threatened and the characters may soon find themselves targets of aliens that wish them to go away and leave things as they are, escalating to lethal force if the characters don't take the hint.

Also, the characters generally have to alert the victims that they are being victimised. In the case of the Chameleons and the Macra, the affected victims are unaware of their existence. In the case of the Krotons, the victims see the aliens as friends and can't comprehend why the Krotons would want to do them harm. In almost every case, there's a victim or victims that will oppose and undermine the characters as well as sympathetic victims that will help them.

HOOKED

There are some adventures where the Second Doctor is baited or forced to participate. The Master of the Land of Fiction seemingly destroys the TARDIS so that the Doctor will take his place, while the Daleks bait the Doctor with temporal anachronisms and the Human Factor so that they can get him to isolate the Dalek Factor for them. The Great Intelligence ensnares the TARDIS in the hopes of capturing the Doctor and draining his mind.

In a hooked adventure, the enemy must have a reason for baiting the Doctor (or other time travellers). Generally this is because the Doctor has something unique that the enemy wants, usually his own mind. Once the characters are hooked, they cannot escape until they face the enemy and figure out a way to thwart him or her.

The characters usually remain free long enough to determine the nature of the enemy while dealing with the enemy's minions. During this time the enemy does all he or she can to catch the time travellers while they discover ways to defeat the enemy.

A common trick is for the enemy to actually want the characters to succeed, or at least allow them to believe that they are succeeding. In such cases you'll want to give the players a chance to figure out that they've been duped in the eleventh hour and give them a chance to turn the tables.

CHAPTER FIVE: THE SECOND DOCTOR'S ADVENTURES,
THE POWER OF THE DALEKS, THE HIGHLANDERS, THE UNDERWATER MENACE

'Well I don't think we're...quite where I expected, but never mind, this looks very interesting'.

While the previous chapter described many of the elements found in Second Doctor adventures, this chapter focuses on his actual adventures, from his first regeneration to his trial at the hands of the Time Lords. The adventures are listed in relative chronological order (from the perspective of the Doctor's timeline). Much care is given to playing or even re-skinning these adventures, making them useful for both players who aren't familiar with the Doctor's past exploits and those who've been peeking in his 500-year diary.

NOW IS THEN; DOES IT MATTER?

Some of the Second Doctor's adventures take place in our recent past, the present, or the near future. However, the Earth's politics and technological developments are different from those he experienced. This presents Gamemasters and players with a decision to make – do you want to play authentically in the Second Doctor's era, or do you want to set the same adventures within the context of the world as it is now?

Upgrade 2.1

Updating the setting of the Second Doctor's Earth-bound adventures requires some work in advance of the game, to adjust the details so that the story works in today's context. This could involve changing names of countries or organisations, and thinking about how our technological advances could affect the resolution of the adventure. The mobile phone alone has revolutionised our personal communications. There are more details on this in the description of each of the Second Doctor's adventures, in the following chapters.

Once that work is done, however, your games will be much easier to run. Everyone will be on the same page with regards to the setting, and there's no risk of arguments breaking out over the availability of GPS.

Keeping it real

Playing the Second Doctor's adventures as he experienced them is the most nostalgically satisfying approach, and also means that the Gamemaster doesn't have to do as much work to adapt the adventures for his or her players. The hard part is keeping a consistent presentation of the setting, especially in regards to the limits of technology.

If you are playing in the Second Doctor's era as part of an on-going campaign, and your players have already visited Earth, they will probably encounter some contradictions and anachronisms, especially in the history of the late 20th and 21st centuries, international politics and technology.

These can be explained as small changes to the timeline, or consequences of the Time War. The differences could even be part of a story arc – finding out what has caused them might reveal a terrifying plan to revert the universe to an earlier timeline, allowing the Daleks to launch an(other) overwhelming pre-emptive strike on a certain junkyard in London...

CHARACTER STATISTICS

Major characters in each story have statistics embedded in the adventure in which they appear. Aliens whose statistics don't differ from those in **Chapter Four: Enemies** are not repeated here. Similarly, characters that easily fall into stock character types (also included in the **Enemies** chapter) are also not repeated. You may wish to adjust these statistics in individual cases when a particular trait may seem obvious. Governor Hensell, for example, has an Adversary, Bragen, who is constantly undermining him. Also, if a particular character turns out to play a major role in the adventure then you may wish to grant her more story points. Continuing the example, Governor Hensell should have 4 story points.

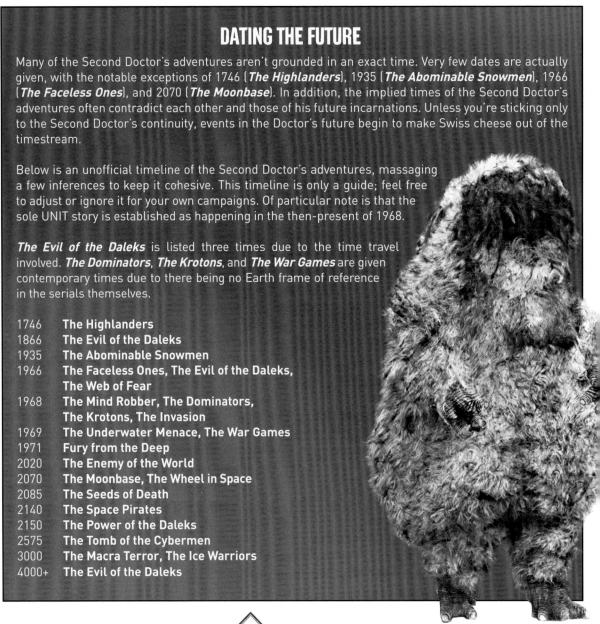

DATING THE FUTURE

Many of the Second Doctor's adventures aren't grounded in an exact time. Very few dates are actually given, with the notable exceptions of 1746 (*The Highlanders*), 1935 (*The Abominable Snowmen*), 1966 (*The Faceless Ones*), and 2070 (*The Moonbase*). In addition, the implied times of the Second Doctor's adventures often contradict each other and those of his future incarnations. Unless you're sticking only to the Second Doctor's continuity, events in the Doctor's future begin to make Swiss cheese out of the timestream.

Below is an unofficial timeline of the Second Doctor's adventures, massaging a few inferences to keep it cohesive. This timeline is only a guide; feel free to adjust or ignore it for your own campaigns. Of particular note is that the sole UNIT story is established as happening in the then-present of 1968.

The Evil of the Daleks is listed three times due to the time travel involved. *The Dominators*, *The Krotons*, and *The War Games* are given contemporary times due to there being no Earth frame of reference in the serials themselves.

1746	**The Highlanders**
1866	**The Evil of the Daleks**
1935	**The Abominable Snowmen**
1966	**The Faceless Ones, The Evil of the Daleks, The Web of Fear**
1968	**The Mind Robber, The Dominators, The Krotons, The Invasion**
1969	**The Underwater Menace, The War Games**
1971	**Fury from the Deep**
2020	**The Enemy of the World**
2070	**The Moonbase, The Wheel in Space**
2085	**The Seeds of Death**
2140	**The Space Pirates**
2150	**The Power of the Daleks**
2575	**The Tomb of the Cybermen**
3000	**The Macra Terror, The Ice Warriors**
4000+	**The Evil of the Daleks**

THE POWER OF THE DALEKS

'Why do human beings kill other human beings?'

⊙ SYNOPSIS

Vulcan colony, the Future (prior to the Dalek Invasion of Earth)

Having watched the Doctor collapse in the TARDIS after the destruction of Mondas and the Cybermen, Ben and Polly observed his regeneration. The new incarnation of the Doctor explained that he'd been 'renewed' and while Polly accepted this, Ben remained sceptical. The new Doctor also had a period of adjustment, referring to his old incarnation in the third person.

The TARDIS landed on the planet Vulcan and the three decided to explore, finding a world of rocky terrain with bubbling pools of mercury. Splitting up, the Doctor met a confused man claiming to be the Earth Examiner, whose ship had landed off-course away from the main colony. Their meeting was observed by a shadowy assassin, sent to eliminate the Examiner. A shot rang out, killing the Examiner and knocking the Doctor unconscious. Ben and Polly found him, but they both fell victim to the mercury fumes.

The three travellers were discovered by members of the Earth colony and taken inside. Deputy Governor Quinn and Security Chief Bragen believed that the Doctor was the Earth Examiner, given that he had the Examiner's badge in his possession. The colonists weren't expecting the Earth Examiner for another two years and believed his appearance was due to a 200 year old alien ship discovered by the colony.

The Doctor played along with the ruse and used it to gain access to the alien ship. The travellers secretly explored the inside of the ship and discovered two dormant Daleks! There was space for a third one but it was missing. The travellers were discovered by an upset Chief Scientist Lesterson. The Doctor got Lesterson to admit that he'd already explored the interior of the ship, but he denied the presence of a third Dalek. It was also obvious that the colonists didn't know about the Daleks.

The Doctor discovered sabotage and, in spite of his insistence that the Daleks were involved, Governor Hensell believed it to be the work of colonial rebels. Quinn, having been present at the sabotage and admitting he summoned the Earth Examiner, was accused of being a rebel and replaced by Bragen as Deputy Governor.

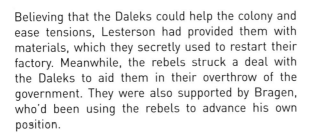

Believing that the Daleks could help the colony and ease tensions, Lesterson had provided them with materials, which they secretly used to restart their factory. Meanwhile, the rebels struck a deal with the Daleks to aid them in their overthrow of the government. They were also supported by Bragen, who'd been using the rebels to advance his own position.

The Daleks helped Bragen and the rebels take control of the colony. They killed the Governor, leaving Bragen in control. Bragen then pinned the murder on the rebels in order to eliminate them. By this point, however, the Daleks had increased their numbers enough to wipe out the entire colony. They were only stopped by the Doctor, who overloaded the main circuits and cut power to the colony, destroying the Daleks in the process. The remaining colonists, both loyalist and rebel, decide to work together to rebuild the colony.

CONTINUITY

This is the first of the Doctor's adventures that takes place immediately after his regeneration. The Doctor shows signs of post-regenerative complications, as he refers to his previous self in the third person and relies on notes that his previous incarnation left in his 500-year diary. Notably the Daleks recognise him, but whether this is due to them understanding his true nature or the fact that the Second Doctor later meets them in the past is uncertain. The colonists have never heard of the Daleks, probably placing this adventure before the Dalek conquest of Earth. As these Daleks require an external power source and one is seen slowly regaining power at the episode's end, it's possible that these Daleks either overcame their reliance on external power or managed to send a message to other Daleks, who created the mobile power dishes seen during the invasion.

◎ RUNNING THE ADVENTURE

While it features the Daleks, this adventure has political intrigue at its heart. Security Chief Bragen schemes his way to become Deputy Governor and, eventually, Governor of the Colony, and then turns on the rebels that helped put him in charge. This contrasts with the Daleks who, although scheming to rebuild their army and exterminate the colony, never fight amongst themselves. They manipulate the humans into doing what they want by pretending to be their robotic servants.

The Doctor becomes part of this intrigue by pretending to be the Earth Examiner, who was killed on arrival.

He does this at first to learn why the Examiner was killed, knowing full well that only the murderer would see through the ruse, but also uses his new authority to investigate the Daleks. This bit of mistaken identity is used in future adventures and a good way to get the characters immediately involved in an adventure without the usual 'just when things go wrong you turn up; why should we trust you?' arguments.

The crucial point here is whether a character goes through the charade of actually being the Earth Examiner or would rather concoct some other scheme to get access to the facilities on Vulcan. When a character sees the Examiner's badge, remind him that such a badge gives authority and access. If your players are slow on the uptake, then you could ask for the expenditure of a Story Point and suggest the ruse to them, but don't push this course of action if they are happily concocting their own scheme.

Even if your characters choose to be simple tourists, they'll soon spot a Dalek and realise that something bad is going on. By this point, the Daleks are well into their plan and the characters may gain an audience with the Governor or Deputy Governor (whoever is filling the seat at that point) by claiming to be experts on the Daleks. Alternatively, the characters may be drafted by the rebels, who'd want outside support for their cause.

If the characters get an audience with the Governor, they will learn about the crashed space ship. Presuming they want to see it Lesterson won't object, as he is indeed making a charade of opening it for the first time. You may wish to allow the characters to spot the Daleks on this first go around, as they, unlike the Doctor, are unlikely to stop the test even if they suspect it is a Dalek vessel based on the markings inside.

How the adventure progresses from this point is up to the characters. Bragen wants Quinn out of the way and hatches a plan to discredit him by cutting off communication with Earth. He also deals with Hansell later. Lesterson excitedly offers the Daleks to the colony in order to ease its workload. He won't take any action against them and undermines any attempt by the characters to destroy them. The rebels want the Daleks for themselves. Meanwhile, the Daleks slowly build their strength and numbers and prepare to exterminate everyone in the colony. The characters have to stop the Daleks in time.

One solution is to overload the electricity cables, but the players should be encouraged to try their own ideas. Perhaps they could unite the colony against the Daleks, or use the Daleks' limited mobility and power dependency against them by fighting a guerrilla war.

THE OTHER TENTH PLANET?

'Vulcan' is an interesting choice of planet name and it has nothing to do with living long or prospering. Since the 19th century, astronomers have postulated the presence of a planet between Mercury and the Sun that was dubbed 'Vulcan' by French mathematician Urbain Jean Joseph Le Verrier. While Einstein seemingly disproved Vulcan's existence in 1915, many astronomers continued to believe that Vulcan might exist.

While **The Power of the Daleks** seems to place Vulcan outside the Solar System, you could elect to put Vulcan within the Solar System. Practicality aside (it's difficult to see how humans would survive on a planet that close to the sun), placing Vulcan within the solar system allows the colony to thrive much earlier, perhaps as early the 21st century. It also explains how Earth can be radioed so quickly and why visits from Earth are limited to every two years (as the travel time likely takes half a year, round trip).

As the Daleks are seen to be not quite dead at the conclusion of this adventure, they may eventually overtake a solar system Vulcan or at least be in a position to observe the Earth and its suitability for Dalek purposes. Once this is broadcast back to Skaro, the Dalek Invasion of Earth begins.

WHAT IS PRODUCED ON VULCAN?

All we learn from this adventure is that Vulcan is home to an Earth colony that has a group of dissatisfied colonists. We don't know what the purpose of the colony is nor do we know why conditions are so bad as to foment a rebellion. We don't even know whether the rebellion is a serious movement or simply a small group of agitators.

What we do know is that Vulcan itself is almost inhospitable, with mercury swamps and plants that spew poisonous gas. With this in mind, two things seem certain. First, we know that Vulcan isn't an emergency colony (Earth is alive and well), so whatever brought the colonists here is worth risking one's health to acquire and second, that if this is a working colony then if the workers are feeling oppressed than it must be due to their working conditions or compensation.

Perhaps the colonists are gas miners. The mercury swamps are obviously dangerous and a colonial government that is cutting corners to save money could be putting the workers at risk in both the mining and refining processes.

FURTHER ADVENTURES

- As the TARDIS leaves a nearby Dalek slowly raises its eyestalk. This could be the last gasp of a power-drained Dalek, or it could be that the Doctor ultimately failed; the Daleks were damaged but not destroyed. Is someone else supplying them with power and, if so, how and for what reason? Perhaps an outside force wants to take over the colony and, through the Daleks, has a cheap way to do so? If so, it wouldn't be too long before the Daleks turned on them and would the Doctor be so willing to help those that eliminated the first colony?

- At the conclusion of this adventure the colonists have no power and Vulcan isn't exactly hospitable. The colonists aren't sure if the power can be restored, perhaps necessitating an evacuation. It's quite possible that, without the Doctor's advice, the evacuating vessels take the Daleks with them and bring them to Earth. Perhaps the characters visit Earth in the mid-22nd century to find that the Daleks are alert and scheming again, this time to take over the Earth!

- Vulcan's unknown resources could be of interest to another enemy, perhaps the Cybermen or the Ice Warriors. This new threat could either visit Vulcan prior to the discovery of the Daleks or immediately thereafter. Perhaps the characters return and find that the desperate colonists have reactivated the Daleks to aid them, incorrectly reasoning that a threat to the colony is a threat to the Daleks.

DEPUTY GOVERNOR QUINN

AWARENESS	4	PRESENCE	3
COORDINATION	3	RESOLVE	4
INGENUITY	3	STRENGTH	3

SKILLS
Convince 2, Fighting 2, Knowledge 3, Marksman 1, Subterfuge 2, Technology 2

TRAITS
Adversary (Major): Bragen is actively working to remove Quinn from power.

TECH LEVEL: 6   STORY POINTS: 3

LESTERSON

AWARENESS	2	PRESENCE	3
COORDINATION	3	RESOLVE	4
INGENUITY	6	STRENGTH	2

SKILLS
Craft 5, Knowledge 6, Science 6, Technology 5

TRAITS
Insatiable Curiosity: Lesterson allows his curiosity about the space ship get the better of him.
Obsession (Major): Lesterson desperately wants to ease conditions for the colony and is willing to overlook major concerns in order to achieve that goal.
Stubborn: Lesterson believes that his work is helping the colony and can't be swayed from reviving the Daleks.
Technically Adept: Lesterson is a good scientist and is able to comprehend some of the Dalek technology.

TECH LEVEL: 6   STORY POINTS: 3

REBEL

AWARENESS	3	PRESENCE	4
COORDINATION	3	RESOLVE	4
INGENUITY	3	STRENGTH	3

SKILLS*
Convince 3, Fighting 2, Marksman 2, Subterfuge 4, Survival 1, Technology 2, Transport 2
*Individual rebels will have a skill level of at least 4 in any skill crucial to their occupation or profession.

TRAITS
Brave: Rebels are willing to risk the consequences in order to achieve their goals.
Obligation (Major): Rebels are obsessed with changing conditions in the colony.

TECH LEVEL: 6   STORY POINTS: 2

SECURITY CHIEF BRAGEN

AWARENESS	5	PRESENCE	5
COORDINATION	4	RESOLVE	5
INGENUITY	4	STRENGTH	3

SKILLS
Athletics 3, Convince 5, Fighting 3, Knowledge 3, Marksman 3, Subterfuge 5, Survival 3, Technology 3, Transport 2

TRAITS
Obsession (Major): Bragen wants to run the colony and will use every means at his disposal to get it.
Selfish: Bragen cares little for who he needs to step on in order to acquire power.
Voice of Authority: Bragen commands authority when he speaks. He gets a +2 to Presence and Convince rolls to get people to do what he wants.

TECH LEVEL: 6   STORY POINTS: 6

THE HIGHLANDERS

'I've never seen a silent lawyer before.'

⊘ SYNOPSIS

Scotland, 1746

The TARDIS arrived in Scotland just after the Battle of Culloden. The travellers soon met a Scottish family and a piper, Jamie McCrimmon, fleeing from the English. The Doctor tended to the Laird's wounds while his daughter Kirsty and Polly fetched clean water. Unfortunately, the rest of the group were captured by English soldiers while they were gone.

The Doctor assumed the guise of Doctor von Wer, a German doctor sympathetic to the English King, in order to curry favour with Lt. Algernon Ffinch. Unfortunately Ffinch's Sergeant didn't fall for the ruse and while Ffinch was chasing the women, believing one of them may be disguised as the rebel Scottish prince, the Sergeant tried to hang the prisoners. He was stopped by Solicitor Grey, who wanted the able-bodied men to sell as slaves in the West Indies.

The Doctor, along with Ben, the Laird, and Jamie were taken with the other prisoners to a gaol in Inverness in preparation for transportation to America. Kirsty and Polly followed them, embarrassing Lt. Ffinch into aiding them. Ffinch was unaware of the slavery plot, a scheme devised by Solicitor Grey and his accomplice, Captain Trask of the *Annabelle*. The Doctor met Captain Trask and learned that he was an arms smuggler before he turned on his partner Willie Mackay, who was now a prisoner on the ship. The Doctor then used his disguise to trick Trask and escape.

In order to make the plot legal, Solicitor Grey offered the prisoners the choice of being hung unless they swore evidence against their comrades or agreed to a seven year term working plantations in the West Indies. They all signed, but Ben tore up the contract and made a daring escape. He met the Doctor and Polly and the three smuggled weapons onto the *Annabelle*.

Armed with the weapons, the prisoners revolted and took over the ship. Trask was thrown overboard while Solicitor Grey was captured. The freed Highlanders

DOCTOR WHO

decided to pilot the boat to France. The travellers returned to England with Jamie, who'd volunteered to guide them back to the TARDIS. Grey escaped, but his attempt to convince Lt Ffinch to arrest the travellers backfired when Ffinch used the evidence against Grey to arrest him instead.

Jamie led the travellers back to the TARDIS. After hearing gunshots in the distance and worried that Jamie might have escorted them at the cost of his own life, the travellers convinced Jamie to accompany them.

CONTINUITY

The Doctor uses a variety of disguises in this adventure, most notably as the German Doctor von Wer ('Doctor of Who').

RUNNING THE ADVENTURE

This is the Second Doctor's only pure historical adventure and therefore acts as the blueprint for how the Second Doctor would handle such adventures. As with many of the First Doctor historicals, this adventure involves some of the characters getting captured and the others working to free them without causing damage to the timeline.

It's important to note here that the Doctor isn't too worried about altering the timeline and does whatever is necessary to save himself and his companions, including interfering with a major historical plot point (the lives of scores of Scots change based on his decisions). The Doctor never questions whether or not he should be interfering; Grey and Trask are doing evil and must be stopped.

This is the first time we see the Second Doctor in 'magician mode'; he dons several disguises, subtly influences people, and comes up with a cache of weaponry just when its needed. While Ben and Polly get to do a lot on their own, it isn't because the Doctor can't; he's just as physically capable and critical to the success of the adventure.

The adventure begins with the characters being captured. If they are captured by the Highlanders, they are led back to the cottage where they meet the Laird. The English then capture them along with the Highlanders. In the Doctor's adventure, some of the characters are collecting water when the English arrive and remain free. Splitting the group in this way can add tension and drama to your game but, as you can only focus on one group at a time, you

need to make sure that neither group is out of the action for too long. If the characters evade Jamie and Alexander in the first place, they can always be picked up by an English patrol instead.

The goal for the adventure is freedom. Ideally, this should include freedom for those captured alongside the characters too, and that's a bit trickier. If the Highlanders stay in Scotland they will be fugitives – the only true freedom they can hope for is to escape on a ship like the Annabelle. Opportunities for escape could present themselves very early on in the adventure, on the road to Inverness. If the characters get free quickly, the Highlanders could appeal for help in making a more thorough getaway to the continent, or to more remote parts of their homeland.

If you want Jamie to become part of the crew then he'll elect to help them find their way back to the TARDIS regardless of where the characters are freed.

While a historical adventure, there is never really a threat of changing history. None of the people that the characters meet are important in the grand scheme of things. The driving motives of the adventure are to rescue the Doctor and Ben and expose a slavery scheme.

HIGHLANDERS AND ALIENS?

While the Highlanders that the Doctor meets saw the Jacobite Rebellion as an English-Scottish war, this was an oversimplification. The Government Army had Scottish and Irish units while the rebels had some English and French units. The war was over the proper successor to the crown. Therefore this adventure seems slightly inaccurate by portraying it as a Scottish rebellion and presuming that any Englishman helping the Jacobites is a deserter.

Similarly, Ffinch takes great pride in arresting Solicitor Grey and implying that he has a terrible fate in store for being branded a slave trader. In fact, slave trading is perfectly legal in Great Britain until the Slave Trade Act of 1807 and in any event the Scotsmen are being processed as indentured servants, not slaves.

Rather than ignore the slight historical accuracies you might choose to embrace them. In this case the Doctor (or any character that can Feel the Turn of the Universe) will realize that something is very wrong with this war. Is this the work of an alien influence (the Master, the Meddling Monk, and the Sontarans make likely candidates) and, if so, can the Doctor set things right?

Or has the TARDIS truly fallen into an alternate universe?

FURTHER ADVENTURES

- When the Time Lords exiled the Doctor to Earth, they returned Jamie to his own time with only the knowledge of his first adventure with the Doctor (presumably he remembers escorting the Doctor, Ben, and Polly back to the TARDIS and believes they left without him). However, there is still a war going on and Jamie is last seen chasing an English soldier. It is entirely possible that Jamie gets arrested, necessitating a rescue by the characters. It could be an interesting challenge for the player of the Doctor to outwardly downplay his affection for Jamie while doing everything he can to help him.

- Captain Trask escaped at the end of this adventure. It's quite possible he set up shop elsewhere; the plantations in the Caribbean still need workers. Whether he hatches another scheme to recruit indentured servants or turns

to the African slave trade, the characters need to stop him. As a turn of events, Captain Trask could run afoul of an alien artefact, ironically causing him to turn to the characters for help.

- The Doctor ends Solicitor Grey's scheme and sets an entire ship of Scots free without worrying about how he affected the timeline. This could come back to haunt him, if one of the rescued Scots or their descendants become pivotal during a 'fixed point in time' and change it.

PERKINS, GREY'S HENCHMAN

AWARENESS	2	PRESENCE	3
COORDINATION	2	RESOLVE	3
INGENUITY	3	STRENGTH	2

SKILLS
Fighting 1, Knowledge 4, Marksman 1

TRAITS
Cowardly

TECH LEVEL: 4   **STORY POINTS: 2**

KIRSTY MCLAREN

AWARENESS	4	PRESENCE	4
COORDINATION	4	RESOLVE	4
INGENUITY	2	STRENGTH	2

SKILLS
Athletics 2, Craft 4, Fighting 1, Knowledge 3, Marksman 1, Subterfuge 3, Survival 4

TRAITS
Attractive: Kirsty is attractive and gets a +2 bonus on rolls in which her appearance would matter.

TECH LEVEL: 4   **STORY POINTS: 7**

SOLICITOR GREY

AWARENESS	4	PRESENCE	2
COORDINATION	2	RESOLVE	4
INGENUITY	4	STRENGTH	2

SKILLS
Convince 4, Fighting 2, Knowledge 5,
Subterfuge 3

TRAITS
By the Book: In spite of his illicit activities
Grey does try to play by the rules and will
accommodate someone that uses the rules
against him, even if it thwarts his plan in the
short term.
Dark Secret (minor): Grey is a slave trader of
sorts and would get in serious trouble if the
authorities ever discovered his scheme.
Selfish: Grey cares little for the welfare of
others so long as his own pockets are full.
Voice of Authority: In spite of his arrogant
manner, Grey commands authority when he
speaks. He receives a +2 bonus on Presence
and Convince rolls.
Weakness (Major): Grey is a greedy man and
his greed often blinds him to the obvious (he
lets the Doctor pull the wool over his eyes twice
with the promise of reward).

TECH LEVEL: 4   STORY POINTS: 6

LAIRD COLIN MCLAREN

AWARENESS	4	PRESENCE	4
COORDINATION	5	RESOLVE	4
INGENUITY	3	STRENGTH	4

SKILLS
Athletics 4, Convince 4, Fighting 6, Knowledge 3,
Marksman 3, Survival 4

TRAITS
Tough

TECH LEVEL: 4   STORY POINTS: 5

CAPTAIN TRASK

AWARENESS	4	PRESENCE	2
COORDINATION	4	RESOLVE	4
INGENUITY	2	STRENGTH	3

SKILLS
Athletics 5, Fighting 5, Marksman 4, Survival 4,
Transport 5

TRAITS
Adversary: Trask has betrayed Willie Mackay
and the latter is awaiting an opportunity to get
even.
Selfish: Trask swapped the smuggling trade
for the windfall of the slave trade, even though
he had to step on Mackay in the process.

TECH LEVEL: 4   STORY POINTS: 8

LT. ALGERNON FFINCH

AWARENESS	2	PRESENCE	4
COORDINATION	3	RESOLVE	3
INGENUITY	4	STRENGTH	3

SKILLS
Athletics 3, Convince 3, Fighting 4, Knowledge 3,
Marksman 4

TRAITS
Attractive: Ffinch is attractive and gets a +2 bonus
on rolls in which his appearance would matter.
Charming: Algernon is an aristocrat and his
polite manner is pleasing to most. He gets a +2
bonus on social rolls where charm is a factor.
Eccentric: As a foppish gentleman, Ffinch's
mannerisms can be off-putting at times.
Weakness (Major): Ffinch is extremely worried
about his pride and reputation and allows
himself to be blackmailed.

TECH LEVEL: 4   STORY POINTS: 6

THE UNDERWATER MENACE

'Nothing in the world can stop me now!'

⊙ SYNOPSIS

Atlantis, after 1968

While exploring a volcanic island somewhere in the Atlantic Ocean, the travellers were captured by primitive warriors, although the island didn't seem to be wholly cut off from the modern world as Polly had discovered a discarded souvenir from the 1968 Olympics. The travellers were led to a reception area in an underwater complex where they met an Atlantean priest, Lolem. Lolem informed them that they were to be sacrificed to the Atlantean god Amdo.

Taking stock of his surroundings, the Doctor deduced that the base was the work of Professor Zaroff, a brilliant scientist who had disappeared during the Cold War. The Doctor talked a serving girl, Ara, into taking a message to the Professor. Zaroff interrupted the sacrifice and took the travellers to his quarters. He explained that he was allied to the Atlanteans, and planned to raise Atlantis. The Professor sent Ben and Jamie to work in the mines while Polly was taken by Zaroff's assistant, the surgeon Damon, to be converted into a Fish Person to help farm the plankton.

The Doctor learned from Zaroff that the latter wanted to raise Atlantis from the sea. His plan, however, called for cracking the Earth's crust in order to drain the water, which would instead destroy the world.

Zaroff was aware of this, but wanted to do it anyway, simply because he could.

Ben and Jamie learned that the Atlanteans have been kidnapping shipwreck survivors and putting them to work as miners or Fish People. They also learned that the farmed plankton can't be stored; it rots within hours. The Doctor escaped from Zaroff and found Polly, who'd been rescued from the operating table by Ara, a sympathetic serving girl. The Doctor attempted to convince King Thous of the Atlanteans about Zaroff's duplicity, but the king handed him over to Zaroff.

Ben and Jamie fled through the tunnels and arrived in time to help the Doctor by using a device inside the head of the Amdo sculpture to make the priests believe Ben is Amdo. The Doctor decided that the best way to get the Atlanteans to cooperate was to disrupt their food supply. They managed to capture Zaroff but he escaped after informing them that the plan was already in motion and couldn't be stopped. Ben and the miners convinced the Fish People to strike. A concerned King Thous summoned Zaroff to demand answers, but Zaroff shot him instead. Fortunately, the wounded king was discovered by the Doctor and tended to by loyal Atlanteans while the Doctor and Ben went after Zaroff. They found Zaroff in his laboratory and the two managed to foil the experiment, flooding the lower levels of Atlantis but otherwise leaving the planet unharmed. Trapped, Zaroff drowned.

A recovered King Thous pledged to rebuild an Atlantis free of the superstitions that so easily duped them while granting the Fish People their freedom.

CONTINUITY

The idea of cracking through the Earth's crust is revisited in **Inferno**. While done on dry land (and only completed in a parallel universe) in that adventure, the result of the completed experiment is just as catastrophic.

This is the second story in a row where the Doctor uses a 'secret' to garner an audience with a villain only to reveal that there is no secret once the audience is granted.

The TARDIS does not to allow the time travellers to communicate in Atlantean when they meet the first set of guards. The simplest reason is that the guards don't want to speak to them, but another reason might be that the effects of decompression have affected the TARDIS' ability to influence their minds until they've adjusted. Still another reason might be that the TARDIS is unfamiliar with Atlantean and needs to sample it before adjusting the time traveller's brains. In any case, the Doctor and his Companions have no trouble understanding Atlanteans throughout the rest of the story (and it's doubtful that they've all switched to English for the convenience of four people).

This is the first appearance of Atlantis. The Atlanteans worship a god named Amdo, who doesn't appear in any Earth pantheon. They have preserved their ancient culture in undersea air-filled caverns along the Mid-Atlantic Ridge. Zaroff has introduced advanced technologies to them, including electric power and the ability to convert a human into an amphibian. While aware of the world above (the Atlanteans kidnap shipwrecked passengers and crew as well as work with Professor Zaroff), the Atlanteans seem unwilling to migrate to surface cultures. Instead, they wish to see their own continent returned to the surface. After Zaroff is defeated, the Atlanteans are determined to remain beneath the sea.

⊙ RUNNING THE ADVENTURE

This adventure has a very 1960s Cold War superspy vibe to it. Ships are sinking in the Atlantic, the survivors taken to fuel a madman's plan. The madman is a Cold War scientist who disappeared decades ago and each side blamed the other for it. He's joined forces with local primitives that believe he is helping them while the madman plots to destroy the world. In furtherance of this plan he's performing genetic experiments on some of the castaways, turning them into underwater slaves.

At its core, this is a very basic adventure theme that can be used countless times over. A civilization in distress reaches out to a saviour, willing to overlook (or is unaware of) the saviour's past. In the meantime the 'saviour' works towards his own ends, which spell doom for the very people he promised to save. The characters have to stop the madman while convincing the people to turn against him.

FISH PEOPLE

The Fish People are humans altered by Professor Zaroff to gather and farm food for Atlantis. While the procedure is described to Polly as surgical in nature, the Second Doctor believes it to be genetic engineering (hence his comment on "controlling the world from a test tube"). Since the Second Doctor knows of Zaroff's previous work, it's safe to assume he recognizes the genetic engineering for what it is.

The humans chosen for conversion are from among those shipwrecked near the island connected to Atlantis. As there are many adult Fish People, it's also safe to assume that Zaroff has 'manufactured' a few shipwrecks to keep the supply high. There are also no Fish People children, so either the Fish People are sterilized upon conversion or their children are kept out of sight. If the Fish People can breed true then they could create their own society.

It has taken Professor Zaroff many years to perfect his experiments, and so the Fish People vary a bit in appearance. His earliest experiments did not alter the Fish Person's eyesight and such Fish People tend to wear diving masks or goggles when swimming. The earlier Fish People still have an affinity for land and can often be found shopping in the Atlantean markets.

Later Fish People have more fins and scales and large, unblinking eyes. These Fish People are better suited to their aquatic environment and rarely leave it.

Considering they were once shipwrecked survivors forced to undergo a radical medical procedure, Fish People are surprisingly well-adjusted. They mingle freely with the Atlanteans and use sign language and gestures to shop in the markets, as the procedure that changed them also took away their human vocal chords.

Created into slavery, the Fish People are surprisingly docile. This may be due to a survivor's complex, as they are so grateful for being saved that they overlook the imbalance in their current condition. Still, if angered, they can be deadly foes underwater, as their quick movements and independence from air-breathing makes it difficult to outfight them.

NOTHING IN THE WORLD CAN STOP ME NOW!

Professor Zaroff is a madman. He believes that his experiment will destroy the world, yet he will do it simply because he can. If you want to make Zaroff a sympathetic adversary, then you can ratchet down his megalomania to that of a wounded scientist that is tired of the scientific community telling him that he can't raise Atlantis from the sea. He firmly believes that he can without destroying the world. The Doctor's (or other character's) attempts to dissuade him only make the Doctor the latest in a long line of naysayers and are easily dismissed by Zaroff.

It's also possible that Zaroff is suffering from some personal tragedy that has sent him over the edge. Perhaps he lost a loved one as a result of Cold War politics, or some other scientist that wronged him is on the verge of making a great discovery and Zaroff wants to pre-empt his or her glory.

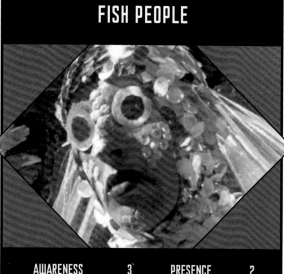

FISH PEOPLE

AWARENESS	3	PRESENCE	2
COORDINATION	3	RESOLVE	2
INGENUITY	1	STRENGTH	3

SKILLS
Athletics (Swimming) 3, Fighting 1, Knowledge (Underwater) 2, Survival (Underwater) 3

TRAITS
Alien Appearance: While surgically-altered humans, Fish People have fins, gills and scales. Some wear diving masks or goggles that give them an even more alien appearance. A few actually do have altered, unblinking eyes.
Enslaved: The Fish People are surgically altered to serve the Atlantean people as underwater farmers. While they could technically leave, they seem unwilling to do so without outside guidance. This may be a psychological problem
Environmental: Fish people are able to survive underwater and are more comfortable underwater than on land.

TECH LEVEL: 5   STORY POINTS: 1-2

AN ALIEN TWIST

Professor Zaroff's experiment, while destructive, is very useful for some of the more martial powers in the galaxy, especially the Daleks or the Sontarans. They may invade in order to extract the Professor before he kills himself or offer to keep him safe while he conducts his experiment. Such enemies would, of course, resent the presence of interfering characters. Another possibility is that Professor Zaroff is the Master or another alien that wants to destroy the world for some other reason (perhaps the Slitheen arrive early, or the Cybermen want to prevent the destruction of Mondas). Finally, it's possible that Zaroff has engineered a giant octopus to attack approaching vessels and cause shipwrecks, providing Atlantis with a regular source of miners and Fish People.

FURTHER ADVENTURES

- Zaroff's machine didn't succeed in destroying the world, but it did cut through a Silurian bunker. An emergency plan activated and a Silurian team has entered Atlantis to take it over (perhaps the Silurian leader's name sounds like 'Amdo,' leading the Atlanteans to bend their knees to their new reptilian overlords).

- After the Doctor defeats Zaroff and the lower caverns of Atlantis are flooded, the Atlanteans leave the Fish People to their own devices. None of the Doctor's future travels on Earth ever mention them, so it's likely that they've either died out in the near future or remained incognito. Perhaps they've moved into the submerged sections of Atlantis and rediscovered some of Zaroff's research. Maybe they wage war with the Atlanteans. Maybe they create their own community and occasionally capsize boats to increase their numbers. Maybe they've moved into an old Silurian bunker. The possibilities are endless.

- There are many that would like Dr Zaroff's process for creating aquatic people, but the notes are buried beneath the sea and the Atlanteans don't want anyone traversing the lower levels;

they are the crypts of the dead. Unfortunately, Zaroff's experiment had penetrated enough crust to emit low levels of Stahlman gas, which has been poisoning local fauna. Mutated crabs, fish, and cephalopods now plague the Atlantic. Unless the hole is plugged, Zaroff's dream of a devastated Earth may soon come to pass.

PROFESSOR ZAROFF

AWARENESS	4	PRESENCE	4
COORDINATION	2	RESOLVE	5
INGENUITY	8	STRENGTH	2

SKILLS
Convince 4, Craft 4, Fighting 3, Knowledge 6, Marksman 3, Medicine 8, Science 6, Subterfuge 3, Technology 7

TRAITS
Boffin: Zaroff has invented a machine that can punch a hole through the crust of the Earth.
Eccentric (Major): It only takes a few minutes of conversation with Zaroff to realise that he's completely mad.
Obsession (Major): Zaroff is so obsessed with proving that he is the greatest scientist of all time that he's actually quite eager to destroy the world to prove it.
Technically Adept: Zaroff is ahead of his time as far as technology is concerned and gets a +2 bonus to any Technology roll.

EQUIPMENT: Pistol

TECH LEVEL: 5   **STORY POINTS: 9**

DAMON

AWARENESS	3	PRESENCE	2
COORDINATION	2	RESOLVE	3
INGENUITY	4	STRENGTH	2

SKILLS
Athletics 1, Convince 2, Craft 4, Fighting 2, Knowledge 5, Marksman 1, Medicine 6, Science 6, Subterfuge 2, Survival 3, Technology 3, Transport 3

TRAITS
Biochemical Genius: Damon gains Areas of Expertise for the Science Skill in Biology and Chemistry and has used this trait to create the Fish People.

TECH LEVEL: 4   **STORY POINTS: 7**

KING THOUS

AWARENESS	3	PRESENCE	4
COORDINATION	2	RESOLVE	4
INGENUITY	2	STRENGTH	3

SKILLS
Athletics 2, Convince 4, Fighting 2, Knowledge 3, Marksman 1, Survival 2

TRAITS
Obligation (Major): Thous is the hereditary leader of Atlantis and feels a duty to protect his subjects.
Stubborn: Thous is a noble and used to being listened to, not swayed. He gets a +2 on Resolve rolls to resist coercion or hypnotism.
Voice of Authority: Thous is king of his domain and gets a +2 on Presence and Convince rolls to get people to do what he wants or gain their trust.

TECH LEVEL: 4   **STORY POINTS: 6**

ATLANTEAN PRIEST

AWARENESS	2	PRESENCE	3
COORDINATION	2	RESOLVE	3
INGENUITY	3	STRENGTH	2

SKILLS
Athletics 2, Convince 4, Craft 2, Fighting 1, Knowledge 3, Survival 2

TRAITS
Voice of Authority: As the servant of Amdo, Atlantean priests get a +2 on Presence and Convince rolls to influence people or gain their trust.

TECH LEVEL: 4   **STORY POINTS: 4**

CHAPTER SIX:
THE MOONBASE, THE MACRA TERROR, THE FACELESS ONES

THE MOONBASE

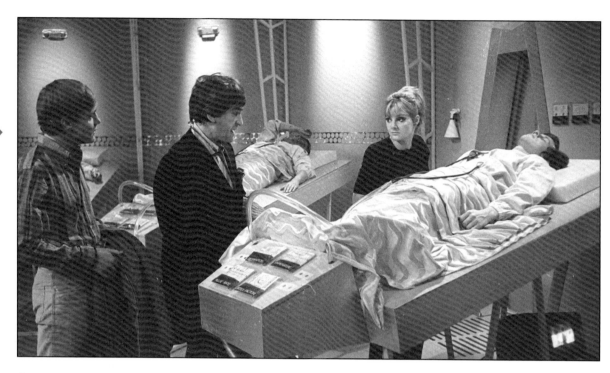

"International Space Control Headquarters Earth calling Weather Control Moon. Come in please".

◯ SYNOPSIS

The Moon, 2070

While attempting to go to Mars, the Doctor instead landed the TARDIS on the moon. The four travellers explored the moon's surface and Polly noticed a glow (a Cybermen ship landing) as Jamie accidentally jumped too far, knocking himself unconscious but discovering a moon base. Jamie was taken by the occupants and the other travellers followed them inside.

The Moonbase housed the Gravitron, a gravity device that controlled weather patterns on Earth. The crew was on edge as a mysterious plague had left them short-handed for the last two weeks; even the Chief Medical Officer contracted it. Space Control put the base under quarantine until the plague could be identified.

The Doctor, Ben, and Polly met Moonbase leader Hobson and his crew, a European team of scientists responsible for keeping Earth's conditions ideal for crop growth and eliminating weather catastrophes. Hobson hoped that the travellers were from a relief

ship, but even though he discovered that they weren't he still hoped the Doctor could fill in for his medical officer and possibly determine the cause of the plague.

Several strange events soon shook the Moonbase. The crew realised that someone was listening to their conversations while Ben noticed that someone disappeared in the storage area. Jamie and Polly discovered that a Cyberman was stealing victims from the sickbay and taking them somewhere. Finally, the crew was having difficulty controlling the Gravitron, disrupting Earth's weather.

The Cybermen soon made their presence known after the Doctor discovered that the sugar supply had been tainted and was the source of the plague. Two Cybermen quickly established control of the base and used helmet-controlled crew members, all prior victims of the plague, to operate the Gravitron. Polly discovered that her nail polish remover could gum up the Cybermen's breathing grill and the travellers use 'Cocktail Polly' to destroy the Cybermen.

Hobson regained control and prepared for another attack from the Cybermen ship. A Cybermen patrol crossed the surface with a laser cannon. They also reactivated the captured altered humans and made them use the Gravitron to knock an Earth relief ship off-course. The Moonbase crew tried to regain control but the Cybermen punctured the dome, causing the air to be sucked out as two more Cybermen ships landed.

The Moonbase crew managed to plug the hole and reset the Gravitron to affect the moon. They were now protected from the laser cannon and used the Gravitron to fling the Cybermen and their ships off the moon. The crew was ecstatic until they realised they had a lot of work to do repairing the Gravitron. The travellers used this opportunity to slip away back to the TARDIS.

The TARDIS scanner has a 'time scanner' setting that enables the operator to get a glimpse of the near future. The Doctor uses it here to see what the next destination holds and it shows a Macra shrouded in mist.

CONTINUITY

Starting in 2050, Earth's weather is controlled by the Gravitron on the moon. The Gravitron is eventually replaced by Earthbound regional weather manipulation stations and the Moonbase is refitted to handle the coordination of T-Mat traffic soon after.

The Cybermen are eager to destroy the Earth relief vessel, implying that human weapons are a threat to them. The Cybermen know the Doctor, in spite of his change in appearance. The most likely explanation is that they have records from *The Invasion* or the unseen visit to Planet 14.

Most people don't take sugar in their coffee in the future, probably due to the prevalence of artificial sweeteners.

The theme of the Doctor pretending to have something he doesn't continues in this adventure. The Doctor claims to have found something useful in his analysis just to keep Hobson at bay a while longer. Once again the Doctor is forced to reveal that he has no information (although ironically he discovers the cause as he admits his failure).

◎ RUNNING THE ADVENTURE

This adventure marks the first proper 'base under siege' adventure of the Second Doctor's tenure (*The Power of the Daleks* and *The Underwater Menace* don't qualify because, although they take place in secluded areas, the threat is obviously from within). All of the tropes of a proper 'base under siege' adventure are here; a team of scientists with a definite hierarchy (most importantly someone the Doctor must convince to trust him or else complicate his attempts to solve it), a mystery as to the nature of the menace, enemy agents within the base preparing for invasion, a direct assault that, while largely repelled, still enables some of the threat to get inside, and a quick and dirty solution that ends the menace once and for all.

It's important in the base under siege adventure that the characters don't have aliases that draw off suspicion; in order for the atmosphere to be effective the characters have to be amongst the suspects and are usually the most likely ones. What the characters should have working to their advantage is the expertise needed to combat the threat (it helps if the local expert is neutralised). In this case the Doctor helps with the scientific investigation (with the Chief Medical Officer down) and is knowledgeable about the Cybermen.

Hobson, the Controller, while thankful for the Doctor's help, has a difficult time trusting him and questions the Doctor's every move, especially after people start disappearing. He also follows the time-honoured tradition of keeping things quiet until he understands what's going on, lest he upset his superiors on Earth. It is only after the Doctor is proven correct about the threat that Hobson changes his tune.

Finally, the Cybermen, while superior fighters, are killed by a chemical concoction and later pushed off the moon via a modification to the Gravitron.

Both of these tools are easily obtainable within the Moonbase and, in the case of the Gravitron, the weakness is telegraphed in advance. Most notable is that the conventional solution, an armed security detail from Earth, is kept from being deployed

WHERE ARE THESE CYBERMEN FROM?

The Cybermen that appear in **The Moonbase** look significantly different to the invaders from Mondas. They appear to be even more robotic and don't need to breathe (the chest unit keeps them alive, but isn't 'breathing' in the traditional sense). They are of the same model as the Cybermen found on Telos in a few centuries' time. Since these Cybermen are of the same model as those seen in **Tomb of the Cybermen** then it creates a chicken-or-the-egg argument as to whether these Cybermen hail from Mondas or migrate there sometime after 2070.

One possibility is that these Cybermen were designed for deep space survival and equipped with independent power sources. Once Mondas was destroyed, these Cybermen decided to marshal their forces in order to conquer Earth as a new home world. Lacking significant numbers, they needed the Gravitron to destroy the Earth population. Concurrently, another faction of Cybermen do the same with the Space Wheel.

Another possibility is that these Cybermen aren't human at all, but a similar humanoid race. This would explain the three-fingered hands and their apparent contempt for humanity (presumably they'd lump the unfortunate Mondasians into the same category) as well as the callous way they propose to destroy it. The Mondasian Cybermen still considered Earthlings as a kindred race, albeit an imperfect one.

LIQUID PLASTIC

This liquid comes in a spray can. If it hits a Cybermat it completely encases it in plastic. If used against a Cyberman's chest unit it causes great damage.

Traits: One Shot, Inflict Major Weakness
Each application acts as a major weakness against a Cyberman's physical attributes, inflicting 4 damage each Action Round. Unless the Cyberman has some way to purge its chest unit of the poison, it keeps taking this damage until it is destroyed.
Cost: 2 Story Points

NEUROTROPE X

This poison, when injected, causes the victim to collapse unconscious with large black tendrils (following nerve bundles) covering the body. This makes the victim more susceptible to control by the Cybermen.

Traits: Anyone that consumes Neurotrope X is completely incapacitated and can be controlled by the Cybermen as per the Possession trait.
Cost: 3 Story Points

GRAVITRON
SPECIAL GADGET

The Gravitron array is a huge artificial gravity projector. It projects a gravitational beam that alters the tides and currents of Earth's oceans, which in turn affect Earth's weather. With the Gravitron, hurricanes can be dispersed harmlessly, and rainfall can be directed to ensure optimum conditions for growing crops. The Gravitron is a joint project of all of Earth's governments, and is the centrepiece of a delicate web of negotiations and agreements. After all, the Gravitron can also be a devastating weapon. If misaligned even slightly, it could flood low-lying countries or trigger cataclysmic typhoons and tsunamis.

The massive machine is powered by a huge thermonuclear reactor with an operating temperature of four million degrees centigrade. The howling of the reactor is also dangerous, and even short exposure to the sonic feedback can drive an operator insane. The crew of the Moonbase are the elite of Earth – only they can be trusted to operate such a vital machine.

Using the Gravitron without training is a a *Very Difficult* task, but success allows the operator to repel or attract the target of the gravitational beam. Failure, however, could have catastrophic consequences...

Cost: 4 Story Points

THE REWRITE

Have you ever run an adventure where the basic plot was sound but it just fell apart and you wanted a do-over? Or have you ever run an adventure that went so well that you want to recapture the magic with the same group of players again? Look no further than this adventure.

One thing almost immediately apparent about **The Moonbase** is how closely it tracks to the previous Cybermen outing **The Tenth Planet**. Both feature an isolated multi-national base in a hostile environment with an easily agitated leader, both have a subplot involving people in danger, both involve a plan to destroy the Earth, and both involve defeating the Cybermen with a large weapon that exploits a key weakness.

All of that said, **The Moonbase** has a much different feel to its predecessor. The Cybermen have undergone a complete redesign, their efforts are specifically targeted at the base, and they use more subtle methods to weaken the Moonbase crew. While pointing out the similarities between the two stories makes the connection obvious, the casual viewer isn't likely to notice it.

If done well, a Gamemaster can take this lesson and apply it to any of the Second Doctor adventures. Simply pick an adventure you like, file off the serial numbers, and re-run it. As the adventure synopses and other information for the Second Doctor's adventures are quite extensive, you can use most of the information for an original adventure. Unlike **The Moonbase**, you don't even need to use the same enemy.

As one example, you might take **The Power of the Daleks** entry and keep the basic structure intact but change the particulars. Rather than finding a Dalek ship in an alien swamp, an oil rigging team in the Arctic of the near future finds an Inuit artefact in the polar ice. One of the engineers at the rig, Dr. Felicia Thompson, cleans the artefact and finds herself under the sway of the Great Intelligence. She begins to modify maintenance robots to help build extra-dimensional pyramids. Meanwhile, her assistant, Martin Kalvak, is secretly working against the oil rig because he believes it's drilling through sacred ground. The Great Intelligence leads him to believe that he can use the maintenance robots to expose more artefacts.

As the Great Intelligence grows in influence, it is preparing to pit the two sides against each other and wipe them out so that it can manifest on Earth without

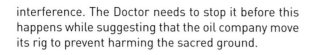

interference. The Doctor needs to stop it before this happens while suggesting that the oil company move its rig to prevent harming the sacred ground.

FURTHER ADVENTURES

- While the Cybermen were bounced off the moon, they weren't all destroyed, especially as they don't need to breathe while marching across the lunar surface (similarly, they can operate in the vacuum of space in **The Wheel in Space**). Lacking the numbers for a full Earth invasion, the Cybermen try another desperate manoeuvre; they hijack a relief ship and try to enter the Moonbase through it, using the hypnotised relief crew to operate the Gravitron.

- While the Doctor helped the Moonbase crew convert the Gravitron into a weapon out of necessity, its utility as a weapon has now been demonstrated. Perhaps the characters discover an Earth criminal using a private Gravitron to extort power and wealth from a vulnerable civilisation, or perhaps Earth space forces have added the Gravitron to their arsenal.

- If the Cyberman poison is called Neurotrope X – or Neurotrope 10, in other words – then is there a Neurotrope 11, or Neurotropes 1-9? The Cybermen might have needed to capture other people in the past to carry out the experiments needed to produce the toxin, and the player characters might stumble across this grisly research. If the poison can only be used in conjunction with sugar, then the Cybermen might set up a secret base on a sugar cane plantation – or in a chocolate factory!

MOONBASE CREW*

AWARENESS	3	PRESENCE	3
COORDINATION	3	RESOLVE	4
INGENUITY	4	STRENGTH	2

SKILLS
Athletics 3, Craft 3, Fighting 1, Knowledge 3, Marksman 1, Science 4, , Survival 3, Technology 4, Transport 2

TRAITS
Biochemical Genius: Moonbase Crewmen that are scientists get a +2 on Science rolls within their areas of expertise.
Technically Adept: Moonbase Crewmen that are technicians get a +2 on Technology rolls within their areas of expertise.

TECH LEVEL: 5   **STORY POINTS: 3**

* When hypnotised by the Cybermen, they also have the **Enslaved** and **Networked** traits.

HOBSON

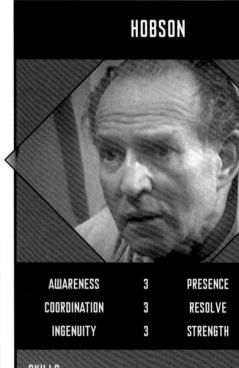

AWARENESS	3	PRESENCE	5
COORDINATION	3	RESOLVE	4
INGENUITY	3	STRENGTH	3

SKILLS
Athletics 2, Convince 5, Craft 4, Fighting 1, Knowledge 2, Marksman 1, Science 3, Subterfuge 1, Technology 5, Transport 2

TRAITS
Technically Adept: Hobson gains a +2 on any Technology roll to fix a broken device.
Voice of Authority: Hobson is the controller of the Moonbase and gets a +2 on Presence and Confidence rolls to influence others or gain their trust

TECH LEVEL: 5   **STORY POINTS: 10**

THE MACRA TERROR

'Doctor, that was it – that thing in the picture! That was the claw! They're in control!'

⊘ SYNOPSIS

Earth Colony, centuries into the future

Despite seeing a giant claw on the scanner, the travellers were pleasantly surprised to discover that they'd landed on a future Earth colony with the atmosphere of a holiday camp. The residents seemed very cheerful, performing songs extolling the virtues of hard work. While attending, the travellers helped subdue a fleeing colonist, Medok. The Pilot of the colony thanked them for their assistance as Police Chief Ola took Medok away. The travellers were also thanked by the Colony's Controller via telescreen, although the young man's picture is static.

In spite of all the pampering the Doctor felt that there was something amiss and went to speak with Medok. The prisoner told him that creatures stalk the colony at night. The Doctor freed him but was apprehended himself. His ignorance of the colony's ways saved him from being sent to "work in the pits", and the Pilot instead sends him to the labour centre to learn about their culture. The travellers learned that the colony exists to mine and refine a toxic gas, although no one seems certain of why they need it.

A strict curfew was enforced that night and everyone was to remain indoors while the police hunted the dangerous Medok.

The Doctor snuck out and met Medok hiding in a construction site, where they encountered a large Macra before being caught by the police. Medok 'confesses' that he manipulated the Doctor so that the Pilot would show leniency, and the Controller ordered the Pilot to brainwash the new travellers.

The brainwashing attempt was made but only Ben was affected; the others fled and the Doctor found the Pilot, discovering that he was brainwashed as well. The Doctor confronted the Controller on the telescreen and demanded to meet him. The screen revealed a frightened old man being dragged away by a giant claw. The Pilot, not comprehending what had happened, ordered the travellers to the gas pits.

The travellers investigated the pits while assigned various jobs and discovered that the crab-like Macra were actually in control of the colony. The Macra needed the gas to survive and conditioned the colonists to pump it for them. The Doctor found his way to the Pilot and manipulated him into seeing the Macra for what they truly were. Horrified, the Pilot finally broke his conditioning.

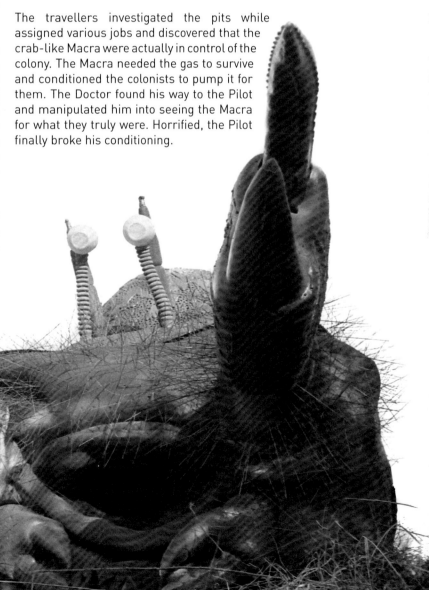

The Macra influenced Ola to suffocate the travellers with the gas, but the Doctor turned the tables and destroyed the Control Room with the help of the now recovered Ben. With the Macra destroyed, the Pilot held a festival in their honour and some colonists proposed making the Doctor the new Pilot. The travellers danced their way back to the TARDIS and left.

CONTINUITY

Beauty pageants in the future have shaken off vestiges of royalty. Rather than beauty queens, the winner of such a pageant is known as a 'beauty president'.

At least some Earth colonies enjoy independence in the future, although outdated terms such as 'colony' and 'pilot' continue to be used. 'Pilot' stems from the original leader of the colony, the pilot that brought them there.

⊙ RUNNING THE ADVENTURE

This adventure explores the hidden dangers of a seemingly utopian society. Much is made of the utopian nature; the travellers are immediately welcomed and refreshed, the community seems happy and content, there is a sense of equality (e.g. they hold beauty pageants for the title of 'Beauty President,' 'Pilot' is a less-authoritarian term for 'Governor'), and the people work for work's sake.

There is a strong allegory about communism as well. The travellers are attended to according to their needs and expected to work for the common good of the colony. The Controller is a 'big brother' figure who is never seen but presents a picture of perfect health. The colonists' minds are filled with propaganda and anything that doesn't fit the Party's (i.e. the Macra's) goals is edited out as if never existing. Dissenters are arrested and re-educated.

Predictably, it is soon revealed that this communist utopian society has a rotten core that reveals that the colonists are slaves to a system that only cares about their usefulness. The Macra need gas to survive and are willing to go to any lengths to ensure that the colonists provide it.

While obviously fuelled by Cold War fears, *The Macra Terror* serves as an example of a utopian society that needs a veil lifted and a threat removed. One could easily replace the communist community with one based on any religion or philosophy that has seemingly achieved perfect harmony. Imagine a world that serves as a religious retreat, with priests and acolytes performing strange tasks or meditations that are actually aiding the Macra or an agrarian paradise where the Macra have machines doing the mining but occasionally take a farmer or two for their dinner.

Rather than giant crabs and gas mines, you could cast the colony as a true 'resort world.' All of the colonists work as resort staff and the world is open to other races as well. The Macra are a 'group mind' of several thousand small crabs. They keep the colony functioning in order to use the guests and staff as a food source.

Every so often, the Macra kill someone and then use mental control to edit everyone's minds so that they don't remember the deceased. The Macra hypnotise some visitors to induce them to choose to remain at the colony in order to and replenish those consumed.

MACRA

The Macra are giant crab-like creatures with claws that can surround a human body. They live beneath the ground and survive on a particular (and unnamed) gas. Without the gas, the Macra become sluggish and even inert. Macra only come to the surface at night. Whether this is due to a physiological need or just to keep from being seen (stretching their legs safely in the dark) is unknown.

The Macra infested a human colony like a parasite, using advanced technology to hypnotise the population and force them to mine the gas that Macra need. The affected humans don't understand why they are mining the gas nor do they accept the existence of the Macra. Where this technology comes from and how the Macra learned to use it is unknown.

MACRA

AWARENESS	2	PRESENCE	4
COORDINATION	3	RESOLVE	3
INGENUITY	3	STRENGTH	12

SKILLS
Athletics 3, Convince 5, Fighting 3, Survival 3

TRAITS
Additional Limbs: The Macra have six legs and two huge, clawed appendages and gain a +4 to their effective speed.
Alien
Alien Appearance: They look like giant crabs.
Armour (Major): The Macra's shell reduces their damage by 10.
Dependency (Gas): The Macra needs to feed on gases to survive.
Fear Factor (3): The Macra are very scary and gain a +6 on rolls to actively scare.
Huge (Minor): A Macra gains +2 to Strength and +1 to Speed, while those trying to spot them gain a +4 and those trying to hit them gain a +2.
Natural Weapon (Claws): The Macra's claws are especially deadly and add +2 to the Macra's strength when using them to inflict damage.
Weakness (Bright light): The Macra remain underground or otherwise hidden during daylight hours. If exposed to daylight or other bright light they become blinded instantly, reducing their Awareness to 0.
Weakness (Fresh Air): The Macra need a particular gas to survive. If deprived of it, they quickly lapse into lethargy.

TECH LEVEL: 6   STORY POINTS: 5-8

It's possible that the Macra have rudimentary natural hypnosis abilities and use this to force the original colonists to build the machines, but there's no evidence of such an ability.

Macra can speak English and use it to issue commands to the colony, but this may be through a translator built into the control centre. Whether Macra eat humans is also a matter of debate, as the Macra seem to hunt humans that they come across (although one leaves Medok's body unmolested after killing him, presumably to continue hunting Jamie).

MACRA INFLUENCING ENGINE

The Macra have fully integrated a hypnosis machine into the communications network of the colony. Every night subliminal messages are fed to the humans as they sleep. A character can resist with an Ingenuity and Resolve roll (Difficulty 15). The longer a victim is exposed to the Macra influence, the bigger the changes in their personality. Here, the Macra use it to brainwash everyone into having the Bad Traits By The Book, Obligation (to serve Control) and Eccentric (mandatory happiness). A single failed resistance roll means the character gains one of these as a Minor Bad Trait. Repeated failures add on the missing Bad Traits or upgrade them to Major Traits (so, six failures in a row turns a character into a brainwashed, gas-mining happy camper like the rest of the citizens of the colony.)

Cost: 2 Story Points

HISTORICAL NOTE: HOLIDAY CAMPS
The Macra-infested colony is reminiscent of traditional Holiday Camps, which had their heyday from the middle of the 20th century until the end of the 1970s and offered families meals and varied entertainments on a strict timetable. Holiday Camps are resorts that cater to low-income working families, who would rent chalets and spend their holiday swimming in the pool, dancing, enjoying the beach (if a seaside resort), or participating in events.

Events are generally scheduled by age group; parents can leave their children for hours at a time as they are participating in their own events. The focus of the activities was on having fun, and many of them were somewhat out of the ordinary. The list on any

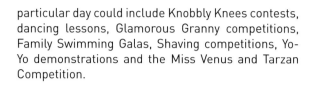
CHAPTER SIX: THE MACRA TERROR

particular day could include Knobbly Knees contests, dancing lessons, Glamorous Granny competitions, Family Swimming Galas, Shaving competitions, Yo-Yo demonstrations and the Miss Venus and Tarzan Competition.

As with the Macra colony, service personnel at holiday camps tended to be incredibly cheery and exuberant. The camps are heavily moderated and even have a form of 'night watchmen' that tour the chalets and ensure that nothing naughty is going on. The Doctor later visits such a camp in his seventh incarnation in **Delta and the Bannermen** (this is worth viewing if you want to get an idea of how to run an adventure in a holiday camp).

More generally, this is a great example of how to turn something cheery into something sinister. The Holiday Camp is actually a mine for toxic gas. Smashing together happy, cheerful entertainments with ghastly or unpleasant purposes makes for wonderful settings – consider, say, a circus that is also a mercenary military unit, or a playground that doubles as a Cyber-conversion experiment, or a seaside resort that eats people.

FURTHER ADVENTURES

- In **Gridlock** the Doctor learns that a devolved Macra has inhabited the gaseous bowels of New Earth. How do the Macra travel through space? What caused their devolution? Is someone leading the Macra to these new hunting grounds? Perhaps the white Macra (the leaders) are still intelligent?

- In spite of looking like giant crustaceans the Macra are obviously intelligent and capable of technological feats. Perhaps they were once

a civilised space-faring race and **The Macra Terror** shows them in a devolving state. This certainly explains why Medok recalls their race name. Perhaps the characters meet the Macra during this earlier period and discover that they are, at this point, a force for good (similar to the Ice Warriors in **The Curse of Peladon**).

- If the Macra do find a gas-rich world then they need to attract colonists to mine it for them. Perhaps a colony ship in distress receives information on a paradise-like world? The characters arrive aboard the ship and note that the colonists are certain that this world is well-suited for a colony, but the characters know it to be ill-suited. Is there a Macra agent on board hypnotising the crew? What awaits them when they land?

MEDOK

AWARENESS	4	PRESENCE	2
COORDINATION	3	RESOLVE	4
INGENUITY	2	STRENGTH	3

SKILLS
Athletics 3, Convince 1, Fighting 3, Knowledge 1, Subterfuge 3, Survival 3, Technology 1, Transport 2

TRAITS
Eccentric: Medok is considered eccentric by the rest of the colony and his own (justified) paranoia makes him just as eccentric to anyone else.

Enslaved: Medok is aware of his enslavement but is ultimately powerless to free himself. Unlike the other Colonists, Medok accepts the existence of the Macra.

Indomitable: Medok's mind is closed to being coerced or hypnotised.

Obsession (Major): Medok is obsessed with getting anyone in the colony to acknowledge the Macra threat.

TECH LEVEL: 6   STORY POINTS: 6

THE TIME SCANNER

The Time Scanner (which is not the same thing as the Time-Space Visualiser installed by the First Doctor) gives glimpses of the ship's next destination. It is normally used as a navigation aid when the Time Lord has full control of his vehicle, but during this era in the Doctor's adventures, when the TARDIS moves seemingly at random, it gives glimpses of the ship's immediate future. The Gamemaster can use the Scanner to foreshadow upcoming adventures, or give the players clues about things to do in the next adventure. For example, if the Scanner shows a scene of two technicians talking about the upcoming arrival of the Earth Examiner, then the players could take this cue to impersonate the Examiner and his assistants when they arrive.

THE PILOT

AWARENESS	3	PRESENCE	5
COORDINATION	3	RESOLVE	4
INGENUITY	3	STRENGTH	3

SKILLS
Athletics 1, Convince 4, Fighting 1, Knowledge 2, Marksman 1, Subterfuge 3, Survival 2, Technology 2, Transport 2

TRAITS
Enslaved: While the Pilot doesn't realise it, he and other colonists are slaves to the Macra. Part of this conditioning involves total denial that the Macra exist.
Voice of Authority: The Pilot has the respect of the colony and gets a +2 on Presence and Convince rolls.

TECH LEVEL: 6   STORY POINTS: 8

POLICE CHIEF OLA

AWARENESS	4	PRESENCE	3
COORDINATION	4	RESOLVE	4
INGENUITY	3	STRENGTH	4

SKILLS
Athletics 4, Convince 3, Fighting 3, Knowledge 2, Marksman 1, Subterfuge 3, Survival 3, Technology 2, Transport 2

TRAITS
By the Book: Ola adheres strictly to the laws of the colony and has trouble thinking "outside the box."
Enslaved: While Ola doesn't realise it, he and other colonists are slaves to the Macra. Part of this conditioning involves total denial that the Macra exist.
Tough: Ola is made of stern stuff and ignores 2 points of any damage taken.

TECH LEVEL: 6   STORY POINTS: 8

THE FACELESS ONES

'You wanted to know what was the secret of Chameleon Tours. Well Inspector, see for yourself!'

⊙ SYNOPSIS

Gatwick Airport, 1966

After the TARDIS arrived on a runway in Gatwick Airport, Polly stumbled into a storeroom owned by Chameleon Youth Tours and observed a pilot, Spencer, shooting a man with a futuristic pistol. Polly fled and brought back the Doctor and Jamie. The Doctor determined that the man was electrocuted by an alien weapon. As they left, Polly was kidnapped with a freeze ray.

Spencer and the other members of Chameleon Youth Tours were actually members of an alien race that had lost their forms in a nuclear war, reducing them to shapeless blobs. They were kidnapping people in order to use their likenesses, achieved by wearing wirelessly linked armbands. In order to cover up the

kidnappings the aliens were mailing fake postcards that indicated that the passengers had reached their destinations.

The travellers, aided by the sister of a kidnapped passenger and a police investigator, gathered evidence and attempted to convince the Commandant of the airport about the scheme. The Commandant didn't understand the motive but agreed to help. The inspector boarded a plane and discovered a futuristic cockpit before being captured by the aliens.

The Doctor, Jamie, and the missing man's sister found a secret office where the Doctor discovered traces of alien gas. Unfortunately, Spencer discovered and paralysed them, then set up a laser beam to kill them. The three managed to deflect the laser with a mirror and freed themselves.

The Doctor investigated the medical unit and discovered that Nurse Pinto was an alien and had been using the unit to affix armbands and map human likenesses onto other aliens. He barely managed to escape when another alien tries to electrocute him. Jamie stowed away on a Chameleon flight and was taken to a space station orbiting the Earth. He learned that the kidnapped humans were being miniaturised for easy transport.

The Doctor confronted one of the aliens and got him to reveal the truth. This alien was killed for revealing their secrets, but not before the Doctor learned that the bodies of the currently mimicked people were still nearby. He also learned that removing the armbands, while harmless to humans, killed the aliens. The bodies were found in the car park and the Doctor forced the aliens to negotiate. After killing their uncompromising leader, the other aliens agreed to leave with a little scientific aid from the Doctor.

As the travellers prepared to leave, Ben and Polly discovered that they were on Earth on the same day that they left, meaning that they could easily return to their normal lives. The Doctor wished them well before telling Jamie that he couldn't find the TARDIS.

CONTINUITY

As luck would have it (or perhaps a glitch with the Fast Return Switch), the TARDIS has actually landed the day before it left with Ben and Polly for the first time (meaning that, for two days, there are two Doctors (of different incarnations) and two Bens and Pollys on Earth. There are also two threats (or three, since the Daleks are busy setting their trap for the Doctor), as WOTAN and the Chameleons hatch their plots at the same time.

RUNNING THE ADVENTURE

After an adventure revolving around the evils of communism **The Faceless Ones** puts the spotlight on the excesses of democracy. The Chameleons prey on the new-found mobility of young travellers to be able to afford to see the world. It also displays ruthless capitalism; the Chameleons, obsessed with their own survival, see humans as little more than a new wardrobe and, in the grand scheme, as a species that can afford to lose tens of thousands of individuals.

This adventure is also a rather blatant allegory on the horrors of nuclear war. The Chameleons are obviously fallout victims, and their bad behaviour is now affecting the next generation (the Chameleons prefer to take young people).

At its very core, this is a simple bait-and-switch adventure. The Chameleons are offering trips to the Continent, but the characters discover clues and evidence that things aren't what they seem. Unlike **The Macra Terror**, there is no brainwashing involved, although there are secret agents mimicking people – another Cold War theme popping up there! If a player

character gets abducted like Polly, then the best thing to do is get the player to play the Chameleon duplicate. You can either secretly inform the player that their real character is temporarily out of action and that they are playing a sinister copy, or let all the players in on the secret and trust in their ability to split in-character and out-of-character knowledge.

CHAMELEON ARMBANDS

A Chameleon Black Armband is matched with a Chameleon White Armband. The wearer of the black armband takes on the appearance of the person wearing the matching white armband. Some of the host's personality may be transferred to the wearer as well. If the matching white armband is removed prior to the removal of the black armband, then the wearer of the black armband disintegrates.

Traits: Mimic Appearance, Restriction: Injury (if the white armband is removed from the mimicked victim then the wearer gets a lethal (4/L/L) shock), Restriction: Single Appearance (the wearer of the black armband can only take on the appearance of the one wearing the white armband).
Cost: 1 Story Point

CHAMELEON MINIATURISATION DEVICE

This gadget miniaturises a victim into the shape of a small doll or action figure. Victims are normally placed in suspended animation first. The process is reversible.

Traits: Stuns victim (S/S/S) and shrinks them to doll size.
Cost: 2 Story Points

CHAMELEONS

The Chameleons are a race that damaged their genetics in a thermonuclear war (or, as they put it, they lost their identities in a colossal explosion). While they once looked human, the Chameleons are now humanoid blobs of twisted, bloated flesh. Through technology they can copy the forms of other human-like beings and imprint it on their own, but the continually mutating genes in their bodies mean that the Chameleon needs constant reinforcement from the host body. To this end, Chameleons have gone to various human-like worlds and steal young people so that they can mimic their form.

'Chameleons' is not the name of the race; it is the name the Doctor dubbed them as they were operating a scheme at Gatwick Airport under the guise of 'Chameleon Tours'. The Chameleons entice young people to sign up for tours to exotic places and then fly them into space, drugging them and miniaturising them in the process. Their goal is to collect 50,000 people to stabilise the appearance of their own race. The space shuttles disguised as airplanes are armed with laser cannons for defence.

The technology used by the Chameleons to copy a physical form sometimes transfers mental and/or social traits as well. A Chameleon might begin to have feelings for one human or start disliking a Chameleon wearing the image of the copied human's rival.

While the Chameleons have agreed to the Doctor's request that they solve their problem through other means, it's possible that the length of time needed to find an alternative will convince at least some Chameleons to return to abducting members of other races.

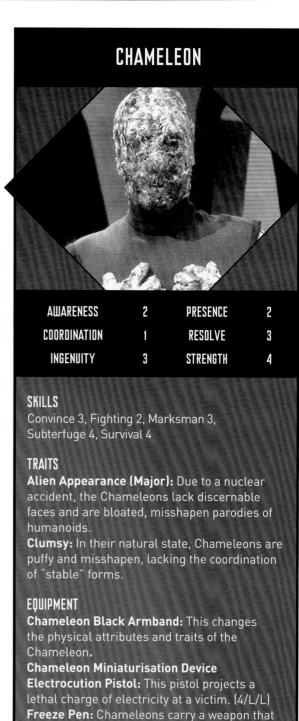

CHAMELEON

AWARENESS	2	PRESENCE	2
COORDINATION	1	RESOLVE	3
INGENUITY	3	STRENGTH	4

SKILLS
Convince 3, Fighting 2, Marksman 3, Subterfuge 4, Survival 4

TRAITS
Alien Appearance (Major): Due to a nuclear accident, the Chameleons lack discernable faces and are bloated, misshapen parodies of humanoids.
Clumsy: In their natural state, Chameleons are puffy and misshapen, lacking the coordination of "stable" forms.

EQUIPMENT
Chameleon Black Armband: This changes the physical attributes and traits of the Chameleon.
Chameleon Miniaturisation Device
Electrocution Pistol: This pistol projects a lethal charge of electricity at a victim. (4/L/L)
Freeze Pen: Chameleons carry a weapon that can put a victim in suspended animation (a knockout of indefinite length). This weapon is often disguised as a normal small object such as a pen. (S/S/S)

TECH LEVEL: 6   **STORY POINTS: 3-6**

PACKAGE HOLIDAYS

Interestingly, after an adventure in the future modelled on the Holiday Camp, the Doctor returns to the present and gets involved in an adventure that features the pastime that is replacing Holiday Camps; the package holiday.

Prior to the internet and price shopping, tour companies offered all-inclusive trips that, for one low price, a traveller could pay a tour company to handle travel, accommodations, meals, and tours. All the traveller had to do was arrive at the airport on time.

CHAMELEON FUN

Through some jiggery-pokery it may be possible to fine-tune the Chameleon armbands to eliminate the threat to the white armband wearer and allow her to remain conscious while the black armband wearer takes on her appearance. This could be very useful in subterfuge, as one person could be in two places at once (providing an alibi) or someone with a useful skill can utilise it in an area where only her companion has access. It's certainly possible that the bands fell into the hands of UNIT or Torchwood, as well as less scrupulous collectors like Henry van Statten.

FURTHER ADVENTURES

- The Doctor promised to help the Chameleons find a cure for their condition. What if it doesn't work? The Chameleons won't be so trusting of the Doctor or Time Lords in general the next time they meet. Finding a cure might require the Doctor to travel back to the time when the Chameleons lost their identities in a gigantic explosion.

- Having the Chameleons visit Earth (or a similar planet) in an earlier period changes their methodology. Entire villages could disappear overnight with no one being any the wiser. Perhaps the Chameleons have manufactured a plague to which their victims are immune (their water supply is laced with the antidote) and while the area is quarantined the Chameleons swoop in and kidnap their victims. Chameleons could pose as local lords, soldiers, or physicians in order to maintain the ruse.

- Not all Chameleons are likely to sign up to the Doctor's proposed solutions, especially if they are less than perfect. Individual Chameleons may snatch a body and effectively live in exile, or an enterprising Chameleon may run a black market for healthy bodies.

SAMANTHA BRIGGS

AWARENESS	4	PRESENCE	3
COORDINATION	4	RESOLVE	4
INGENUITY	3	STRENGTH	2

SKILLS
Athletics 2, Convince 3, Fighting 1, Knowledge 2, Marksman 2, Subterfuge 2, Survival 1, Technology 2, Transport 1

TRAITS
Argumentative: Samantha's assertiveness sometimes land her into trouble, where she often bursts into tears once she's realised it.
Attractive: Samantha gets +2 to rolls in which her appearance would be a factor.
Inexperienced: Samantha doesn't have a great deal of life experience and gets easily frustrated.
Insatiable Curiosity

TECH LEVEL: 5   STORY POINTS: 9

DETECTIVE INSPECTOR CROSSLAND

AWARENESS	4	PRESENCE	4
COORDINATION	3	RESOLVE	4
INGENUITY	3	STRENGTH	3

SKILLS
Athletics 3, Convince 4, Craft 1, Fighting 3, Knowledge 3, Marksman 3, Medicine 2, Science 3, Subterfuge 4, Survival 2, Technology 3, Transport 2

TRAITS
Insatiable Curiosity

TECH LEVEL: 5   STORY POINTS: 6

CAPTAIN BLADE (HUMAN DUPLICATE)

AWARENESS	3	PRESENCE	4
COORDINATION	3	RESOLVE	4
INGENUITY	4	STRENGTH	3

SKILLS
Athletics 3, Convince 4, Fighting 3, Knowledge 4, Marksman 4, Medicine 2, Science 2, Subterfuge 4, Survival 3, Technology 3, Transport 5

TRAITS
Alien
Voice of Authority: Blade is in charge of the Earth operation and gets a +2 on Presence and Convince rolls.

EQUIPMENT
Pilot uniform, electrocution gun, paralysation pen

TECH LEVEL: 5   STORY POINTS: 3

CHAPTER SEVEN:
THE EVIL OF THE DALEKS, THE TOMB OF THE CYBERMEN, THE ABOMINABLE SNOWMAN

THE EVIL OF THE DALEKS

'You will take the "Dalek Factor." You will spread it to the entire history of Earth!'

SYNOPSIS

London, 1966 and 1866; Skaro, the Future

In 1966, Dalek agents stole the TARDIS and deliberately left clues for the Doctor and Jamie to follow. This led to an antiques store owned by Professor Waterfield, a time traveller from 1866. He sold 'Victorian antiques' that were actually everyday Victorian knick-knacks transported through time. The Doctor and Jamie snuck inside and discovered an alien platform in a hidden room. They were knocked out using a gas trap and Professor Waterfield brought them back to 1866.

Waterfield, along with his partner Thomas Maxtible, woke up the Doctor. They explained that they'd built a time machine with mirrors and attracted the attention of the Daleks. The Daleks were holding Waterfield's daughter Victoria hostage in order to ensure their compliance. The Daleks wanted the Doctor's aid in isolating 'the Human Factor,' or what made humanity so resilient that they defeated the Daleks every time.

The Daleks forced the Doctor to use Jamie in an experiment to free Victoria. The Daleks also used a mind-controlled human, a mute muscleman named Kemel, to challenge Jamie. During an altercation Jamie saved Kemel and the two became friends. They rescued Victoria, but Jamie was separated from them. A Dalek forced Kemel to take Victoria through the mirrored cabinet back to Skaro.

Through the experiments performed on Jaime, the Doctor synthesised the Human Factor and implanted

it into three Daleks, who he named Alpha, Beta and Omega. These Daleks began acting like children, playing with the Doctor, until they received a summons to Skaro. Jamic found the Doctor and they searched for Victoria, while Maxtible tried to convince Waterfield to join him; Maxtible's reason for aiding the Daleks was that they promised him the secret of turning metal into gold. When Waterfield refused, Maxtible knocked him to the brink of unconsciousness and left for Skaro.

The Daleks left a bomb behind but the Doctor and Jamie found Waterfield and the three escaped through the mirrored cabinet just in time. They entered a Dalek city where they were soon captured and reunited with Victoria, Kemel, and Maxtible. The Daleks had no intention of giving him the secret of atomic transmutation, and instead imprisoned him with the other humans. He had, however, discovered something useful – the Daleks had brought the TARDIS to Skaro.

The three humanised Daleks were spreading the human factor through the city and Skaro was soon at the brink of civil war. The Doctor was brought before the Dalek Emperor, who informed the Doctor that his real plan was to isolate the Dalek Factor and have the Doctor spread it through human history in the TARDIS. The Doctor duped the Emperor into creating even more humanised Daleks before escaping during the confusion. Kemel was killed by Maxtible, who had been infected with the Dalek Factor. Waterfield was killed saving the Doctor from extermination, and the Doctor promised to look after Victoria for him.

The Doctor, Jamie, and Victoria escaped to the edge of the city where they watched the civil war rage within. The Doctor noted that this might be the end of the Daleks before the three left in the TARDIS.

CONTINUITY

The Dalek Emperor is seen for the first time. He is guarded by black Daleks. It is unknown whether this Dalek Emperor is actually Davros.

There's some uncertainty as to whether Maxtible and Waterfield's mirrored time machine worked or simply tapped into Dalek Time Corridor technology. We presume the latter, as the time mats that the Doctor uses to get back to 1866 and from there to Skaro are Dalek devices.

This is the first adventure where two different Dalek factions vie for control.

RUNNING THE ADVENTURE

Once again, the Daleks use time travel against the Doctor, but this time they aren't simply trying to kill him. They acknowledge the genius of their enemy and force him to help them become an even greater threat. Normally, this task would fall to a supporting character, usually a mad genius or well-meaning dupe (Professors Maxtible and Waterfield seem to fit this role, but they are simply pawns in a greater game).

This adventure answers the question of why an old enemy wouldn't simply kill the characters once they are in their grasp. Tension is added by using the other characters in the experiments to make the enemy stronger, with a real risk of death. Finally, there's a chance that the character's meddling actually does change the enemy for the better (the Daleks that put the Master on trial in **Doctor Who: The Movie** could be the triumphant humanised Daleks), or eliminate their threat, as Skaro descends into a civil war that the Doctor believes will be the end of the Daleks.

Finally, this is an adventure about conversion. For the first time, being a Dalek is presented as something more than a Skaro mutant that is forced to live in a casing. It is a 'brainwashing' method that can be applied to anyone; similarly, a sense of humanity can be instilled in the Daleks.

WHAT ARE THE DALEK AND HUMAN FACTORS?

The Dalek and Human factors are distillations of the essence that makes one a Dalek or Human. They are presented as opposites in this adventure, although they are basically enhancements of particular virtues; the Human Factor seems to encourage 'good' emotions, while the Dalek Factor engenders hate, xenophobia, and slavish devotion to the Dalek hierarchy.

The question here is whether these factors are nature versus nurture. As cyborgs, the Daleks created by Davros in **Genesis of the Daleks** have partially computerised brains (one lacked the ability to recognise 'pity'). As Daleks can survive outside their casings, at least for short periods, it makes more sense that the 'databank' is a teaching machine or hypnosis technique. Taking this a step further, the arches in this adventure are primarily hypnosis machines that instantly rewire the brain with mental conditioning.

THE FACTORS

Dalek research – aided by the Doctor – distilled the essence of humanity into the Human Factor, the root of our compassion and adaptability and determination and creativity. By isolating the Human Factor, the Daleks were able to create its inverse, the Dalek Factor. Either Factor could be imprinted onto a living creature by means of the Factor Arch.

HUMAN FACTOR (SPECIAL GOOD TRAIT)

Possession of the Human Factor increases the character's Resolve by 1, and gives the traits Empathic or Brave. It also makes the possessor more compassionate. Most importantly, it gives an extra 2 Story Points. The Human Factor costs 4 Character Points.

DALEK FACTOR (SPECIAL GOOD TRAIT)

The inverse Dalek Factor increases the character's Ingenuity, Resolve and Marksman scores by 1, and gives the traits Obsession and Obligation (Serve the Daleks). Furthermore, the character gets a free Story Point every adventure that can only be spent on furthering the cause of conquering and exterminating lesser species to ensure the ultimate victory of the Daleks. Gaining the Dalek Factor costs 2 Character Points.

FACTOR ARCH (SPECIAL GADGET)

The Factor Arch is a biodata modification imprinter that projects the Dalek Factor or Human Factor onto any creature that passes through it. A character may resist imprinting by making an Ingenuity + Resolve test against Difficulty 21. If the imprinting succeeds, the character immediately gains the appropriate Factor. If he does not have the Character Points spare to purchase it, he must do so as soon as he gains the necessary Experience Points.

Human characters may not possess the Human Factor, Daleks can't have the Dalek Factor, and imprinting one Factor cancels out the other.

DID THE DALEKS TRAP THE RIGHT DOCTOR?

How exactly did the Daleks know that the Doctor would be in London at a particular point in 1966? While it's possible that the Daleks took a look at 'tomorrow's Times' and caught a reference to the Doctor (or more likely an 'anonymous helper') solving a strange kidnapping scheme at Gatwick, it's more likely that the Daleks had knowledge of WOTAN's attempt to take over the world. It stands to reason that the trap was set for the First Doctor and they mistakenly took the Second Doctor's TARDIS. The plot thickens when one notes that the authorisation signature was signed 'J. Smith.' Given his propensity to play long games and chess matches, perhaps the Seventh Doctor had a hand in duping the Daleks to take the wrong TARDIS?

MIRRORED TIME TRAVEL

Professors Waterfield and Maxtible have created a time machine by lining a room with mirrors. Somehow, the lightbeams reflected in this room managed to tap into a time corridor and connected 1866 to Skaro. While it is likely that a Dalek time corridor provided the main link between Earth and Skaro, there is certainly something odd going on with mirrors and time travel. UNIT use mirrors as a part of their time machine in **Turn Left**, while the Doctor traps one of the Family of Blood behind all mirrors in another adventure. Waterfield may be like a caveman who bangs two shiny warm rocks together, then feels sick – he's discovered uranium, radiation and radiation poisoning all at once, but has no context to describe his discovery.

Mirrored time travel could have all sorts of implications. Perhaps an old mansion has enough carefully placed mirrors that ascending a staircase a certain way can transport someone from 1966 to 1666. Perhaps someone in the past is using mirror technology to glimpse the future and make a profit (or at least make the right decisions) in the past. Perhaps a time traveller is slowly going insane as she continues to make adjustments in order to make her future perfect.

TIME CORRIDOR

The Daleks have developed a Time Corridor, an artificial link between two fixed points in time via a stable quantum wormhole through the vortex. You simply step in one end of the Corridor and are whisked to the other end in the blink of an eye, protected from the ravages of the vortex by the quantum energy field of the Corridor itself. The Time Corridor can create a stable destination point, but provides no means with which to return until a fixed 'gateway' can be installed at that destination. These fixed gateways allow travelers to journey from one end of the corridor to the other instantaneously, and one can see from one side to the other and step through as easily as walking through a door.

The quantum tunnel created by a Time Corridor is vulnerable to vortex turbulence. Like solar flare interference with radio communications, massive shifts in the flow of the vortex can make a Time Corridor unstable and even the most stable connections have to be reset from time to time after a time-surge washes away the quantum tunnel and everything in transit inside it. The Daleks have monitoring equipment to keep track of these sorts of natural forces but they are still a hazard.

Time Corridors are also navigational hazards in vortex travel. Unwary Time Travel Capsules 'fall' into them, getting sucked into an artificial plug-hole in the vortex and forcibly deposited at its end. It can be very difficult for even a TARDIS to break free from their pull once caught inside, and the worst part is that once you've materialized at the corridors destination, it's practically impossible to take off again while the Corridor is still active without damaging your Time Travel Capsule.

Traits: Transmit, Vortex, Restriction (Gates Required, Loss of Corridor*)
* On a Disastrous Failure when using the Time Corridor, anything or anyone transported is lost.
Cost: 7 Story Points

For descriptions and game information on the Daleks, see page 34 in the Enemies chapter.

FURTHER ADVENTURES

- Skaro is now a dead world, with the Daleks having destroyed themselves. An archaeological expedition comes to Skaro and unearths the Dalek Factor arch, which is still in working condition. While powering it up, some scientists are accidentally converted into Daleks. Can they be stopped before they unearth more Dalek technology and resurrect the true Dalek race?

- A mirrored time machine is relatively 'low-tech'. It's certainly possible for someone else to invent one. What happens when an opportunist takes items from a more advanced time back to the past or uses her knowledge of the intervening years to become the most powerful person on the planet? For that matter, what happened to the 1966 end of Waterfield's time machine?

- A colony is in trouble from an impending cataclysm and reaches out for help. The Daleks answer and seemingly have altruistic motives. Is this a group of humanised Daleks that survived the civil war, or are they regular Daleks playing a ruthless game for reasons that benefit them?

THEODORE MAXTIBLE

AWARENESS	3	PRESENCE	4
COORDINATION	2	RESOLVE	4
INGENUITY	6	STRENGTH	3

SKILLS
Athletics 2, Convince 4, Craft 4, Fighting 2, Knowledge 5, Marksman 2, Medicine 2, Science 6, Subterfuge 3, Technology 6, Transport 4

TRAITS
Boffin: Maxtible can create gadgets through jiggery-pokery.
Obsession: Maxtible is determined to learn how to turn lead into gold.
Technically Adept: Maxtible gets a +2 on Technology rolls and can operate gadgets.
Unattractive: Maxtible is a bear of a man with a shaggy mane and wild stare. He gets a -2 in most social situations but a +2 to rolls when intimidating someone.

TECH LEVEL: 4   STORY POINTS: 6

EDWARD WATERFIELD

AWARENESS	3	PRESENCE	3
COORDINATION	2	RESOLVE	2
INGENUITY	6	STRENGTH	2

SKILLS
Athletics 1, Convince 2, Craft 5, Fighting 1, Knowledge 5, Marksman 2, Medicine 2, Science 6, Subterfuge 3, Technology 6, Transport 4

TRAITS
Boffin: Waterfield can create gadgets through jiggery-pokery.
Technically Adept: Waterfield gets a +2 on Technology rolls and can operate gadgets.

TECH LEVEL: 4   STORY POINTS: 6

KEMEL

AWARENESS	3	PRESENCE	2
COORDINATION	3	RESOLVE	3
INGENUITY	3	STRENGTH	5

SKILLS
Athletics 5, Fighting 5, Knowledge 3, Marksman 1, Subterfuge 3, Survival 3, Technology 1, Transport 1

TRAITS
Mute: Kemel cannot speak.
Tough: Any damage that affects Kemel's attributes is reduced by 2

TECH LEVEL: 4   STORY POINTS: 3

THE TOMB OF THE CYBERMEN

'You belong to us. You shall be like us.'

⊘ SYNOPSIS

Telos, at least the 26th century

The TARDIS landed on the desolate planet of Telos. The travellers discovered an Earth archaeological expedition led by Professor Parry that was looking for the lost city of the Cybermen. They found an electrically-charged entrance that the Doctor was able to open after the unfortunate death of the first expedition member that touched it. Inside was a large control room with a couple other doors; the expedition split up to explore them. Klieg, an intellectual expedition member, remained in the main control room to try and open a large hatch.

Kaftan, the sponsor of the expedition, conspired with Klieg. She tried to eliminate Victoria by trapping her in a sarcophagus-like Cybermen revitalising chamber while Jamie was almost killed by a weapon testing device that killed another expedition member. Jamie also discovered a tiny Cybermat, which Victoria put in her purse. Captain Hopper arrived and announced that the rocket ship was sabotaged. As he couldn't

trust anyone he wanted them to remain in the control room while the repairs were completed. The sabotage was actually carried out by Kaftan's large mute servant Toberman.

With subtle help from the Doctor, Klieg managed to open the hatch and the men descended. They discovered a honeycomb of extremely cold corridors. Upstairs, Kaftan drugged Victoria asleep and closed the hatch, trapping the rest of the expedition below before she was stunned unconscious by Victoria's Cybermat. Below, the expedition discovered the suspended animation chambers of the Cybermen and Klieg woke them up after shooting and killing a protesting expedition member. Klieg revealed that he was a member of the Brotherhood of Logicians and needed the Cybermen's physical power to create a new, logical order.

The Cybermen advanced on the expedition with their Cyber-Controller, the leader of the Cybermen. Klieg attempted to forge an alliance, but the Cyber-Controller rejected him. Instead, the Cyber-Controller revealed that the entire tomb was a trap; the Cybermen were out of supplies and needed intelligent beings to convert; the series of tests to obtain entry had confirmed them to be suitable for conversion. Luckily, Captain Hopper was able to open the hatch and mount a rescue; only Toberman was captured as the rest of the team made it through the hatch and closed it.

Kaftan and Klieg were isolated while the expedition members were still barred from returning to the ship. The Cybermen send Cybermats through the vents to attack the expedition. The Doctor neutralised the threat, but Kaftan and Klieg used a Cyberman weapon to establish control and re-opened the hatch. Klieg bargained with the Cyber-Controller, who ascended into the control room with a partially-converted Toberman. The Doctor tried to sabotage the Cyber-Controller's revitalisation but failed; the Cyber-Controller was only seemingly destroyed when the Doctor appealed to Toberman's humanity after the Cyber-Controller killed Kaftan and the giant tossed the Cyber-Controller into a control panel. Other Cybermen emerging from the hatch were destroyed while the rest retreated to the chambers to conserve power.

The Doctor took Toberman with him into the corridors in order to refreeze the Cybermen. Klieg attempted to stop him, wanting to be the new Cyber-Controller, but was killed by a Cyberman. Toberman destroyed the Cyberman and the Doctor completed the task. Unfortunately, the Cyber-Controller was not quite dead and attacked the expedition as it fled. Toberman sacrificed himself by closing the door and electrocuting himself along with the Cyber-Controller. Once again, the Cybermen were entombed for eternity.

CONTINUITY
Kaftan and Klieg belong to a group known as the Brotherhood of Logicians. The Brotherhood wants to restructure Earth civilization based on pure logic. The Brotherhood will use force to achieve their goal and hope to use the Cybermen as their army.

The Cyber-Controller simply called 'the Controller' in this adventure; however, in **Attack of the Cybermen** it is revealed that 'Cyber-Controller' is his title. A remnant of the Cybermen remains frozen on the planet Telos until they are later awakened prior to **Attack of the Cybermen**.

Small food cubes are carried in place of actual food. Whether this is standard food is unknown but artificial food was created by the time of the New Ice Age.

Kaftan offers £50 to the first person that opens the outer doors. This is probably not British currency as we know it today as it seems a trivial amount, especially with at least five centuries of inflation. It's possible that either the British pound was re-valued, or this may be a different type of currency altogether (a galactic pound?).

The Doctor claims to be around 450 Earth years old in this story. This would make him half the age he gives to Rose Tyler in his ninth incarnation.

◎ RUNNING THE ADVENTURE
Tomb of the Cybermen is essentially an early 20th century pulp serial rewritten for science fiction. There is an ancient tomb sitting in a desolate area, mummies that can be summoned and returned to torpor through ritual (in this case a control panel), and a questionable prize. We even have scarab beetles in the form of Cybermats. The sponsors of the expedition are treasure hunters that want to plunder the tomb rather than study it and their grandiose plan to conquer Earth echoes the mad world conquerors of pulp fiction.

Added to this is the drama of a rival expedition and puzzles that must be solved in order to get into the main treasure room. Here, the 'rival expedition' is actually different factions within the same expedition. Its sponsors, Klieg and Kaftan, clearly have a different agenda than Professor Parry and, should they succeed, their plans spell doom for the rest of the expedition. The puzzles require all factions to work together and the 'treasure' is the mummies themselves, or the Cybermen.

THE TOMB
After several defeats, the Cybermen attempt to attract brilliant minds by entombing their army in a freezer that can only be opened by solving a number of logical problems. The main doors to the buried tomb are trapped; discerning the electrical trap (damage 6/L/L) requires an Awareness and Technology roll (Difficulty 15), while disarming it requires an Ingenuity and Technology roll (Difficulty 18). If the trap is disarmed or simply sprung then the doors may be safely opened. They are, however, heavy, and require great strength to open. This can

be accomplished with a Strength and Resolve roll (Difficulty 18). This opens the doors into the main control room.

There are three exits from the control room; a door on either side as well as a large hatch that leads below. The hatch is quite evident but the doors are hidden, requiring an Awareness and Ingenuity roll (Difficulty 18) to notice them. A character studying the walls looking for hidden doors can find them with an Awareness and Subterfuge roll (Difficulty 15).

Opening the hatch requires a high level of mathematics knowledge working the levers on the control panel. A character that makes an Ingenuity and Science roll (Difficulty18) can figure out how to open and close the hatch. Besides the hatch, there are plenty of rooms to explore behind the doors. The characters may find the weapon development room and the Cybermen rejuvenation chamber.

Once the characters manage to get the hatch open, they can descend into the maze of corridors that lead to the Cybermen tombs. Once the Cybermen are thawed, however, the adventure changes to confrontation. The Cybermen Controller reveals the plot and takes at least one member of the expedition hostage to begin conversion.

THE MATTER OF TELOS

The importance of Telos is a bit over-inflated where the Cybermen are concerned; it is only referenced in this adventure; it goes unmentioned in the other three instances where the Cybermen met the Second Doctor. This makes sense if the Cybermen landed on Telos after the events of the other four adventures (if we include all of the First and Second Doctor's adventures with them), which take place in the 20th and 21st centuries.

If we take the Cybermen Cyber-Controller at his word then the Cybermen retreated here after the events of **The Moonbase** (and by extension **The Wheel in Space**) because they were out of supplies, which were dwindling after the destruction of Mondas (for which the Cybermen blame the Doctor, but he was really little more than a knowledgeable observer). It's likely that Telos had been scouted in advance when Mondas passed by or the more militaristic Cybermen came upon it during their explorations. Earth was still a tempting target, but the Cybermen were foiled at every opportunity. By retreating to Telos, they'd hoped to await more intelligent specimens from Earth in order to convert them and hopefully mount a successful invasion of Earth. It took 500 years for the humans to find them.

A WORTHY SUCCESSOR?

One of the strangest aspects of this adventure is that the Cybermen seem to be waiting for "advanced brains" to repopulate the Cybermen race. It is interesting that the only human they convert in the story is Toberman, who is Kaftan's muscle, as well as the fact that the Cybermen hardly seem picky about who they convert in other encounters with them. So why do they set up elaborate tests here?

Underneath all of their metal and plastic, the Cybermen are still organic beings. Like all organic beings, they'll eventually grow old and die. It's possible that what the Cybermen are looking for in this instance is another Cybermen Cyber-Controller (or Cyber-Controllers) to replace their aging leader. It certainly explains why they're willing to remain in suspended animation (thus preserving the current Cybermen Cyber-Controller's life) until a suitable candidate comes along. His or her friends, of course, will be converted into regular Cybermen.

FURTHER ADVENTURES

- In spite of the evidence, Klieg is not dead. The Cyberman that attacked him used Neurotrope X to make him appear dead. Similarly, the Cybermen Cyber-Controller was also only damaged. Klieg is converted and makes several upgrades to the Cybermen design (including the Cybermen Cyber-Controller). Armed with Klieg's knowledge, the Cybermen know of several colony worlds ripe for conquest and conversion. The characters arrive at one of these outposts just before the Cybermen attack.

- A faction of Cybermen that never got frozen has been perfecting their bodies in preparation for war. The characters arrive at a colony jubilantly celebrating the repulsion of a Cybermen invasion. As the characters examine a Cyberman corpse they make a shocking discovery; this Cyberman would be immune to the glitter guns of the upcoming Cyber-Wars. The characters need to find the remnants of this Cybermen faction and stop them from contacting and upgrading those on Telos.

- The plan of the Brotherhood of Logicians in this adventure seems very – well – illogical. It makes more sense that this is the mad scheme of a couple of members rather than a concerted effort by the group. While Klieg and Kaftan are off chasing old legends, the leadership of the Brotherhood is conducting genetic experiments to create a perfectly logical 'super human'. Of course, the first wave of these new humans 'logically' try to take over Earth.

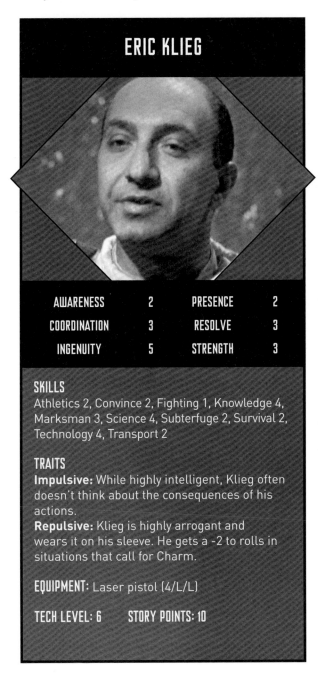

ERIC KLIEG

AWARENESS	2	PRESENCE	2
COORDINATION	3	RESOLVE	3
INGENUITY	5	STRENGTH	3

SKILLS
Athletics 2, Convince 2, Fighting 1, Knowledge 4, Marksman 3, Science 4, Subterfuge 2, Survival 2, Technology 4, Transport 2

TRAITS
Impulsive: While highly intelligent, Klieg often doesn't think about the consequences of his actions.
Repulsive: Klieg is highly arrogant and wears it on his sleeve. He gets a -2 to rolls in situations that call for Charm.

EQUIPMENT: Laser pistol (4/L/L)

TECH LEVEL: 6   STORY POINTS: 10

CAPTAIN HOPPER

AWARENESS	4	PRESENCE	4
COORDINATION	4	RESOLVE	4
INGENUITY	4	STRENGTH	3

SKILLS
Athletics 3, Convince 4, Fighting 3, Knowledge 2, Marksman 4, Medicine 1, Science 3, Subterfuge 3, Survival 3, Technology 3, Transport 5

TRAITS
Brave: Hopper gets a +2 bonus to Resolve rolls when he needs to show courage.
Quick Reflexes: Captain Hopper generally goes first in a round.

EQUIPMENT: Laser pistol (4/L/L), Smoke grenades

STORY POINTS: 10

TOBERMAN, AUGMENTED

AWARENESS	3	PRESENCE	2
COORDINATION	4	RESOLVE	5
INGENUITY	2	STRENGTH	7

SKILLS
Athletics 5, Fighting 5, Knowledge 2, Marksman 2, Subterfuge 3, Survival 3, Technology 2, Transport 2

TRAITS
Cyborg
Fear Factor (1): Seeing Toberman's augmented arm for the first time is unsettling and he gains a +2 on attempts to scare someone.
Indomitable: Toberman gets a +4 to resist or shake off mind-controlling effects.
Tough: Toberman is strong. Subtract 2 points before applying Attribute damage.

TECH LEVEL: 6   **STORY POINTS: 6**

KAFTAN

AWARENESS	4	PRESENCE	4
COORDINATION	3	RESOLVE	3
INGENUITY	5	STRENGTH	2

SKILLS
Athletics 2, Convince 4, Fighting 1, Knowledge 4, Marksman 3, Medicine 2, Science 4, Subterfuge 2, Survival 2, Technology 4, Transport 2

TRAITS
Eccentric: Kaftan acts in an odd manner that makes her distinctive.
Resourceful Pockets: Kaftan always has something useful in her bag.

EQUIPMENT: Laser pistol (4/L/L), Strong sedative (S/S/S)

TECH LEVEL: 6   **STORY POINTS: 6**

PROFESSOR PARRY

AWARENESS	5	PRESENCE	3
COORDINATION	3	RESOLVE	3
INGENUITY	4	STRENGTH	2

SKILLS
Athletics 3, Convince 3, Craft 3, Fighting 1, Knowledge 5, Marksman 1, Medicine 2, Science 3, Survival 3, Technology 2, Transport 2

TRAITS
Sense of Direction: Parry gets a +2 on rolls to figure out directions.

TECH LEVEL: 6   **STORY POINTS: 6**

TOBERMAN

AWARENESS	3	PRESENCE	2
COORDINATION	4	RESOLVE	5
INGENUITY	2	STRENGTH	6

SKILLS
Athletics 5, Fighting 5, Knowledge 2, Marksman 2, Subterfuge 3, Survival 3, Technology 2, Transport 2

TRAITS
Indomitable: Toberman gets a +4 to resist or shake off mind-controlling effects.
Tough: Toberman is strong. Subtract 2 points before applying Attribute damage.

TECH LEVEL: 6   **STORY POINTS: 6**

THE ABOMINABLE SNOWMEN

'Come in, my child, come in. You have no alternative.'

⊙ SYNOPSIS

Tibet, 1935

The TARDIS arrived in the Himalayas, offering the Doctor an opportunity to return a holy Tibetan bell, a ghanta, which he'd taken for safe keeping from a monastery in 1630. After finding large footprints near the TARDIS, the Doctor decided to return the relic to the Det-Sen Monastery alone. On the way down the mountain he discovered a dead body near an abandoned tent, and found a bag and rifle which he took with him. On arrival at the monastery, the Doctor was accosted by the monks and an English explorer named Travers, whose rucksack and rifle the Doctor was carrying. Travers accused the Doctor of killing his companion, changing his earlier story about a creature attacking them. Khrisong, the leading warrior amongst the monks, didn't really trust Travers, but as some monks had also been killed recently he decided to imprison the Doctor until the monks decided what to do with him.

Jamie and Victoria soon got bored waiting in the TARDIS and went to explore. After seeing the strange tracks outside the ship, they came across a timber-propped cave, and ran inside when a large, furred creature approached. Jamie found a pyramid of silver spheres at the back of the cave. As the creature entered the cave, Jamie knocked out a support beam and brought down part of the roof onto it. Jamie pocketed one of the spheres, and they noticed that the buried creature was stirring. Jamie and Victoria fled the creature and headed after the Doctor to warn him.

Although the monks disagreed over the Doctor's fate, Khrisong decided to act. He tied the Doctor to the monastery gate to see if the Yetis would rescue him, proving that he was in league with them. After the Doctor was taken from his cell, a young monk named Thonmi found the ghanta and realised that the Doctor had returned it. He took it to the Abbot, Songsten, and they were joined by their master – the lama, Padmasambhava. The lama learned that the Doctor had returned the relic, and asked that he be treated with respect and kindness. The Abbot ordered that the Doctor be released.

Travers left the monastery and met Jamie and Victoria, who agreed to show him the Yeti's cave in return for him first taking them to the monastery. The Doctor was freed, and examined the silver sphere while Jamie told him what had happened in the cave. Jamie and the monks captured a Yeti for the Doctor to study, but they didn't notice a discarded silver sphere, which began to move and emit a strange electronic sound. The Doctor discovered that the Yeti was a robot with a mysterious flap-covered cavity in its chest, and deduced that its control unit must have been dislodged.

The Doctor convinced Khrisong of the need to find the sphere while, in the inner sanctum, Padmasambhava moved Yeti figurines around a map of the monastery. Outside, several Yetis matched his movements. The lama instructed Songsten to take a transparent pyramid to the cave in order to fully manifest the Great Intelligence.

Khrisong found a sphere on the mountainside but the Yetis attacked and retrieved it, injuring the warrior monk in the process. He was saved by the Doctor, who realised that, with the right equipment, he could track who was controlling the spheres and the Yetis. In order to do this he needed to get back to the TARDIS. Jamie accompanied him and they found a Yeti guarding it. Fortunately it lacked a control sphere, but the one Jamie and the Doctor carried tried to enter it. They prevented it by plugging the Yeti's cavity with a rock. They retrieved the tracking device and returned to the monastery. On the way they were confronted by five Yetis tracking the sphere they held, but escaped by throwing it away – the Yetis ignored them and chased after the silver ball instead.

Meanwhile, Abbot Songsten took the pyramid to the cave and activated it, causing a foamy Great Intelligence to start oozing out. A hidden Travers watched this happen. Via the Abbot, Padmasambhava ordered the monks to leave the monastery. When they don't obey, he summoned the Yeti to scare them away. Victoria stumbled across the lama in his sanctum and saw that he was controlling the Yeti. The Yeti toppled the monastery's holy statue and killed a monk before the lama moved them back outside. He hypnotised Victoria and sent her to urge the monks to leave the monastery. Upon hearing that his old friend Padmasambhava was still alive, the Doctor went to meet him and learned that the old man had encountered the Great Intelligence while astrally

projecting, and had been possessed by it. The Lama appeared to be exhausted from the effort of trying to resist the Intelligence's control, and seemed to die. The Doctor left and helped Victoria recover from her hypnosis. Travers had returned from the cave, and told the Doctor what had happened in the cave.

The Abbot, who is now also controlled by the Great Intelligence, killed Khrisong before being over-powered. The Doctor ordered everyone apart from himself and his companions to flee so that he could deal with the threat. Returning to the inner sanctum, they found Padmasambhava alive and under the Intelligence's control.

As more Yetis came to the defence of the possessed Lama, the Doctor distracted the Great Intelligence while Jamie and another monk destroyed the control sphere, causing all the Yeti's sphere's to explode and the robots fell to the ground. Realising the relevance of the pyramid in the cave, the Doctor urged Jamie to destroy the one in the sanctum. Jamie did so, causing the other pyramid in the cave to explode, destroying part of the mountain. Defeated, the Great Intelligence was expelled from Earth, and Padmasambhava died peacefully in the Doctor's arms.

As the travellers said goodbye to Travers, he spots a real Yeti in the distance...

CONTINUITY

The Doctor has been to the Det-Sen Monastery on previous occasions. He took the ghanta in 1630 and is only now returning it. Padmasambhava is still the lama of the monastery.

There are actual yetis in the Himalayas, but they are shy, reclusive creatures. They are generally friendly towards the Tibetan monks.

The Doctor apparently no longer wants to learn how to play the bagpipes as he doesn't want Jamie fixing his broken set.

⊙ RUNNING THE ADVENTURE

To a modern gamer, there are many elements to this adventure that seem rather Lovecraftian. There is a disembodied horror from beyond space and time that is controlling a monk that tried to attain a higher level of existence – the monk's lifespan has been considerably increased as a result. There are strange robots built with a level of technology unknown in 1935 (even the year falls within the span of Lovecraft's writings) as well as alien machines that somehow breach the walls of reality and manifest the Great Intelligence as a formless blob.

It is very easy to reinterpret this as a horror adventure (one in which the characters win, of course). The Great Intelligence is a genuine threat and may be beyond the characters' capabilities to stop should it actually manifest. It can hypnotise people, making it difficult to tell friend from foe and the Yetis fill the role of shaggy, horrific beasts.

Rather than mechanical robots and pyramids, you could make the Great Intelligence's powers more overtly psychic. The Yeti, for example, don't need to be robots. They could be psychic manifestations, hypnotised real Yeti, or even giant snow-puppets animated with psychic energy. In such a case it probably wouldn't take the Great Intelligence two hundred years to manifest (although the revamp of the pyramids in the next paragraph could take decades or even centuries to accomplish).

Also of interest are the pyramids. Perhaps this is now a crystalline structure which holds the mental energy of victims. The Great Intelligence needs to collect enough mental energy to escape its extra-dimensional prison, allowing it to manifest on Earth. This is why it's so interested in the Doctor; it can 'fill the rest of the tank', as it were, and manifest after draining the Time Lord.

A LESSON FROM THE WEATHER

At the beginning of this adventure the TARDIS scanner clearly shows a snow-covered landscape. When the Doctor and his companions do go outside there isn't a snowflake to be found. While it's possible that the TARDIS scanner actually gave them a visual of a Tibetan mountainside a bit into the future (after a snowfall), there is a lesson to be learned for Gamemasters; if you bother to set up atmospheric conditions be sure to utilise them during play.

Imagine how much more creepy and hostile this adventure would be if it was snowing. It would be much more difficult to move around and there would be an even greater sense of isolation. The Yetis become vague shapes in a snowstorm and victims would be covered, only to be discovered by kicking them with one's foot. Snow tracks are easier to follow but can get covered over by more snow. Characters dress differently for inclement weather. And, if the snow is high enough, it could be difficult to get away from an advancing Yeti.

FURTHER ADVENTURES

- At the conclusion of this adventure Travers spots a real Yeti, which is slimmer and more docile than the robotic Yetis. As it turns out, the 'real' Yeti are a sentient race that had also been harmed by the robotic Yetis. Unfortunately, either Travers or another hunter kills one, causing the rest of the Yetis to react in revenge and to reclaim the body. The hunter is staying in an isolated village, where the characters arrive to find the town under siege.

- The Great Intelligence may contact other ascended minds at other points in history and utilise local legends to keep people away. It may contact a New Age priestess in the Pacific

Northwest, utilising Sasquatches as guards or it may contact a Druid deep in a British forest, creating fae-like robots to scare away intruders.

- In the near future the Great Intelligence is using an immersive online computer game to contact an appropriate mind, using an elaborate series of puzzles to 'open the mind' of a potential host. The game is secret and a legend amongst gamers. Unfortunately, the Great Intelligence wants to keep it secret and those that find its game and fail die along with their avatars.

EDWARD TRAVERS

AWARENESS	3	PRESENCE	4
COORDINATION	4	RESOLVE	4
INGENUITY	5	STRENGTH	3

SKILLS
Athletics 4, Convince 3, Craft 3, Fighting 2, Knowledge 4, Marksman 3, Medicine 1, Science 4, Subterfuge 2, Survival 4, Technology 2, Transport 2

TRAITS
Brave: Travers gets a +2 on rolls when he needs to show courage.
Charming: Travers has natural charm and gets a +2 on rolls when using it.
Obsession: Travers is obsessed with finding a Yeti and believes that others are trying to beat him to it. Worse, he believes that others are capable of killing in order to beat him to it.

TECH LEVEL: 5   STORY POINTS: 12

KHRISONG

AWARENESS	4	PRESENCE	4
COORDINATION	5	RESOLVE	4
INGENUITY	2	STRENGTH	5

SKILLS
Athletics 5, Convince 2, Craft 2, Fighting 5, Knowledge 3, Marksman 3, Medicine 1, Survival 3

TRAITS
Brave: Khrisong gets a +2 on rolls when he needs to show courage.
Tough: Khrisong is tough. Damage is reduced by 2 before being applied to his attributes.

EQUIPMENT: An assortment of martial weapons, usually a sword (damage Strength +2).

TECH LEVEL: 4   STORY POINTS: 6

SONGSTEN

AWARENESS	3	PRESENCE	4
COORDINATION	3	RESOLVE	3
INGENUITY	4	STRENGTH	2

SKILLS
Athletics 2, Convince 4, Craft 2, Fighting 2, Knowledge 4, Marksman 1, Medicine 2, Science 2, Subterfuge 3, Survival 3

TRAITS
Enslaved: Songsten is under the control of the Great Intelligence.

STORY POINTS: 8

CHAPTER EIGHT:
THE ICE WARRIORS, THE ENEMY OF THE WORLD, THE WEB OF FEAR

THE ICE WARRIORS

Caught and initially accused of being scavengers, the Doctor, Jamie, and Victoria were granted a little leeway by base leader Clent when the Doctor saved the ioniser from overloading. Clent theorised that overpopulation killed most of the plants, leading to this new ice age. The drilling team returned to the base with the humanoid, an Ice Warrior named Varga, in tow.

While the Doctor and the base crew attended a meeting, the Ice Warrior thawed out and took Victoria hostage. The Ice Warrior raided the medical centre for supplies and was spotted by an ex-crewman, Penley, who was stealing supplies to aid Storr, another ex-crewman that was injured in an avalanche. The Doctor believed that the humanoid was an alien and probably trying to find his ship. If it was nearby, the ioniser might accidentally hit it and spark a nuclear explosion.

Varga freed his associates from the ice and they burrowed to their ship. He released Victoria to contact the humans and learned that they were interested in his ship's engines. The attempt to recapture Victoria failed and Jamie was injured. Victoria was trapped by cracking ice and she was saved by Storr, but he wanted to join the Ice Warriors. They killed him instead.

'This is a decision for a man to take, not a machine. The computer isn't designed to take risks, but that is the essence of man's progress. We must decide.'

⊙ SYNOPSIS

Brittanicus Base, Great Britain, the Future

It is Earth's future, when a new Ice Age threatens to cover most of the planet. To combat this threat the Earth government created a network of ionisers to slow the glacial advance. One of these ionisers was located at Brittanicus base, a converted mansion in Great Britain. The base drilling crew discovered a humanoid shape in a glacier just as the TARDIS arrived nearby.

The Doctor entered the Ice Warrior ship to negotiate with Varga. He offered to free their ship with the ioniser, but Varga believed the humans wanted to destroy him. He also needed their resources to fuel his ship, which the Doctor learned was an ion drive and therefore not susceptible to explosion. To accomplish this, Varga prepared his ship's sonic cannon and threatened to use it if his demands weren't met.

Penley rescued Jamie and returned to the base but Clent tranquilised them and attempted to negotiate with Varga, who left the ship with the other Ice Warriors except for Zondal, who remained to guard the Doctor and Victoria. Inside the ship, the Doctor used ammonium sulphide to subdue Zondal and rewired the sonic cannon to injure the Ice Warriors inside the base. The Ice Warriors retreated back to the ship as the Doctor and Victoria returned to the base.

The Ice Warriors attempted to take off while the base crew, now with Penley and Jamie awake, overrode the computer and used the ioniser against the ship. The ship exploded and the Earth was safe, leaving the World Computer to keep working on holding back the glaciers.

CONTINUITY

Earth has entered a new Ice Age that came early due to efforts to solve a worldwide famine. Humanity has taken all available farmland to make their homes; food is artificially produced. Ionisation technology is being used to keep the glaciers from advancing any further. The world is run by the great World Computer.

The Arctic cities built in the 26th century apparently haven't solved the population problem. Perhaps they were too small and new ones can't be built fast enough.

The humans don't seem to recognize the Ice Warriors in spite of their attempt to conquer and transform Earth in the 21st century. Perhaps the incident is far enough in the past, records were lost during the Dalek Invasion, or a Time War ripple erased the earlier invasion.

◯ RUNNING THE ADVENTURE

This adventure comes wrapped in an environmental message; the problem of the new Ice Age is inadvertently man-made, as Earthlings in the future wiped out too many plants and damaged the natural order of the planet. They are reduced to using artificial means to maintain some semblance of the Earth that they remember.

Environmental and other catastrophes are a great way to add plot elements and background scenery to your adventures. Pick an environmental issue such as global warming, peak oil, or over-fishing, and wrap an entire adventure around it. The issue need not be the focus of the adventure; in The Ice Warriors the main threat comes from aliens and their spaceship buried in the ice, not the advancing glaciers. The glaciers and the means to stop them simply add interesting plot elements to the same story.

WHY WOULD A LACK OF PLANTS DIMINISH CARBON DIOXIDE?

The explanation of the lack of carbon dioxide on Earth due to a severe depletion of plant life seems backwards; if anything the lack of plants would decrease oxygen and increase the amount of carbon dioxide, resulting in a world that chokes animal life and invites plant life to grow again. It's the kind of issue that could pull your players out of the story as they debate scientific plausibility.

However, the idea that something prematurely started a new ice age and that a network of machines is necessary to combat the glaciers is an exciting and plausible situation. This new ice age can be the result of the Earth crying out in rage after centuries of artificial weather manipulation. Alternatively, perhaps the artificial food creator eats up carbon dioxide. There's also the possibility of a nuclear winter, created either through war (perhaps the

AMMONIUM SULPHIDE PHIAL (MINOR GADGET)

A common 'stink bomb' that gives off a scent similar to rotten eggs, ammonium sulphide is a potent stunning weapon when released in the face of an Ice Warrior.

Traits: One Shot, Restriction (only usable against certain races), against an appropriate race it acts as a stun weapon, and lethal if enough is breathed (S/S/L)
Cost: 1 Story Point

aftermath of World War IV), scientific exploration (someone's finally drilled too deep and the Earth erupts like never before), asteroid impact, or simply a cure being worse than the disease (a way to combat global warming is so effective that the opposite effect occurs). It's your game, pick one and run with it!

THE DANGER OF FANATICISM

Most of the Brittanicus Base crew have a slavish devotion to the World Computer, which they believe is infallible. There are two points about this that are extremely relevant. The first is unchecked fanaticism, in which people so strongly believe that someone has their best interest in mind that they willing go along with anything he or she says and shut out any dissenting viewpoints. In this case, it is the cold logic of the World Computer that the crew puts their faith in; the machine effectively runs the world government.

The second point is the lack of humanity on the part of the World Computer. Science fiction is filled with examples of computers deciding that humanity is not nearly as important as some other goal, either for a greater 'good' or simply self-preservation. Here, the computer would rather sacrifice a base full of humans, and those protected by this particular ioniser, in order to preserve the ioniser network. It does this even though it doesn't fully understand the nature of the alien threat.

WHY DOESN'T ANYONE RECOGNISE THE ICE WARRIORS?

For anyone remotely familiar with the Ice Warriors, Varga's body in the ice should be immediately recognisable. Evidence indicates that the humans should remember, as the Ice Warriors tried to invade Earth previously (*The Seeds of Death*) and they join the Federation as Martians in the near future (*The Curse of Peladon*). There are two ways to approach this question.

First, it's entirely possible that the Ice Warriors are unknown in this period. *The Curse of Peladon* has the Martian delegate surprised to learn that Earth still retains an aristocratic society; this seems odd for two members of the Federation that live so close to each other.

It is more likely that the Ice Warriors have left Mars and settled on a 'New Mars' somewhere else (or, by the same token, perhaps Earthlings have moved somewhere else). The lack of memory can be explained as a purge of records during the Dalek conquest of Earth.

Second, and more sinisterly, it's possible that the humans at the Brittanicus Base don't recall the Ice Warriors (it was a long time ago, presumably with other alien contacts since, and the Dalek invasion was much more successful), however, the World Computer does recognise them and has taken their abilities into consideration when calculating its response. This viewpoint has support; when Clent asks the computer whether their actions would succeed, the computer goes haywire. This seems the reaction of a machine not wanting to reveal the answer, rather than simply offer an 'insufficient data' response.

FURTHER ADVENTURES

- In the 11th century a small fleet of Norse long ships discovers an Ice Warrior buried in an iceberg floating in the Atlantic. This Ice Warrior quickly takes over the crew and leads them to the New World, where he hopes to discover his ship. One of the Norsemen is a Norwegian prince and his father is preparing to send a large fleet to scour 'Vinland' to find him. A large-scale Nordic invasion would alter Earth's history, and what happened to the Ice Warrior's ship?

- Clent warns that if the ionisers slip then thousands of years of history would be buried under the ice. Even at its current level of advance, a number of nations, including Canada, Great Britain, Norway, Sweden, Finland, and Russia, already lost major cities to the glaciers. Perhaps something that needs to be retrieved is already buried, and the characters join an expedition to find it.

- The World Computer not only keeps the glaciers at bay, it also guides society. Perhaps the World Computer takes its job a bit too seriously and institutes a dictatorship that severely rations resources and curtails human freedoms. The characters arrive in a Computer Police State and must aid the rebels in freeing a docile humanity from its influence.

STORR

AWARENESS	3	PRESENCE	2
COORDINATION	2	RESOLVE	4
INGENUITY	3	STRENGTH	2

SKILLS
Athletics 2, Convince 2, Craft 4, Fighting 2, Knowledge 3, Marksman 2, Science 3, Subterfuge 4, Survival 5

TRAITS
Argumentative
Eccentric
Phobia: Storr is anti-technology and modern medicine and incurs a -2 penalty when broaching the subject.

TECH LEVEL: 5   STORY POINTS: 4

CLENT

AWARENESS	2	PRESENCE	3
COORDINATION	2	RESOLVE	3
INGENUITY	3	STRENGTH	2

SKILLS
Athletics 2, Convince 5, Craft 3, Fighting 2, Knowledge 4, Marksman 2, Science 4, Subterfuge 2, Technology 5, Transport 2

TRAITS
By the Book
Phobia: Clent is afraid to take the initiative if the computer doesn't offer solutions. He gets a -2 on all rolls when he takes initiative or goes against the computer's advice.
Voice of Authority: Clent gets a +2 on social rolls when dealing with the staff at Britannicus Base.

TECH LEVEL: 5   STORY POINTS: 8

ELRIC PENLEY

AWARENESS	4	PRESENCE	4
COORDINATION	3	RESOLVE	4
INGENUITY	4	STRENGTH	2

SKILLS
Athletics 2, Convince 3, Craft 2, Fighting 2, Knowledge 4, Marksman 2, Medicine 4, Science 4, Subterfuge 3, Survival 3, Technology 5, Transport 2

TRAITS
Outcast: Penley is an exile from the ioniser group. He gets a -2 to social rolls when dealing with them.

TECH LEVEL: 5   STORY POINTS: 8

THE ENEMY OF THE WORLD

'A sort of Jekyll and Hyde character, perhaps, our Mister Salamander.'

⊙ SYNOPSIS

Earth, Early 21st Century

The TARDIS landed on an Australian beach in the early 21st century. The travellers were immediately attacked by three men and rescued by an agent, Astrid, who swooped in via helicopter. After the rescue she introduced them to her superior, a man named Giles Kent. Kent explained that the Doctor was attacked because he had an uncanny resemblance to Ramon Salamander, a Mexican scientist that created a Sun Catcher, which regulated the weather and increased food production. Kent believed that Salamander was trying to take over the world and wanted the Doctor's help to expose him.

The Doctor was sceptical, wondering if this was simply a turf war between Kent and Salamander, but Jamie and Victoria convinced him to help. Kent sent Jamie and Victoria to Europe in order to get inside Salamander's circle. Astrid aided Jamie by setting up a fake assassination attempt and allowing Jamie to take the credit in stopping it. Jamie used his new goodwill with Salamander to secure jobs for himself and Victoria as a guard and chef, respectively. Salamander, meanwhile, used his Sun Catcher to make volcanoes in Hungary explode and indict Controller Denes so Salamander could install a puppet leader in his place. Back in Australia, Kent noted to the Doctor that these anomalous natural disasters were created by Salamander to discredit unfriendly government officials and gain power for himself.

With Astrid's help, Jamie and Victoria tried to help Denes escape but he was killed during the attempt and Jamie and Victoria were captured. World Zones Authority Security Chief Bruce, who'd earlier been fooled by the Doctor pretending to be Salamander, was confused by Salamander's relationship to Jamie and Victoria and came to believe a double was involved. Salamander took the two back to Australia while Bruce attempted and failed to catch Kent and the Doctor. Kent convinced the Doctor to impersonate Salamander to save his friends and the Doctor realised that his initial concern was correct: it was a turf war.

Regardless, the Doctor impersonated Salamander to get inside the Kanowa research station in Australia, where Kent believed information to expose Salamander existed. Meanwhile Salamander and Bruce were at odds, since Salamander wanted the Doctor and Kent captured in spite of them not doing anything illegal. It was revealed that the Kanowa research station hid the true power behind Salamander's Sun Catcher; he was holding a group of engineers and scientists in a bunker below ground. These people believed that there was a war on the surface and that the Sun Catcher was a weapon aiding the war effort.

The Doctor rescued Jamie and Victoria while Astrid went below and told the bunker crew that Salamander was lying. Kent was revealed as Salamander's former partner in his scheme and, while the former comrades confront each other, Kent rigs the complex to explode. Jamie encountered Salamander on the way back to the TARDIS, and took him to be the Doctor. His suspicions were raised when Salamander indicated that Jamie should take the ship's controls, something that the Doctor had forbidden. The Doctor returned to the ship at that moment, and in the ensuing struggle Salamander knocked the dematerialisation switch with the TARDIS's doors wide open. The Doctor, Jamie and Victoria held on for dear life as Salamander was sucked into the time vortex.

CONTINUITY

Earth is now run by the World Zones Organisation, a stronger United Nations (this name doesn't stick, as the UN continues to be used in adventures set a bit further in the future). The WZO is concerned about declining resources and is looking for ways to replenish them. Weather manipulation technology plays a key role. It is likely that this weather technology is the precursor to the Gravitron and that the WZO sets up Space Control.

Air travel in the early 21st century is conducted by rocket. These could be scramjets (travelling at 4000 miles an hour, or over 7-8 times faster than a Boeing 747), which are still experimental as of the very early 21st century.

Salamander is considered a saviour due to his weather manipulator helping feed an overpopulated Earth. This is the earliest of many attempts at weather manipulation and new forms of food production throughout the 21st century. The ultimate solution is artificial food.

⊙ RUNNING THE ADVENTURE

The catalyst for the characters getting involved in this adventure is the fact that the Doctor is a dead ringer for Salamander. Unlike a similar coincidence in **The Massacre**, this adventure takes place in the near future, which means all bets are off for changing history (as the Gamemaster is free to rule that future events take their proper course without actual history contradicting her – at least for a few years!).

Having a duplicate of a character adds a number of interesting wrinkles to the adventure:

- It provides a convenient hook for the characters to get involved in an adventure without resorting to the usual 'we're just here to help' explanation, false title ('oh, I'm the Chief Inspector/foreign medical doctor/Earth Ambassador), or psychic paper. The character may be recruited by someone that recognises him as a duplicate and uses him to his advantage.

- The character has the face of the duplicate but none of the memories, mannerisms, or even the voice of the original (although the latter is usually ignored in fiction). She'll need a good Convince skill to carry off being who she's not while covering for the 'gaps' in her knowledge.

- While the character can act as a duplicate, she can't be in two places at once. Unless the character only appears in areas where the duplicate is located, others will begin to suspect when they realise that the same character is miles apart at the same time.

- What goes around comes around. While the character can substitute for the duplicate, the reverse is also true. The character's associates may be duped into believing that the duplicate is the character, much as Salamander convinced Jamie and Victoria long enough to take over the TARDIS (and, to return to the earlier point, Salamander looked like the Doctor but lacked his knowledge; he moved the TARDIS with the doors open).

Optionally, you can do away with the 'evil twin' subplot. In a hyperlinked society of the near future, the PCs already have something of interest to Kent; they lack identities.

It would be fairly easy for someone with government connections to falsify alternate identities and the characters will never be in real danger of having their real identities accidentally 'out' them (this assumes that none of the characters have analogues in the near future...a companion from 2010 might have to explain why she looks like she's 19 when she should be 39 or so).

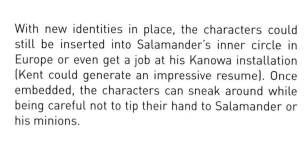

With new identities in place, the characters could still be inserted into Salamander's inner circle in Europe or even get a job at his Kanowa installation (Kent could generate an impressive resume). Once embedded, the characters can sneak around while being careful not to tip their hand to Salamander or his minions.

THE NAME IS SMITH, DOCTOR JOHN SMITH...

Even more-so than *The Underwater Menace*, this adventure is a pastiche of the James Bond films. All of the elements are here; dashing spies, globetrotting, a megalomaniac with a catchy name, a super weapon, and a wild scheme (the nuclear shelter). On the other side of the pond, we'd recognise Mission Impossible elements as well, particularly with a group effort and a member of the group impersonating someone else. Only the convenient duplicate is a bit outside of the box, but masters of disguise aren't exactly uncommon in spy thrillers.

This type of an adventure makes an excellent template for UNIT or Torchwood groups, particularly if the megalomaniac has a little help from aliens or is using alien technology. Even groups using the Doctor and companions may find an adventure in this mould to be a refreshing change of pace from historical, futuristic, and monster-of-the-week adventures.

Another interesting angle is to use Tegan Jovanka. She'd likely be in her 60s or 70s at this point, but being a former companion she may be suspicious of Salamander and would certainly be alarmed to hear of a police box showing up on an Australian beach. She may be working with Kent or, if you're using a shorter version of this adventure, be the characters' main contact and instigator of the investigation into Kanowa station.

FURTHER ADVENTURES

- Salamander was sucked into the time vortex, but that doesn't mean he stays there. If he survived somehow, he could be dumped into any period of Earth history and use his wiles and his scientific knowledge to gain power for himself. The characters could encounter Salamander running an East Indies shipping empire in the 17th century, or aiding the rebels in the Taiping Rebellion.

- The control equipment was destroyed, but the Sun Catcher is still orbiting the planet. It's a ready weapon and possible precursor to the Gravitron. This makes it a tempting target for an alien race bent on Earth's domination or a tool by a renegade Earth faction that wants to act against the world government.

- Very few people knew that the Doctor was a duplicate for Salamander and this could have caused problems had the Doctor remained. The characters arrive in a place where one character resembles a master criminal that has recently disappeared. The 'double' is arrested and tried for his duplicate's crimes while the other characters try to free him and find evidence to absolve him. Also, there is still the question of what happened to the real criminal?

GILES KENT

AWARENESS	3	PRESENCE	4
COORDINATION	3	RESOLVE	4
INGENUITY	4	STRENGTH	2

SKILLS
Athletics 1, Convince 4, Fighting 2, Knowledge 4, Marksman 3, Medicine 1, Science 3, Subterfuge 4, Survival 1, Technology 3, Transport 3

TRAITS
Adversary (Major): Kent's former partner Salamander is trying to destroy him.
Charming: Kent gets a +2 to influence others.
Obsession (Major): Kent wants to take over Salamander's operation for himself.

TECH LEVEL: 5   **STORY POINTS: 3**

ASTRID FERRIER

AWARENESS	4	PRESENCE	4
COORDINATION	4	RESOLVE	4
INGENUITY	3	STRENGTH	3

SKILLS

Athletics 4, Convince 2, Fighting 3, Marksman 3, Subterfuge 4, Survival 4, Transport 3

TRAITS

Attractive: Astrid gets +2 to rolls in which her appearance would be a factor.
Quick Reflexes: Astrid always goes first in the Action Round phase.

TECH LEVEL: 5   STORY POINTS: 6

SECURITY CHIEF DONALD BRUCE

AWARENESS	4	PRESENCE	3
COORDINATION	4	RESOLVE	5
INGENUITY	3	STRENGTH	3

SKILLS

Athletics 3, Convince 3, Fighting 3, Knowledge 2, Marksman 3, Subterfuge 2, Technology 2, Transport 2

TRAITS

Stubborn: Bruce is committed to his job and isn't easily swayed.
Voice of Authority: Bruce commands authority when he speaks. He gets a +2 to Presence and Convince rolls to get people to do what he wants.

TECH LEVEL: 5   STORY POINTS: 8

RAMÓN SALAMANDER

AWARENESS	3	PRESENCE	6
COORDINATION	4	RESOLVE	5
INGENUITY	6	STRENGTH	3

SKILLS

Athletics 2, Convince 5, Fighting 2, Knowledge 4, Marksman 3, Science 3, Subterfuge 5, Survival 3, Technology 5

TRAITS

Adversary (Major): Salamander's former partner Kent is trying to destroy him.
Boffin: Salamander can create Gadgets through Jiggery-Pokery.
Indomitable: Salamander is determined and gets a +4 bonus to any rolls to resist being possessed, hypnotised, or otherwise mentally controlled.
Lucky: Salamander always seems to be able to slip out of sticky situations. When he rolls double '1''s, he may roll again, once only!
Menacing: Salamander gets a +2 bonus on attempts to get people to do what he wants. Characters he has menaced also get a +2 to resist attempts by others to act against him.
Obsession (Major): Salamander wants to rule the world.
Technically Adept: Salamander gets a +2 on Technology rolls to fix broken devices or understand complex gadgets.
Voice of Authority: Salamander gets a +2 on Presence and Convince rolls.

TECH LEVEL: 5   STORY POINTS: 10

THE WEB OF FEAR

'Lethbridge-Stewart. Expect you're wondering who the devil I am, eh?'

⊙ SYNOPSIS

London Underground, 1968

The now elderly Professor Travers managed to reactivate a control sphere. He visited a private museum that contained a deactivated yeti that he had sold to the museum's owner, Silverstein, many years previously. Silverstein refused to sell the yeti back to the professor, despite Travers' insistence that he needed it to experiment with the control sphere. Soon thereafter, the control sphere escaped from Travers' possession, crashed through the window and reactivated the Yeti (reconfiguring it into a Mark II version in the process).

Sometime later, central London was evacuated as a mist appeared, along with a mysterious web-like fungus in the Underground. Those that entered the mist didn't return, and an evacuation was underway. The army was trying to contain the fungus but were being attacked by the Yetis, who were now using web guns.

The Yetis, the mist, and the fungus were controlled by the Great Intelligence, which was once again trying to manifest on Earth. It reached out and tried to capture the TARDIS, but the Doctor managed to land in the Underground. Jamie and Victoria were soon captured by the army, where they meet Travers and his daughter. Travers was shocked that they hadn't aged. Meanwhile, the Doctor followed a cable to explosives and watched as the Yetis used their webs to contain the explosion.

As the webs advanced through the Underground, Anne believed the Doctor might be behind the Yetis. Jamie and some soldiers were trapped by Yetis, but the Yetis were called away. Victoria slipped free and found the Doctor, who'd also bumped into Colonel Lethbridge-Stewart, who'd survived a Yeti attack and was looking for the rest of the army in the Underground. They found the army base at Goodge Street and Lethbridge-Stewart assumed command, although Captain Knight was suspicious of him.

The military and the Doctor worked to buy some time by sealing the base, but there was a saboteur inside that kept a door opened. The saboteur used a Yeti homing device to let a Yeti inside and destroy the explosives inside the locker. A Yeti also attacked Travers and Anne, dragging away the elderly professor. The Doctor and his companions found Anne and told her that her father was taken. Suspicion ran wild amongst the army personnel over who was behind the attack and the sabotage.

The Doctor learned that Travers was working on a control unit for the spheres and convinced Anne to help him complete the work. He also told Lethbridge-Stewart that he was a time traveller and needed his TARDIS back. The Colonel mounted a retrieval operation and the Doctor accompanied him. They were ambushed by the Yetis and failed to get it, but the Doctor did get some electronic components that he needed for the control unit. The army suffers a serious defeat and retreats.

They returned to base and Travers appeared, escorted by two Yetis. Travers had been taken over by the Great Intelligence, and admitted that this was all a trap for the Doctor; the being wanted to take over the Doctor's body. He gave the Doctor twenty minutes to decide and took Victoria to Piccadilly Circus station as a hostage. There, they found a pyramid structure unlike anything they had seen in Tibet. The Doctor and Anne finished work on their control unit and managed to control a Yeti.

The base was overcome by the webs, and the Doctor, Jamie, Lethbridge Stuart and the others were captured and taken to Piccadilly Circus. Jamie hid with a Yeti-controlling microphone, while the Doctor was forced to put on a headset, but managed to tamper with it first. The Great Intelligence revealed itself to be in Staff Sergeant Arnold's body (he had been the traitorous saboteur). The Doctor donned the headset the Intelligence would use to take over his mind, but Jamie used the controlled Yeti to attack the other robots. Despite the Doctor's protests (he was hoping to use the tampered headset to destroy the Great Intelligence for good), Jamie seizes the headset and hurls it into the control pyramid, destroying it and foiling the schemes of the Great Intelligence once more.

CONTINUITY

This is the first appearance of Colonel Lethbridge-Stewart. UNIT is formed partly as a reaction to this adventure and Lethbridge-Stewart's role in defeating the Yeti leads to an offer to lead the British branch of UNIT, which he accepts.

RUNNING THE ADVENTURE

Forget about shaggy giants with web guns, deadly mists, and fungi filling the London Underground; what really makes this adventure sizzle is the 'whodunit' mystery. Specifically, who is working with the Great Intelligence on the inside against the army and the time travellers? Every character in the adventure is painted as a possible mole through suspicious backgrounds, actions, or coincidences. And just when you think you've figured it out, another character comes along and makes your choice less likely.

Time Travellers are, of course, immediately suspect, as they tend to appear out of nowhere with no references and have strange mannerisms and styles of dress (even psychic paper can only help so much). Characters have to solve the mystery while maintaining their innocence.

This type of adventure works well when there is little mystery about the adversary. In this adventure the Doctor, Jamie, and Victoria know why the Yeti

are here and what the Great Intelligence is up to, for the most part. Their efforts to defeat the Great Intelligence are hampered by the confusion, distrust, and sabotage caused by the mole.

If you have a copy of **Defending the Earth: The UNIT Sourcebook**, you could use the battle rules to play out the efforts of the army to resist the spread of the Yetis and the fungus through the underground, perhaps using the names of particular stations as the boxes on the battle grid.

FURTHER ADVENTURES

- The Doctor declares that the Great Intelligence is in space. While this could simply be shorthand for another dimension, it's also possible that the Great Intelligence's efforts in **The Abominable Snowmen** and **The Web of Fear** have enabled it to manifest enough that it is floating in outer space. The characters appear aboard a luxury space liner, where the Great Intelligence takes over the Ood servants to strengthen its manifestation.

- There are a number of crimes being committed in London using Yetis. Is the Great Intelligence back, or has someone else figured out how to control them? The characters are thrust into this mystery when they arrive at the scene of the latest crime.

- During the evacuation, the British Museum was looted of particular artefacts. The characters have the misfortune of arriving in the museum just as the curator notices the theft. The characters are immediately suspected, but there's an additional complication; one of the artefacts taken was alien, and its use alerted its previous owners to its presence. A company of Judoon is dispatched to recover it just as Londoners are returning to the city.

PROFESSOR EDWARD TRAVERS

AWARENESS	3	PRESENCE	4
COORDINATION	3	RESOLVE	4
INGENUITY	5	STRENGTH	2

SKILLS
Athletics 2, Convince 3, Craft 3, Fighting 1, Knowledge 5, Marksman 3, Medicine 2, Science 5, Subterfuge 2, Survival 4, Technology 4, Transport 2

TRAITS
Brave: Travers gets a +2 on rolls when he needs to show courage.
Charming: Travers has natural charm and gets a +2 on rolls when using it.
Obsession: Travers is obsessed with unlocking the secrets of the control spheres.

TECH LEVEL: 5 **STORY POINTS:** 12

ANNE TRAVERS

AWARENESS	3	PRESENCE	3
COORDINATION	2	RESOLVE	4
INGENUITY	4	STRENGTH	2

SKILLS
Craft 3, Knowledge 3, Science 4, Subterfuge 2, Survival 1, Technology 3

TRAITS
Attractive: Anne gets a +2 bonus to any rolls that involve her attractiveness.
Boffin: Anne can create Gadgets through Jiggery-Pokery.
Technically Adept: Anne gets a +2 to any Technology rolls to fix a faulty device or use complex gadgets.

TECH LEVEL: 5 **STORY POINTS:** 6

COLONEL ALISTAIR GORDON LETHBRIDGE-STEWART

AWARENESS	4	PRESENCE	4
COORDINATION	4	RESOLVE	4
INGENUITY	4	STRENGTH	4

SKILLS
Athletics 3, Convince 3, Fighting 3, Knowledge 2, Marksman 3, Subterfuge 2, Survival 3, Transport 3

TRAITS
Brave: Alistair gets a +2 bonus on all rolls in which he needs to show courage.
By the Book: Alistair always follows protocol.
Impulsive: Gets -2 to rolls to resist impulsive reactions.
Indomitable: Alistair gets a +4 bonus to resist mind control.
Keen Senses (major)
Military Rank: UK Army Colonel.
Obligation: UK Military
Quick Reflexes: Alistair usually goes first.
Technically Inept: Alistair gets a -2 penalty when trying to fix computer or electrical equipment.
Tough: Any damage that affects Alistair is reduced by 2.
Voice of Authority: Alistair gets a +2 bonus on Presence and Convince rolls to get people to follow his orders.

TECH LEVEL: 5 **STORY POINTS:** 10

CHAPTER NINE:
FURY OF THE DEEP, THE WHEEL IN SPACE, THE DOMINATORS

FURY FROM THE DEEP

'The mind does not exist. It is tired. It is dead. It is obsolete. Only our new masters can offer us life.'

⊙ SYNOPSIS

England and North Sea, late 20th Century

The TARDIS materialised in the ocean and the Doctor, Jamie, and Victoria floated ashore on a rubber raft. The Doctor was concerned by the amount of sea foam on the beach and found that there were giant pipes pumping gas from the sea for ESGO – Euro Sea Gas. The travellers heard a sound like a heartbeat within the pipes, but were discovered by security guards, shot with tranquilisers and taken to the ESGO refinery. The Chief, Robson, had lost contact with one of their rigs, and pressure in the pipes from the rigs was dropping. He suspected the travellers of sabotage, and ordered them held under guard.

Robson's assistant Harris was more sympathetic but lacked authority to release the travellers; they were locked in a cabin. The Doctor told Harris about the strange sound in the pipes, but he assured them that nothing could get inside and that Robson would never allow the gas to be stopped anyway. Harris asked his wife Maggie to retrieve a file he had left at home that

suggested that the gas flow should be stopped. She did so, but accidentally touched a piece of seaweed that was sitting on his desk. It stung her and, after she threw it away, started foaming.

Contact was briefly re-established with the silent rig, but its chief seemed quiet and evasive before the feed went dead once more.

The time travellers escaped from their cabin and learned that Robson was stonewalling investigations into the strange happenings, despite concerned reports from Chief Baxter and Van Lutyens from the Control Rig about plummeting morale and the strange heartbeat sound in the pipes. The Doctor and Jamie found the Pipeline Room and the Doctor listened to the pipe with his stethoscope, becoming convinced that something was moving within.

Victoria stumbled across someone trying to release the oxygen stored in the refinery and turned off the valves, but was locked in the room as foam and seaweed flooded in through a ventilation grille. The seaweed took a vaguely humanoid form and moved to attack her. The Doctor and Jamie, alerted by her screams, found and released her just in time. The Chief Engineer found that the oxygen tanks

were empty, and Robson again accused Victoria of sabotage. He was convinced that the sounds heard were due to a mechanical fault, and refused to stop the gas flow even though the pressure was still falling.

Harris discovered that Maggie had fallen ill from her sting and requested the Doctor's assistance, as the company doctor was out on a rig. Robson very reluctantly let them go. They found Maggie lying on the floor in a room filled with toxic fumes (breathed on her by Mr. Oak and Mr. Quill, two maintenance workers controlled by a seaweed creature). The Doctor believed she was in a coma and that the toxic fumes were the same as those that attacked Victoria.

The Doctor, Jamie, and Victoria retreated to the TARDIS to run tests on the seaweed and determined that it was alive and produced a toxic gas. A similar creature had been reported by sailors in the 18th century but dismissed as 'sea folklore.' The Doctor surmised that the creature gained intelligence through a parasitic relationship with its victims. The seaweed grew very quickly, and almost overflowed from its box while they weren't looking, but they managed to contain it. They returned to the Harris residence to find Maggie gone and the house covered in weed and foam.

Meanwhile, the workers increased pressure on Robson to shut off the pumps and clean them out. Robson resisted, retreating to his quarters where he was locked in by Oak and attacked by a seaweed creature. Harris released him and Robson fled.

Harris took command and informed the Director about the situation. He told Van Lutyens about the creature he caught a glimpse of in Robson's room, and they connected it with the earlier attack on Victoria. The Doctor and companions arrived and told Harris what they knew. A controlled Robson returned to the rig and attempted to reassert control as the 'lost rig' count climbed to three. Van Lutyens investigated the base of the impeller shaft, which he thought was the source of the problems. He discovered that the chamber was full of foam and weed, and was attacked and taken by the weed creature.

The Director of the Board of ESGO, Megan Jones, arrived and sided with Robson, dismissing the idea of a seaweed creature. She sent helicopters to investigate the other rigs. She was

surprised when the helicopter pilots reported that the lost rigs were covered with sea foam. Robson reacted angrily to Harris' suggestion that the rigs should be bombed, before they received a chilling communication from the Control Rig – a panicking Chief Baxter reporting that the creatures were all around them before the transmission abruptly ended.

The crew fended off a concerted sea creature attack as the Doctor deduced that oxygen must be toxic to it. Victoria was captured by Robson and taken to one of the rigs. The Doctor and Jamie followed in a helicopter. The Doctor met Robson, now under complete control and surrounded by foam and seaweed, who told him that the sea creature intended to spread across the world and conquer humanity. Jamie freed Victoria and, as Robson attacked, Victoria screamed, which seemed to cause the controlled man intense discomfort and allowed them to escape. They all flew back to the refinery – an adventurous journey with the Doctor as an untrained helicopter pilot.

Realising that Victoria's loud screaming had consistently driven off the creature, the Doctor amplified the sound and played it throughout the pipeline. The sea creature was defeated and the ESGO network and staff returned to normal; no one had died. Victoria decided that she had experienced quite enough danger and elected to stay behind with Harris and Maggie, so the Doctor and an especially despondent Jamie left in the TARDIS without her.

CONTINUITY

The sonic screwdriver makes its first appearance and is used as a screwdriver.

In this era, multinational corporations have the power to tranquilise and imprison trespassers. They can also call upon the Royal Air Force if needed.

⊙ RUNNING THE ADVENTURE

Out of all of the Second Doctor's adventures this one comes closest to evoking the feel of a horror movie (*The Web of Fear* comes close, but the mystery aspect outweighs the horror). Here you have the Doctor and his companions entering an isolated base as a mysterious alien creature starts infecting people and turning them against the remaining technicians. They also have to deal with two shaky leaders (the stubborn Robson and the frightened Harris) before finally getting decisive support from Jones. In a subversion of trope, a companion's screams are enough to end the threat.

As with many horror and science fiction movies of the 1950s and 1960s, there's an undercurrent of anti-communism. The Seaweed Creature is portrayed as a composite entity sapping free will from the victims that it incorporates into its colony. It is conquering an off-shore fort and plans to launch an attack on England (and eventually the world). The 'good guys' are capitalists and work hand in hand with the 'Western' British and Dutch (and possibly other) governments. And while the 'communist menace' is defeated, future threats still lurk beneath the waves.

In short, Gamemasters looking to tinge their games with horror will find this adventure very useful to

emulate. Devise a creature based on a current 'fear' and keep it in the shadows until it is time for the reveal and, when that time comes, make it seem shocking and all-powerful. Drop hints about the creature's Achilles' heel throughout the adventure; reveal it in full (with story points if necessary) when the Characters need it most.

With the ambiguously dated setting and the amount of power Robson and ESGO have, it seems that this story is set in the near future with echoes of the cyberpunk genre. The Corporation seems to have its own enclave where its employees live and receive medical care, and it has the right to shoot (with tranquiliser guns) any trespassers and may even imprison them.

Robson has the ability to cut the complex off from the outside world even to non-employees (in a state of emergency one might presume a Corporation could keep its own employees on site, but one can't see the harm in allowing non-employees to leave and return at their leisure). It even appears that the Royal Air Force is available as back-up for the Corporation.

Gamemasters that enjoy running near-future settings can place this adventure in a world where multi-national corporations are truly autonomous entities that work as partners with weaker governments, but effectively control them. In this case Megan Jones is the ultimate authority and Euro Sea has its own military.

Finally, it should be noted that, while this Second Doctor adventure is his most horrific, no one actually dies at the conclusion. The menace is simply wiped away, returning its victims to their normal states.

SEAWEED CREATURE

The Seaweed Creature is a being from the depths of the sea. It is not known if the Seaweed Creature is truly intelligent or even of this Earth. It is also uncertain whether there is a single Seaweed Creature or if it's a colony of creatures with a hive-mind. The Doctor certainly believes it has a nerve centre but does not elaborate.

The Seaweed Creature is relatively harmless so long as it is free from human contact; it was reportedly seen by sailors in the eighteenth century. Once it begins possessing humans, however, it has a desire to expand. The Doctor theorizes that it starts gaining the intelligence of its possessed victims (this leads to the possibility of the Seaweed Creature being some sort of discarded bio-weapon (perhaps from the Sea Devils or the Zygons?)). In its aggressive state the Seaweed Creature wants to expand, incorporating more humans into its collective intelligence until it has taken over the world. In spite of its horrific means of conversion, the Seaweed Creature actually takes care of its thralls and enables them to breathe and survive underwater.

SEAWEED CREATURE

AWARENESS	3	PRESENCE	1
COORDINATION	3	RESOLVE	4
INGENUITY	1	STRENGTH	5

SKILLS
Athletics 5, Fighting 3, Marksman 4, Subterfuge 3, Survival 3

TRAITS
Alien: While possibly terrestrial, the Seaweed Creature is sufficiently alien to humans.
Alien Appearance: The Seaweed Creature is a mass of weedy tendrils surrounded by sea foam.
Environmental (Aquatic): The Seaweed Creature can survive above and below the water.
Natural Weapon (poisonous gas): The Seaweed Creature can emit a poison gas that knocks a victim unconscious (S/S/S) which helps it possess the victim.
Possess: The Seaweed Creature can possess a person by touching them. This possession takes a bit of time to be fully effective.
Telepathy: The Seaweed Creature can mentally contact Seaweed-controlled Human Thralls.
Weakness (Noise, Major): The Seaweed Creature loses 4 attribute levels when it hears Victoria's (or similar person's) scream.
Weakness (Oxygen, Minor): The Seaweed Creature gets sluggish when attacked with pure oxygen. It makes all rolls at a -2 penalty and is unable to advance in the direction that the oxygen is coming from.

STORY POINTS: 8-10

SEAWEED THRALL

AWARENESS	3	PRESENCE	3
COORDINATION	3	RESOLVE	3
INGENUITY	-	STRENGTH	3

SKILLS
Athletics 4, Fighting 3, Marksman 3, Subterfuge 4

TRAITS
Enslaved: A Seaweed Thrall is directly controlled by the Seaweed Creature.
Environmental (Aquatic): A Seaweed Thrall can survive above and below the water.
Natural Weapon (poisonous gas): A Seaweed Thrall can emit a poison gas that knocks a victim unconscious (S/S/S). This leaves the victim exposed to the Seaweed Creature.
Telepathy: Seaweed Thralls can mentally contact the Seaweed Creature.
Weakness (Noise): If the Seaweed Thrall hears Victoria's scream, she momentarily gets her original attributes back and may attempt to free herself from the Seaweed Creature's control (the Seaweed Creature uses its reduced Attributes as it is affected by the scream as well).
Weakness (Oxygen): The Seaweed Thrall gets sluggish when attacked with pure oxygen. She makes all rolls at a -2 penalty and is unable to advance in the direction that the oxygen is coming from.

STORY POINTS: 4-6

COMPANIONS OUT OF TIME

Victoria elected to stay behind at the conclusion of this adventure, over a century into her own future. While this may seem strange, remember that the Doctor had no control over his TARDIS during his first two incarnations (in spite of the Second Doctor's arguments to the contrary). Companions either had to rely on extraordinary luck to get home (like Ben and Polly), choose a place they like well enough when they land (Victoria, Vicki), or determine to stay with the Doctor until forced otherwise (Jamie and Zoe).

While the Doctor rarely checks on ex-companions during his adventures, you could add interesting plot elements by considering what the companions got up to after they left, especially if they settled in a time after their departure or if they settled in a time prior to events they witnessed.

Ben and Polly returned to 1966, which is only a handful of years before **The Underwater Menace**. What if they knew a particular ship was doomed to sink and loved ones were on it? Would it change time if they rescued them? What if they fed information to the government as to Dr Zaroff's whereabouts? How would they prepare for the coming of the Cybermen in 1986 (we know they are alive, as they are alive and well in 2010).

Victoria is on the other end of the scale. She's a teenager living in a world about 100 years into her future. While her classical education would be of some use (and she's probably better-read than her peers), she'd be hopelessly outmatched in other topics. The Second Doctor may have enabled her to take new classes during her time with him or picked her up later and broadened her education (and perhaps dropped her off in a different era). Still, if Victoria remains in the 1970s (or thereabouts)

then she'd likely be around for Salamander's rise to power and, while she is unaware of the events of **The Seeds of Death**, she'd certainly know what an Ice Warrior is.

FURTHER ADVENTURES

* The Seaweed Creature menaced English sailors in the 18th century and gas rigs in the 20th century; it's likely that it surfaced before or will again. The characters could arrive aboard a ship sailing the North Sea in any time period and be menaced, or, with the amount of oil drilling in the North Sea, the Seaweed Creature could attempt a similar strike as the one on ESGO.

* This adventure depicts a world where private security has the right to tranquilise trespassers and hold them for unspecified periods. International Electromatics (**The Invasion**) seems an early adopter of this corporate autonomy, complete with private police, and it is likely that this environment enabled Kent and Salamander to cover their scheme. Any alien invasion/mad scientist/industrial horror adventure could be livened up with corporate controllers and directors making decisions normally left to government officials.

* There could certainly be more than one Seaweed Creature. What if one menaced a country on the other side of the Iron Curtain? The characters, presuming they could be perceived as Westerners, would certainly have a more difficult time defending accusations of sabotage and would have great trouble convincing, for example, Russian officials of their altruism before the Seaweed Creature spreads.

THE WHEEL IN SPACE

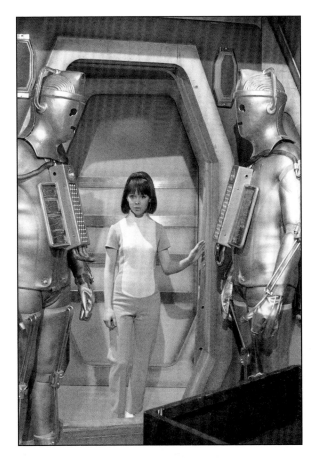

'Logic, my dear Zoe, merely enables one to be wrong with authority.'

⊘ SYNOPSIS

Space Station W-3, 21st century

As the TARDIS began to land, it seemed to be warning the travellers to go elsewhere by flashing images of alternative locations. The ship experienced a power overload which caused an explosion and damaged the fluid links. The Doctor removed the Time Vector Generator and he and Jamie exited onto a deserted spaceship. The ship's engines suddenly fired and the Doctor fell, suffering concussion. A rogue Servo Robot attempted to kill them, but Jamie destroyed it with the Time Vector Generator as the Doctor slipped into unconsciousness.

Nearby, the crew of Space Station W-3, or simply 'the Wheel,' monitored the seemingly adrift ship. The ship was named the Silver Carrier and had been reported missing 2 months ago. It was extremely off-course.

The Controller feared that the ship's autopilot could fire the engines and threaten the Wheel. His concerns were amplified when they detected inexplicable drops in air pressure and small objects, assumed to be meteorites, hitting the hull of the space station. He ordered the rocket destroyed. A debate about whether there might be survivors ensued, and ended when Jamie's use of the Time Vector Generator was detected indicating that someone was aboard the ship.

Two crewmembers spacewalked to the Silver Carrier and retrieved the time travellers. Both were taken to Dr Gemma Corwyn, who revealed that the Doctor had a concussion. Dr Corwyn told Jamie that he might want a tour of the station and suggested crewmember Zoe Heriot as a guide. Meanwhile, Dr Corwyn shared her concerns with the Controller that the Doctor and Jamie might be stowaways or saboteurs working for the Pull Back to Earth movement.

During his tour, Jamie discovered that the crew planned to use the X-Ray laser to destroy the now presumably empty Silver Carrier. Panicked because the TARDIS was still aboard, Jamie sabotaged the X-Ray laser, which left the Wheel defenceless until it could be repaired. Crewmembers working on the laser soon discovered sabotage by the Cybermats – these were the 'meteorites' that the crew had detected hitting the station. Meanwhile, the Silver Carrier proved not to be empty, as two Cybermen emerged from transport containers and reported to the Cyber-Planner, who was aboard a nearby Cybermen ship.

The Doctor woke up and convinced Dr Corwyn that he and Jamie were not saboteurs. Zoe brought them a Cybermat that had been captured in liquid plastic and the Doctor and Jamie recognised it. The Doctor believed that there were Cybermen aboard the Silver Carrier. Unfortunately, two crewmembers had already gone back to the Silver Carrier for replacement parts for the X-Ray laser. They were hypnotised by the Cybermen so that they'd transport the Cybermen onto the Wheel.

The Cybermen killed one crewmember and forced another to repair the laser before sending him to the control room to smash the communications console. He was killed, but the Doctor surmised that mind control was involved. He showed the crew a technique to block further attempts. The Doctor investigated and discovered that the Cybermen wanted to control, not destroy, the Wheel. The Doctor had a crewmember broadcast a particular frequency throughout the station which destroyed the Cybermats.

The crew turned on a force field around the control centre to stop the Cybermen from entering. When it was announced that the X-Ray laser was functional, the Doctor determined that the Cybermen wanted the Wheel protected, it must be the springboard for an invasion of Earth! The Doctor believed that the Time Vector Generator could destroy the Cybermen but it was still aboard the Silver Carrier.

Meanwhile, the Cybermen attempted to poison the air supply but were discovered by Dr Corwyn, who relayed the plan just before being killed, enabling the crew to neutralise that threat. Jamie and Zoe retrieved the Time Vector Generator as the Doctor confronted the Cybermen and confirmed their plan. He destroyed one with an electrical field. He then helped tie the Time Vector Generator into the X-Ray laser.

The Cybermen launched a desperate attack against the Wheel by spacewalking troops to the station. The crew used the modified X-Ray laser to destroy their ship, while Jamie and a crewman used liquid plastic to destroy the remaining Cyberman on board and repelled the rest into space with the Wheel's force field. The Doctor took the mercury he needed to fix the TARDIS and discovered that Zoe had stowed away on board.

CONTINUITY

The Cyber-Planner takes the place of the mobile Cyber-Controller. It functions as an admiral in this adventure.

This is the first occurrence of the Doctor using "Dr. John Smith" as an alternate name. Jamie dubs him this when pressed for a name by Dr. Corwyn.

In his first encounter with the Daleks on Skaro, the Doctor falsely claims that the TARDIS' mercury fluid link is low. Here, it actually is a problem.

Scotsmen stop wearing kilts around the year 2000, although it's become trendy amongst Scandinavian men. The term "kiltie" describes Scandinavian kilt-wearers, although it's not clear whether this is a derogatory term.

Some schools are starting to give children intensive lessons in logical thinking, which has the side-effect of muting their students' emotions. This may be the origin of the Brotherhood of Logicians.

The humans aboard the space station have never heard of Cybermen or Daleks. While this establishes that the story takes place before the Dalek Invasion, it doesn't explain why they've never heard of the Cybermen.

Perhaps the two Cybermen invasions of Earth in the latter 20th century were dismissed by the crew's parents and grandparents as nightmares best forgotten, or classified by the government. Or, yet again, blame time ripples and eddies in the space-time continuum.

The sidearm of choice during this period is the blaster, which is a form of laser pistol. Bernalium is used to power the X-Ray laser and is usually stored in rods.

Bennett initially believes that the Doctor and Jamie are part of the 'Pull Back to Earth' movement, which wants to end the space programme. It's possible that this group helps foster the creation of the Travel Mat, which actually does achieve that aim for a while.

The Wheel has internal and external force fields. The exterior force field can deflect meteorites (and Cybermen) while the interior force fields prevent people from getting inside the operations centre (and presumably other sensitive areas of the station).

⟳ RUNNING THE ADVENTURE

This is the first adventure that really showcases the precariousness of space travel in the middle of the 21st century. The Cybermen have a large invasion fleet, but they need to rely on a signal from a Space Wheel at the edge of the Solar System to guide them to Earth without incident. Otherwise, they risk missing Earth and possibly getting pulled into the sun.

If you want to retain this feel for 21st century adventures then most Transport tasks are only **Very Easy – Routine** if the character has a signal to follow. Absent the signal, task ratings become at least **Difficult** and more likely **Very Difficult** or **Improbable.** Missing this roll usually dooms the craft to getting lost in deep space or plunging into the sun.

If it's your player characters making the roll, you should have a back-up plan unless you want them to seal their fates. Perhaps there's an enemy on board, an emergency beacon, a separate transmission, or a rescue ship in the vicinity. It's also possible that the missing signal could be rebroadcast and enable the characters to plot a new course with it. Finally, you can give them something to aim at; maybe they don't have a transmission leading them to Earth but if they can see Jupiter and the Sun out the window then they can at least head towards the inner solar system.

DAMN THOSE MERCURY LINKS!

Once again, the mercury links explode, stranding the travellers in a dangerous situation. You can use the mercury links as a catch-all reason to stop the player characters from leaving in the Tardis *and* as a McGuffin that they have to chase down. Maybe the only source of mercury on the planet in the laboratory of the sinister alchemist who's drugging the king, or perhaps the characters get captured by a mad computer while searching for mercury supplies.

Mercury's only liquid between around -40°C and 350° C – does that mean that the Tardis could be disabled easily by freezing it? The fate of the ship near the cold sun in **Amy's Choice** (see *The Eleventh Doctor Sourcbook*) does suggest extreme cold can shut down the console.

A MISSING BROADCAST?

As the Silver Carrier drifted towards the Space Wheel, the Controller determined to destroy it with the X-Ray laser. If not for Jamie, the laser would have destroyed it, fortuitously but inadvertently trumping the Cybermen's plan. While one could argue that the

Cybermats had already sabotaged the X-Ray Laser (their machinations covered over by Jamie's actions), they weren't even launched until after the Doctor and Jamie had been taken from the ship; the Wheel crew almost blew up the ship before that.

What makes the most sense is that the Servo Robot was programmed to pre-empt the attack, but the Doctor and Jamie's boarding distracted it. Given the servo robot's hostility, it probably believed that they were space pirates or unauthorised intruders (otherwise it would have helpfully informed them that it had supplies on board that were useful to the Wheel).

ANOTHER MYSTERY OF THE WHEEL

One of the most curious things about this adventure is the fact that the crew of the Wheel have all been given drugs to prevent mind control (giving them a +2 to resist mind-controlling effects) as well as a Silenski capsule implant to monitor their brainwaves. The obvious question is why. Is there something about being in deep space that makes the mind more open to suggestion? Has humanity encountered a race that uses hypnotism as a weapon or has humanity itself developed hypnotism to the point of it being an effective tool against others?

One possible and sinister interpretation is to string certain elements of this adventure together. Bennett is a capable leader until confronted with things that seem irrational. Zoe is a product of a scholastic emphasis on logic. Perhaps the drugs are designed to help humanity become more logical and rational-minded as well as 'edit' dangerous experiences and information. Does the government of Earth want to delete the previous invasions of the Cybermen from human memory? If so, then why?

FURTHER ADVENTURES

- The remnants of the Cyber-fleet spread out and head towards the centre of the Solar System, hoping to find Earth. One ship does encounter an Earth freighter and the Cybermen intend to board it and use its signals to lead the rest of the fleet to Earth. The characters arrive on the freighter just before the boarding.

- The Pull Back to Earth movement could be anything from a well-meaning group that believes humans shouldn't be leaving the circle of life that is Earth, or it could be violently militant. If the latter, then the characters could arrive on a

space liner or colony that is being sabotaged by Pull Back to Earth agents.

- The meteorite trick with the Cybermats could work well in other circumstances. The Cybermen send a bunch of Cybermats to Earth during the Cold War to disrupt the communications of one side and detonate a nuclear bomb, making it appear that the other side made a first strike. The Cybermen plan to watch from the safety of orbit. Thanks to the modifications they made on Mondas, the Cybermen have terraforming machines to rebuild the Earth's ecosphere after the war.

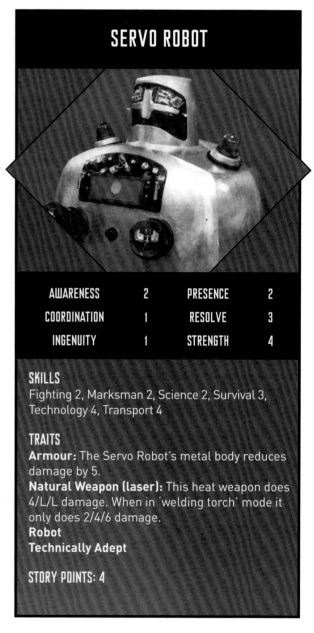

SERVO ROBOT

AWARENESS	2	PRESENCE	2
COORDINATION	1	RESOLVE	3
INGENUITY	1	STRENGTH	4

SKILLS
Fighting 2, Marksman 2, Science 2, Survival 3, Technology 4, Transport 4

TRAITS
Armour: The Servo Robot's metal body reduces damage by 5.
Natural Weapon (laser): This heat weapon does 4/L/L damage. When in 'welding torch' mode it only does 2/4/6 damage.
Robot
Technically Adept

STORY POINTS: 4

THE DOMINATORS

'An unintelligent enemy is far less dangerous than an intelligent one, Jamie.'

⊙ SYNOPSIS

Dulkis, Unspecified

A Dominator spaceship left its fleet and landed on a radioactive island on the planet Dulkis. The two Dominators aboard, Navigator Rago and Probationer Toba, wanted to enslave the natives and use the planet to power their fleet. Using their robotic servants the Quarks, Toba killed a group of Dulcians on an unauthorised trip to the island leaving only their pilot Cully, who managed to seek shelter, unharmed. The TARDIS landed nearby and the Doctor was delighted that they could relax and enjoy themselves – he had visited peaceful, pacifist Dulkis before. The Doctor, Jamie, and Zoe heard the Dominators destroy Cully's ship and began to explore, finding a museum to war – a reminder of Dulkis before its pacifism. Here they met a group of students and their Educator, Balan.

The island had been used to test a nuclear blast, but the research team was shocked to discover that there was no longer any radiation present. Unbeknownst to them, the Dominators had sucked it all into their ship – they needed radiation to power thie vessels. Cully arrived at the shelter and told everyone about the Dominators; he suggested going to the capital. Unfortunately, Cully was considered a con man and Balan believed that he was in league with the time travellers perpetuating a joke.

The Doctor and Jamie headed back to the TARDIS and learned that the Dominators were drilling through the planet's surface before being captured and taken to the Dominators' ship. The Dominators tested them and the Doctor and Jamie pretended to fail all of the intelligence tests. They were then let go. Meanwhile, Cully took Zoe to the capital to speak with the Council. Predictably, the Council, led by Cully's father the Director, believed that Cully had conspired with Zoe to prank them.

Cully and Zoe returned to the island, where they, along with the academic team, were captured by the Dominators. They were all taken to a drilling site to clear debris. The Doctor and Jamie went to the capital, where the Council still refused action. They felt that the Dominators could take what they wanted from the island and leave. They only started grasping what was happening when their attempt to contact Balan failed.

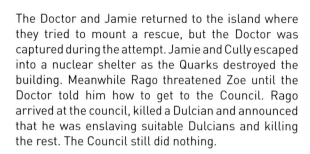

The Doctor and Jamie returned to the island where they tried to mount a rescue, but the Doctor was captured during the attempt. Jamie and Cully escaped into a nuclear shelter as the Quarks destroyed the building. Meanwhile Rago threatened Zoe until the Doctor told him how to get to the Council. Rago arrived at the council, killed a Dulcian and announced that he was enslaving suitable Dulcians and killing the rest. The Council still did nothing.

Toba killed Balan while interrogating the prisoners about the attackers before being admonished by Rago. Rago contacted the Fleet Leader who decided that none of the Dulcians were worth saving, while Jamie and Cully arrived and freed the prisoners. The Doctor wondered why there were four drilling sites at the corners of a square and one in the middle. He realised that the Dominators planned to turn the entire planet into radioactive magma that they could harvest for energy to power their ships. The final part of their plan was to drop a 'seed device' into the drilling area. The device was already near to critical mass. Jamie realised that the shelter they were hiding in was close to the drilling area, and they tunnelled through to the central bore hole to prevent the coming disaster.

The Dominators dropped the nuclear seed into the central hole, but the Doctor caught it on the way down. He snuck it onto the Dominators' ship, which exploded during take-off. Cully and the students headed to the capital via capsule while the time travellers remained behind. Unfortunately, the rockets from the other drilling holes created an active volcano and the time travellers found themselves racing a sheet of lava to get to the TARDIS...

CONTINUITY

Weapons haven't been used on Dulkis for 172 years (when the atomic test took place). The Doctor visited Dulkis prior to this and is unaware of the atomic test that irradiated the Island of Death. The Doctor enjoyed his visit to Dulkis and didn't want to leave.

While the Dulcians have turned to pacifism, they maintain working weapons in at least one effectively abandoned museum. These weapons later prove useful against Quarks. Useful discarded technology also appears in **The Seeds of Death**, where part of the solution involves using a rocket from a little-regarded private museum.

The Dominators can suck all of the radiation from a localized area and convert it to power. Such a technology would be very beneficial to planets irradiated by war or accident.

Unlike in **The Underwater Menace** and **Inferno** (but not, presumably, **The Dalek Invasion of Earth**), a breach of a planet's crust does not necessarily result in a destroyed world. This may be due to the particular geology of Dulkis.

The sonic screwdriver can burn through metal and brick.

⊙ RUNNING THE ADVENTURE

What should the characters do when they arrive at a place where the locals seem unwilling to save themselves? The Dulcians seem so unwilling to do anything and are willing to give up whatever it takes for the Dominators to simply leave their world.

If the Dulcians had even the slightest military or police power then they'd make short work of two Dominators and a few Quarks, especially considering the power restrictions the Dominators seem to be working under. It's a wonder that the Doctor simply doesn't shrug and leave with his companions in the TARDIS. Certainly that might be the position of your players when presented with a similar situation?

The most important thing you need to do in this type of situation is present the pacifist world as sympathetic rather than simply stubbornly naive. Here are a few ways to accomplish that.

- Provide a credible backstory. The Dulcians aren't simply biologically wired to be pacifists; they had violence and wars in the past. They overcame it and built a utopian society. The Dulcians are also unaware that aliens exist, or at least that aliens would want anything from them, so they have no reason to maintain a defence system.

- Provide sympathetic characters. While the Dulcian Council seems unwilling to do anything, the characters meet the rebellious Cully and some scholars that are directly in the line of fire. These Dulcians are more open to resistance as they are being preyed upon.

- Make it difficult to simply pack up and leave. The characters have access to the TARDIS, but between separate trips to the Council, being captured, and getting buried in rubble it's difficult for the characters to take off in the TARDIS.

- Make the villains as unsympathetic as possible. The Dominators are callous and cold. Rago cares nothing for the Dulcians; he admonishes Toba for not properly conserving energy and wasting opportunities. Toba kills people every chance he gets. If nothing else, the characters shouldn't want to let the Dominators win, no matter how they feel about the Dulcians.

DOMINATORS

The Dominators are a humanoid race of conquerors whose empire spans ten galaxies. They pride themselves in assessing problems with cold detachment and practicality; more emotional members of their race aren't allowed to advance to positions of authority. Dominators are generally accompanied by their robotic servants, the Quarks.

Judging by the two Dominators that the Doctor encountered, it would seem that the Dominators are a naturally aggressive and impulsive species whose officers pride themselves in being able to hold their emotions in check. Still, even the cool officers can lose their temper if their patience is challenged, and their violent streak re-emerges.

Due to their brutal efficiency, Dominators tend to try to get the most done with the least amount of resources. This makes capturing victims preferable to killing them, as slavery is more efficient than relying on the Quarks for physical labour. Sometimes, this can lead to mistakes (such as scanning Jaime's vital signs and presuming that the Doctor's will be the same).

The Dominators travel in saucer-shaped spacecraft usually manned by a crew of two Dominators and three Quarks. The spacecraft can absorb and convert local radiation into fuel, the nuclear destruction of a planet is enough to refuel an entire fleet.

DOMINATOR NAVIGATOR

AWARENESS	3	PRESENCE	4
COORDINATION	4	RESOLVE	4
INGENUITY	3	STRENGTH	4

SKILLS
Athletics 2, Convince 2, Fighting 4, Knowledge 3, Marksman 4, Medicine 2, Science 3, Technology 4, Transport 3

TRAITS
Armour (Minor): A Dominator's combat suit provides some protection, reducing damage by 5.

Fear Factor (1): While they look like tall humans, Dominators have a manner and reputation that strikes fear in the hearts of others. They gain a +2 on attempts to instil fear in their enemies.

Indomitable: Dominators have disciplined minds and gain +4 on attempts to resist any type of mental control.

Obsession (major) – Efficiency: Dominators are obsessed with efficiency and will only conduct actions that they don't deem wasteful.

Stubborn: Dominators believe that they are better than other races and they don't value their opinions or experience. They receive +2 to resist Convince attempts.

Voice of Authority: Dominators demand to be obeyed and there are harsh consequences when their orders aren't complied with. They receive a +2 on Presence and Convince rolls to get people to do what they want.

TECH LEVEL: 7   STORY POINTS: 3-5

Notes: Higher-ranking Dominators have Obsession (Efficiency) as a major bad trait.

DOMINATOR PROBATIONER

AWARENESS	3	PRESENCE	4
COORDINATION	4	RESOLVE	4
INGENUITY	3	STRENGTH	4

SKILLS
Athletics 2, Convince 2, Fighting 4, Knowledge 3, Marksman 4, Medicine 2, Science 3, Technology 4, Transport 3

TRAITS
Armour (Minor): A Dominator's combat suit provides some protection, reducing damage by 5.

Fear Factor (1): While they look like tall humans, Dominators have a manner and reputation that strikes fear in the hearts of others. They gain a +2 on attempts to instil fear in their enemies.

Indomitable: Dominators have disciplined minds and gain +4 on attempts to resist any type of mental control.

Stubborn: Dominators believe that they are better than other races and they don't value their opinions or experience. They receive +2 to resist Convince attempts.

Voice of Authority: Dominators demand to be obeyed and there are harsh consequences when their orders aren't complied with. They receive a +2 on Presence and Convince rolls to get people to do what they want.

TECH LEVEL: 7   STORY POINTS: 3-5

QUARKS

Quarks are the robotic servants and enforcers of the Dominators. They aren't very fast and require a lot of power although they can re-energise themselves and are capable of great destruction. They have two folding arms which can stun and disintegrate opponents as well as destroy large structures. The Dominators also use the Quarks as portable batteries to power their mobile equipment. Due to the power drain multiple Quarks are often used for this purpose.

DULCIANS

The Dulcians appear human, but have larger brains and two hearts. They are physically weak compared even to humans, although this may be the result of the lack of conflict in their society. Most are pacifists, refusing to fight even when attacked.

The Dulcian character package gives +1 Ingenuity, -1 Strength, and the Code of Conduct trait at the cost of 1 Character Point.

QUARK

AWARENESS	2	PRESENCE	3
COORDINATION	2	RESOLVE	4
INGENUITY	2	STRENGTH	7

SKILLS
Convince 2, Craft 3, Fighting 2, Knowledge 3, Marksman 3, Science 3, Technology 3, Transport 3

TRAITS
Arm Cannon: Quarks have energy cannons built into their folding arms. They deliver lethal damage (4/L/L). The cannons can also be set to a stun setting.
Armour (Major Trait): Quarks are heavily armoured and reduce damage taken by 5.
Enslaved: Quarks are a robot slave race and require someone to give them instructions.
Fear Factor (3): With their oddly shaped appearance and deadly weaponry Quarks are a fearsome threat and gain +6 to instil fear in those that oppose them.
Molecular Bonding: Quarks can bond a victim to a metallic surface, much like a magnet. On a successful hit, the victim's molecules are agitated and he suffers a stun effect. He is also irresistibly attracted to the nearest large metallic surface and is bonded to it until the Quark turns the power off.
Power Transfer: Quarks can use their internal energy reserves as batteries, powering up other objects. This can be done without touching the object, but the Quark must be close by. Quarks work in groups to power objects that require a lot of energy; otherwise, a single Quark might drain itself dry. The Gamemaster should determine how long a Quark (or Quarks) can power an item for recharge based on the needs of the plot.

Robot
Scan (Minor Trait): Quarks can scan technological items. They gain a +2 on Awareness and Technology rolls to determine an object's circuitry and function.
Technically Adept
Transmit: Quarks can communicate with each other and their masters remotely.
Weakness (Major Trait): While power providers, Quarks are notorious energy suckers. After a Quark fires its arm cannon four times, it takes 4 points of Coordination and Resolve damage and its arm cannon is only capable of stun damage from that point forward. A Quark must refrain from shooting for 4 rounds to recharge and fire normally again.
Weld: Quarks can weld material with their lower set of arms.

TECH LEVEL: 7   STORY POINTS: 3-6

DOES DULKIS SEEM FAMILIAR?

Dulkis and Gallifrey have many parallels. Both are largely pacifist societies with violent histories. Both have ruling councils reluctant to get involved in confrontations. Both allowed alien races to invade their worlds and appear to do nothing about it, at least initially. Even the Dulcians themselves resemble Gallifreyans, with larger brains and two hearts. Perhaps one of the reasons that the Doctor enjoys Dulkis so much is that it reminds him of home?

FURTHER ADVENTURES

- The Dominators are a warlike race that conquered much of the 'Ten Galaxies.' It shouldn't be long before they cross a race that challenges them, such as the Draconians or Sontarans. The characters could arrive on a battleground between the two races as they work against each other, with an innocent society caught in the middle.

- The characters arrive on Dulkis during their last war, which is devastating the entire world. While many Dulcians are now coming around to the idea of the futility of war, there is at least one faction that has developed a superweapon that they hope will win the war. The characters arrive as the superweapon nears completion; can they prevent the faction from destroying Dulkis?

- Dulkis has a dirty little secret; its people haven't adopted a policy of pacifism; their minds have been altered to weed out aggressive tendencies. This doesn't always fully work (explaining Cully), but normally such deviations are harmless side-effects. Recently, however, some Dulcians are manifesting aggressive emotions and Dulkis has its first serial killer in centuries. Is someone tampering with the mind control, or is Dulcian biology beginning to reject the treatments? If the characters get involved, should they help the Dulcians return to a medicated paradise or force them to live with free will?

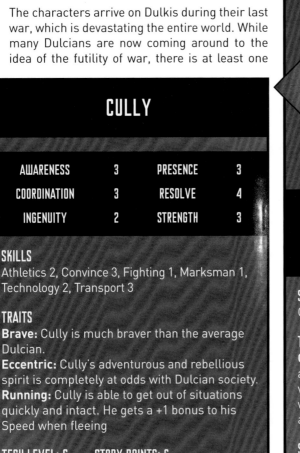

CULLY

AWARENESS	3	PRESENCE	3
COORDINATION	3	RESOLVE	4
INGENUITY	2	STRENGTH	3

SKILLS
Athletics 2, Convince 3, Fighting 1, Marksman 1, Technology 2, Transport 3

TRAITS
Brave: Cully is much braver than the average Dulcian.
Eccentric: Cully's adventurous and rebellious spirit is completely at odds with Dulcian society.
Running: Cully is able to get out of situations quickly and intact. He gets a +1 bonus to his Speed when fleeing

TECH LEVEL: 6   STORY POINTS: 6

DULCIAN

AWARENESS	2	PRESENCE	2
COORDINATION	2	RESOLVE	2
INGENUITY	3	STRENGTH	2

SKILLS
Convince 4, Knowledge 3, Science 2, Technology 2

TRAITS
Obsession (Pacifism): Dulcians are pacifists and won't use violence. When confronted by a violent person, a Dulcian attempts to reason with and understand him (which basically acts as a variation on the Argumentative trait).

STORY POINTS: 2

CHAPTER TEN:
THE MIND ROBBER, THE INVASION, THE KROTONS

THE MIND ROBBER

'Don't worry about fiction. Hang on to real life. You've got to get out!'

NAME CHANGE!

The kidnapped writer of The Mind Robber is generally referred to as 'the Master' during the course of the adventure. The use of this term is problematic, as 'The Master of the Land of Fiction' conjures images of a certain renegade Time Lord. For this reason, the Master of this adventure is referred to as 'the Controller,' as this is the title the Master was to bestow on the Doctor when he took his place. This also eases the confusion between 'the Master' and 'the Master Brain.'

⊘ SYNOPSIS

The Land of Fiction, outside Time and Space.

The lava from the volcano on Dulkis covered the TARDIS and overheated the mercury fluid links, resulting in the Doctor using an emergency unit to save them. This device catapulted the TARDIS beyond time and space. The Doctor warned Jamie and Zoe not to leave the TARDIS, but the two companions were lured outside by images of their homes on the viewer. They found themselves in a misty white void while the Doctor felt an attack on his mind. He managed to fend it off and return his companions to the TARDIS before they could be captured by White Robots.

A strange vibration shook the TARDIS apart and the three time travellers were scattered through a forest. Jamie confronted an English 'redcoat' which shot him, turning Jamie into a frozen two-dimensional image. Zoe was surrounded by walls and plunged into a hole when she went through the sole door. The Controller was watching them but worried about where the Doctor was. He sent clockwork soldiers after him.

The Doctor found his companions after beating a series of riddles while avoiding the clockwork soldiers. He returned Jamie to life, albeit with the wrong face. They met a sailor that the Doctor realised was Lemuel Gulliver of Gulliver's Travels. He could only speak lines that the character said in the novel. Gulliver handed them over to the clockwork soldiers, who took them to the edge of the forest. They were attacked by the mythological Unicorn, but turned it into a statue by declaring that it didn't exist. Continuing on, they found a house, where the Doctor was able to fix Jamie's face, and they discovered the entrance to a Labyrinth. Zoe and the Doctor entered, leaving Jamie behind.

Jamie was pursued by a soldier but received help from Rapunzel, who helped him enter the castle of the Master Brain. He found a room full of computers which showed that Zoe would be turned to stone by Medusa. In the Labyrinth, the two travellers encountered and overcame the Minotaur before confronting Medusa. The Doctor used a mirror to turn the creature to stone, and the computer in the castle displayed a failure reading. The Doctor and Zoe were helped into the castle by a comic strip superhero known as the Karkus, after Zoe subdued him using martial arts.

Reunited with Jamie, they met the Controller, who explained that they were in a Land of Fiction run by the Master Brain. The Master Brain needed a creative mind to run the Land and plucked the Controller from time. Now that the Controller was getting old, the Master Brain wanted the Doctor to replace him. Additionally, the Master Brain planned to take over the Earth. The Doctor refused and Jamie and Zoe were hypnotised to help trap him.

The Controller managed to capture the Doctor and linked him to the Master Brain. The Doctor realised that this gave him control and he engaged in a battle of wits with the Controller. The Master Brain realised that the Doctor was too powerful and ordered the White Robots to kill him. Fortunately, Jamie and Zoe, freed by the Doctor, pushed several buttons on the Master Brain's control panel and overloaded it. The Doctor managed to get the Controller away before the Master Brain exploded.

Everything faded to black as the time travellers and the Controller huddled together. The TARDIS reformed around them.

CONTINUITY

The TARDIS can withstand being buried in hot lava. It also has an emergency switch that can take it outside of normal space-time.

The TARDIS is seemingly destroyed for the first time and the console is separated from the TARDIS for the first time.

The Karkus is an Earth literary superhero created around 2000, probably from middle Europe. He's still popular enough toward the end of the 21st century/ early 22nd century that Zoe recognises him.

⊙ RUNNING THE ADVENTURE

This adventure provides the Gamemaster with a bit of fun, as the Land of Fiction operates by its own rules. There are many other variations on this theme that you can try, from trapping the characters in a virtual reality (such as an online video game), a cartoon world, or even a setting that seems normal but for strange anomalies like magic or superhero powers. The trick is that, once the characters realise their situation, there has to be some way for them to turn the tables and embrace the genre in which they've found themselves. A character may realise that she can cast magic spells or develop superpowers; a character may discover that they can rewrite computer codes; a character may manifest an eraser to rub out enemy cartoons or create helpful objects. In the end, there should also be a controlling force that the characters can overcome to enable them to escape the strange land.

EMERGENCY UNIT

An Emergency Unit is a TARDIS 'booster' – it provides a quick blast of power that jolts the ship out of the normal universe and into a safer dimension. The same effect can be achieved by jettisoning rooms (see the Time Traveller's Companion for more on advanced TARDIS manoeuvres like that.) The unit has a timer built into it. When the timer runs out, the Emergency Unit returns the ship to its previous course.

Emergency Units are one-shot gadgets. A fully-stocked TARDIS carries several such modules.

The Land of Fiction

The Land of Fiction exists outside of normal space-time. It apparently contains all of the fictional works of Earth, past and present, although it is still anchored to the 'present' in terms of its Controller's awareness. Interestingly, all the way back in **The Chase** (see **The First Doctor Sourcebook**), the Doctor mentioned that that the TARDIS could land in bizarre regions like the collective unconscious of humanity. The Land of Fiction may be a part of this mental 'space'.

However, the Controller's castle is protected by quite conventional electronic security systems, and he watches the Doctor through computer monitors. The robots, too, are real as opposed to fictional constructs. If the TARDIS can enter the collective unconscious, then other equally-advanced invaders can do so too. Whoever built the Master Brain and the White Robots intended to conquer Earth or erase humanity by turning the whole species into fiction.

Death of the Author

The Controller encountered by the Doctor and his companions was a writer of boy's adventures, and the fictional constructs and challenges he created reflect that – the travellers face toy soldiers and mythical monsters. Swapping in another author could result in a very different take on the Land of Fiction – what would the Master Brain have done with Agatha Christie, or Shakespeare, or Lovecraft, or Samuel Beckett?

MASTER BRAIN

The Master Brain is a supercomputer that controls the Controller of the Land of Fiction, a realm outside of normal time and space. It is unknown who created the Master Brain but they obviously wanted to remove the Earth's population. It plans a non-violent invasion, enticing humans to come into the Land of Fiction and play out fantasies for the rest of their lives (assuming that the Master Brain doesn't plan to kill them once its plan is accomplished).

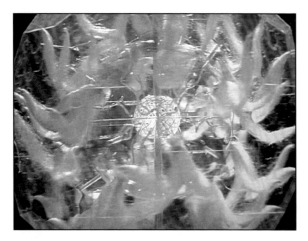

What is known is that the Master Brain lacks creativity. It plucked a paperback writer from early 20th century Earth to act as its creative force, the implication being that the Master Brain has been doing this ever since its creators disappeared. The Controller makes no reference to his predecessor, but there must have been one. Otherwise, if the Master Brain had the ability to pluck humans at will, it would have no need for a Controller.

The Master Brain can pluck images from a victim's mind but it needs the Controller to filter and use them properly. Notably, while the Master Brain takes images from Jamie and Zoe it does not seem to get any information from the Doctor. There are no Gallifreyan literary figures or images in the Land of Fiction.

Once someone is connected to the Master Brain they have control of the Land of Fiction. They can conjure fictional constructs or command existing ones. The previous Controller is used to ensure compliance from a new Controller, but if the new person resists then the Master Brain resorts to brute force. Overloading the Master Brain's computer system causes the Land of Fiction to self-destruct.

A Controller can use the Master Brain to create a fictional landscape that allows victims to interact with it on a physical and literary level. In some cases a victim can evade obstacles by solving logical problems and riddles. The Controller can also make fictional constructs.

MASTER BRAIN

AWARENESS	5	PRESENCE	1
COORDINATION	-	RESOLVE	5
INGENUITY	2	STRENGTH	5

SKILLS
Knowledge 5, Technology 5

TRAITS
Alien
Alien Appearance: The Master Brain looks like a giant brain connected to a computer system.
Cyborg: The Master Brain is a combination of mechanical and biological (possibly synthetic) parts.
Huge (Major): The Master Brain is very large but immobile, making it very easy to hit.
Hypnosis (Major): The Master Brain can hypnotise the Controller in order to ensure compliance.
Immortal (Major): The Master Brain can seemingly live forever barring a violent end.
Indomitable: The Master Brain gets a +4 to rolls in order to resist being controlled.
Networked: The Master Brain is connected to a vast computer system and can send 'eyes and ears' throughout the Land of Fiction.
Psychic: The Master Brain can peer into a victim's mind to extract characters and images.
Slow (Major): The Master Brain cannot move on its own.
Special: The Master Brain can entice victims to enter the Land of Fiction from Earth.
Uncreative (Special): The Master Brain is coldly logical and utterly incapable of imaginative thought.
Weakness (Major): Randomly pressing the buttons and knobs on the computer panel can cause the Master Brain to overload, causing 4 points of Attribute damage each turn.

TECH LEVEL: 10   STORY POINTS: 10

FICTIONAL CONSTRUCTS

Fictional constructs are characters plucked from fiction and given a physical form. They seem unaware of their status and see everything through their own fictional lens.

TOY SOLDIER

AWARENESS	2	PRESENCE	2
COORDINATION	3	RESOLVE	3
INGENUITY	1	STRENGTH	5

SKILLS
Athletics 2, Fighting 3, Marksman 2

TRAITS
Camera Hat: The Master of the Land of Fiction can see what the toy soldier sees through a camera set in its hat. This is also how the toy soldier 'sees', so covering the camera lens blinds the toy soldier.
Invisible to Fiction: Fictional characters do not see the toy soldiers or acknowledge their existence.
Literally By The Book (Minor): A fictional construct can only say words attributed to him from the fiction in which he was created.
Tough: A toy soldier's tin 'skin' offers some protection. All damage against a toy soldier is reduced by two.
Weakness (Major): Once all victims realise that they are fighting against a fictional construct, the fictional construct is either turned into a cardboard cut-out, a statue or vanishes. This weakness only manifests if everyone viewing it realises that it is fictional. If even one person has doubts, then the fictional construct remains. The victims can choose to keep the fictional construct around if they so desire.

EQUIPMENT
Rifle: A toy soldier uses a rifle that was common around the turn of the 20th century - 4/8/12

Bayonet: The toy soldier gets a +2 to damage when using his rifle as a bayonet.

TECH LEVEL: 6   STORY POINTS: 2

Some fictional constructs are limited to using words of dialogue from their sources, while others have more freedom (likely due to drawing from multiple sources or from the Master creating new dialogue for them). They generally aren't adversarial unless being so is true to their literary roots.

A special kind of fictional construct is the toy soldier. Toy soldiers act as extensions of the Controller's will in the Land of Fiction. The Controller can see through cameras in their hats and can give them direct orders.

WHITE ROBOTS

White robots may or may not be fictional constructs but they are the main troops of the Master Brain and seem to exist outside of the fictional landscapes. They also seem to act directly for the Master Brain and not the Controller. They are mute and it is possible that the Master Brain uses them as conduits to collect information from the minds of their victims.

WHITE ROBOT

AWARENESS	4	PRESENCE	4
COORDINATION	3	RESOLVE	4
INGENUITY	1	STRENGTH	5

SKILLS
Fighting 3, Marksman 3

TRAITS
Robot: White Robots are artificial constructs, although they might initially be mistaken for an armoured humanoid.
Natural Weapon (Disorienting beam): White Robots can use the beam to disorient their victims, doing 2/4/6 damage to their Awareness score. White Robots can also increase the power to lethal levels, doing 4/L/L damage.

TECH LEVEL: 6   STORY POINTS: 3-6

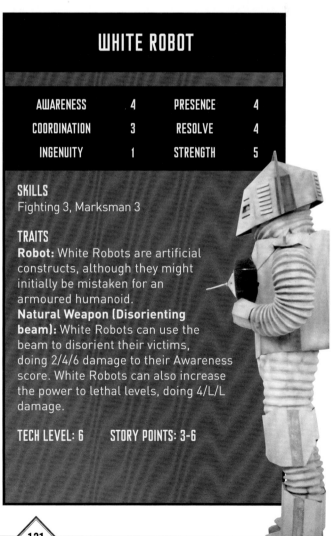

WHO CREATED THE MASTER BRAIN?

The ultimate goal of the Master Brain is to remove the entire population of Earth and bring it to the Land of Fiction so that the planet is left uninhabited. What the Master Brain plans to do with it is not entirely clear. It is implied that the Master Brain was created, so perhaps this is a unique way of invading worlds.

If the Master Brain truly needs someone with an exceptional mind like the Doctor, then it follows that the Makers of the Master Brain must be highly intelligent as well. The usual suspects are the Celestials, the Daemons, Light, or even the Time Lords. Alternatively, the Master Brain and the Land of Fiction may have been built as a leisure land. At some point, the Master Brain evolved and perhaps turned on its Makers. This enables any race (even future humanity) to be the Makers.

As a computer, however, the Master Brain still needs a creative spark and, in its evolved state, only a creature of advanced intelligence will do. Why it wants to invade is unclear; this could be a remnant of the Maker's wishes or the desire of a fictional character that the Master Brain absorbed. Perhaps the Master Brain has no plan, and the various lost civilisations of the universe had their populations simply scooped away in the past.

DID THIS ADVENTURE REALLY HAPPEN?

The end of this adventure leads directly into **The Invasion** with no evidence of the Controller on board the TARDIS. While the Controller could simply have been sent back to his own time (likely sometime in the mid-20th century), the time travellers never referred to the events in this adventure. It's possible that they either forgot or it was a mass dream, perhaps brought on by the TARDIS to keep them sane while traversing beyond time and space.

- There are a number of elements to this story that could reflect dreamlike perspectives from the time travellers, especially if looked at through the eyes of another time traveller.

- Zoe never mentions the name of her home city. It also looks rather futuristic (and perhaps even on the moon or a different planet) for the year 2000, which she cites as when she read about the Karkus' adventures.

- Jamie's face is rearranged by the Doctor, which can be seen as an allegory on regeneration. The Doctor considers the change a 'nasty trick,'

which is curious considering that he's used to people changing faces.

- The White Robots look remarkably like 'child-friendly' versions of the Cybermen, who menace the time travellers in the very next adventure. This could be the TARDIS' projection of future danger, viewed through the lens of the Land of Fiction.

- The defeating of the Master Brain could simply be the time travellers struggling to return to normal space or be lost in their delusions forever.

FURTHER ADVENTURES

- The Master Brain was not destroyed. Instead, merely damaged, it rebuilt itself and searched for a new controller. This time around the Land of Fiction is more focused and realistic; the characters may not realise where they are until they've unwittingly subjected themselves to it.

- The Controller was returned to Earth, but as the Master Brain has no concept of time it returned him to 1926. Now 20 years too old, the Controller uses his knowledge of future fiction to generate income; he soon becomes the most famous author on the planet and his stories inspire a generation of scientists and engineers. The characters arrive in the middle of World War II, but it is a very different war. Rocket planes jet through the sky and infantry soldiers carry laser rifles. The characters need to return to 1926 to fix time, but first they need to get back to the TARDIS, from which they were separated.

- The characters arrive on Earth in the 35th century and discover a Draconian scientific colony. The Draconians have never met a live Earthling, as they all disappeared in the 22nd century; colonial humans that returned to Earth also disappeared. Archaeological teams have been trying for centuries to figure out why. If the characters look through the archives, they discover that all the humans on Earth disappeared on the date of Zoe's death. Should the characters go back in time to meet Zoe, they discover that she remembers her time with the Doctor, up to when he sent her and Jamie back to their own times so that he could take over the Land of Fiction. As it turns out, the characters are in a parallel universe, and one in which this desperate Doctor wants their TARDIS to help him escape his fate.

THE CONTROLLER

AWARENESS	3	PRESENCE	2
COORDINATION	2	RESOLVE	5
INGENUITY	5	STRENGTH	1

The Controller is an unnamed but prolific British author that wrote 5000 words a week for 25 years, primarily for the Captain Jack Harkaway adventures in *The Ensign* boy's magazine. The Master Brain kidnapped the Controller while he was sleeping in 1926 to run the Land of Fiction.

SKILLS
Convince 3, Knowledge 4 (literature, puzzles), Subterfuge 4

TRAITS
Voice of Authority (Minor Good Trait): +2 bonus to Presence and Convince rolls

TECH LEVEL: 4   STORY POINTS: 5

GULLIVER

AWARENESS	3	PRESENCE	4
COORDINATION	3	RESOLVE	3
INGENUITY	3	STRENGTH	3

SKILLS
Athletics 3, Fighting 2, Knowledge 3, Marksman 1, Medicine 4, Science 2, Survival 3, Transport 3

TRAITS
Literally By The Book (Minor): A fictional construct can only say words attributed to him from the fiction in which he was created.
Weakness (Major): Once all victims realise that they are fighting against a fictional construct, the fictional construct is either turned into a cardboard cut-out, a statue or vanishes. This weakness only manifests if everyone viewing it realises that it is fictional. If even one person has doubts, then the fictional construct remains. The victims can choose to keep the fictional construct around if they so desire.

TECH LEVEL: 4   STORY POINTS: 4

THE KARKUS

AWARENESS	3	PRESENCE	2
COORDINATION	4	RESOLVE	3
INGENUITY	2	STRENGTH	8

SKILLS
Athletics 5, Fighting 5, Marksman 3

TRAITS
Anti-Molecular Ray Disintegrator*: While primarily used against inanimate objects, the Anti-Molecular Ray Disintegrator is a lethal weapon - 4/L/L.
Literally By The Book (Minor): A fictional construct can only say words attributed to him from the fiction in which he was created.

Weakness (Major): Once all victims realise that they are fighting against a fictional construct, it either turns into a cardboard cut-out, a statue or vanishes. This weakness only manifests if everyone viewing it realises that it is fictional. If even one person has doubts, then the construct remains. The victims can keep the fictional construct around if they so desire.

*The Anti-Molecular Ray Disintegrator can be disbelieved on its own. This only infuriates the Karkus, who then attacks with his great strength.

TECH LEVEL: 5   STORY POINTS: 4

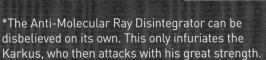

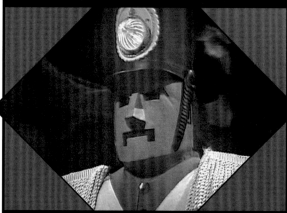

REDCOAT

AWARENESS	3	PRESENCE	2
COORDINATION	3	RESOLVE	3
INGENUITY	2	STRENGTH	3

SKILLS
Athletics 2, Fighting 3, Marksman 3, Survival 2

TRAITS
Face Rifle: The redcoat has a rifle that stuns a character when it hits, freezing him in place. The character's face is also removed and a board appears with various choices for different parts of the face. Once the face is assembled the character is no longer stunned. It's possible to get the face 'wrong'; the character reassembling it must make an Awareness and Ingenuity roll (Difficulty 12) to reconstruct the face properly.
Literally By The Book (Minor): A fictional construct can only say words attributed to him from the fiction in which he was created.
Weakness (Major): Once all victims realise that they are fighting against a fictional construct, the fictional construct is either turned into a cardboard cut-out, a statue or vanishes. This weakness only manifests if everyone viewing it realises that it is fictional. If even one person has doubts, then the fictional construct remains. The victims can choose to keep the fictional construct around if they so desire.

TECH LEVEL: 3   STORY POINTS: 2

MEDUSA

AWARENESS	4	PRESENCE	2
COORDINATION	3	RESOLVE	3
INGENUITY	2	STRENGTH	2

SKILLS
Athletics 2, Subterfuge 3

TRAITS
Literally By The Book (Minor): A fictional construct can only say words attributed to him from the fiction in which he was created.
Stony Gaze (Special): Medusa's gaze turns her victims into stone. If Medusa gets a fantastic result in an opposed Awareness and Coordination roll when the victim has a chance of looking at her, then the victim turns to stone.
Weakness (Major): Once all victims realise that they are fighting against a fictional construct, Medusa turns into a stone statue. This weakness only manifests if everyone viewing it realises that it is fictional. If even one person has doubts, then Medusa remains.

TECH LEVEL: 2   STORY POINTS: 2

RAPUNZEL

AWARENESS	2	PRESENCE	3
COORDINATION	2	RESOLVE	3
INGENUITY	3	STRENGTH	1

SKILLS
Convince 2, Knowledge 2

TRAITS
Attractive: Rapunzel gets a +2 on any roll in which her beauty is a factor.

Literally By The Book (Minor): A fictional construct can only say words attributed to him from the fiction in which he was created.

Ropy Hair (Special): Rapunzel has extremely long hair that can be used as a rope. Due to her fictional nature the laws of physics do not apply and Rapunzel does not need to brace herself or end up with a snapped neck due to characters climbing up her hair.

Weakness (Major): Once all victims realise that they are fighting against a fictional construct, the fictional construct is either turned into a cardboard cut-out, a statue or vanishes. This weakness only manifests if everyone viewing it realises that it is fictional. If even one person has doubts, then the fictional construct remains. The victims can choose to keep the fictional construct around if they so desire.

STORY POINTS: 2

THE MINOTAUR

AWARENESS	2	PRESENCE	3
COORDINATION	3	RESOLVE	5
INGENUITY	1	STRENGTH	7

SKILLS
Athletics 3, Fighting 4, Survival 3

TRAITS
Keen Senses (Smell): The Minotaur gets +2 on Awareness rolls when using his nose.

Literally By The Book (Minor): A fictional construct can only say words attributed to him from the fiction in which he was created.

Natural Weapons (Bite and Gore): The Minotaur's bite and horns grant him a +2 on damage in close combat.

Tough: The Minotaur has a tough hide. All damage is reduced by 2.

Weakness (Major): Once all victims realise that they are fighting against a fictional construct, the fictional construct is either turned into a cardboard cut-out, a statue or vanishes. This weakness only manifests if everyone viewing it realises that it is fictional. If even one person has doubts, then the fictional construct remains. The victims can choose to keep the fictional construct around if they so desire.

STORY POINTS: 4

THE INVASION

'Don't underestimate them, Jimmy. They may look like amateurs, but that man has an incredible knack of being one jump ahead of everyone.'

⊙ SYNOPSIS

London, 1968

The TARDIS materialised near the moon, but immediately came under missile attack. The Doctor took evasive action and the TARDIS ended up on the Earth, but with a damaged visual stabiliser rendering it invisible. Noting the date, the Doctor suggested seeking out Professor Travers for help. They flagged down a passing lorry, but the driver was concerned about security at International Electromatics (IE). He explained that they were inside the IE compound, and that the company had bought out the previous inhabitants from the area. Most of them had joined the company, but some had disappeared. The time travellers took the ride, but got out just before the driver was stopped outside the compound by IE security guards, who killed him.

The time travellers reached London and learned that Travers and his daughter went abroad for a year and lent the house to Professor Watkins and his photographer niece, Isobel, who answered the door. While Watkins could have been helpful with the repairs, Isobel mentioned that he worked for IE and

she hadn't seen him in over a week. The Doctor and Jamie went to the IE London office building, where they slipped past the computer receptionist but were captured and brought before CEO Tobias Vaughn. Vaughn apologised for the rough treatment, and explained that Professor Watkins was at a critical stage of his work and had remained on site. He offered to fix the Doctor's damaged circuit and let them go.

After they left, Vaughn consulted with the hidden Cyber-Planner. The Cyber-Planner recalled the Doctor and Jamie from meeting them on Planet 14. Meanwhile the Doctor and Jamie try to elude the IE security guards tailing them and end up getting captured by UNIT. They were taken onboard a converted Hercules aircraft, the mobile command centre of the newly promoted Brigadier Lethbridge-Stewart. The Brigadier explained that his team had been watching IE, as they'd exploded on the technological scene rather quickly. Unfortunately, UNIT agents sent to assess the situation had either disappeared or become uncooperative.

Meanwhile, Zoe and Isobel went looking for the Doctor and got captured by IE after causing the computer receptionist to melt down by giving it an irresolvable logic problem. Vaughn wanted to use Isobel to encourage Watkins' compliance. The Doctor and Jamie went after them only to be captured by Vaughn after observing several large containers being loaded on a train, including one with Zoe's feather boa caught in the lid. Vaughn took them to the IE factory and allowed the Doctor to meet Watkins. Watkins told the Doctor about the Cerebration Mentor which can affect emotions. The Doctor also noticed a deep space radio transmitter. Vaughn demanded to be told about the visual stabiliser, seeing the TARDIS as a potential escape route if his plans went awry.

The Doctor and Jamie managed to escape and, with UNIT's aid, rescued Isobel and Zoe by helicopter. Vaughn realised that UNIT were a threat to his plans, he contacts Major-General Rutledge and hypnotises him, telling him to stop UNIT operations involving IE.

The Brigadier mentioned that UFOs had been appearing over England in the last year and kept disappearing near the IE factory. The Doctor and Jamie infiltrated IE's London warehouse and learned that the transport cylinders contained Cybermen! They returned to UNIT to find that the Brigadier had been ordered to stand down, and was trying to get the orders overturned by UNIT's HQ in Geneva. Vaughn tested the Cerebration Mentor on a Cyberman and made it go berserk. By now, it was obvious that Vaughn and the Cyber-Planner had different ideas for the aftermath of the invasion.

UNIT freed Watkins, but only after he'd perfected the Cerebration Mentor for Vaughn and learned that Vaughn was a partially-converted Cyberman. The Doctor realised that small IE circuits installed in commercial products could boost a hypnotic signal from the Cybermen ship. He designed a signal jammer that could be worn at the base of the neck, and they were issued to the UNIT force.

The signal was soon broadcast, putting everyone around the world to sleep. Cybermen troops emerged from the sewers and took over London. The Brigadier realised that Russia had a space flight on schedule and this rocket could be armed and used against the Cybermen ship. Directed by Zoe's calculations, British missiles shot down every small Cyberman ship entering the atmosphere. The Doctor met Vaughn and convinced him that the Cybermen were playing him for a fool.

Vaughn agreed to help the Doctor destroy the homing beacon. After destroying the machine in the IE London office, they travelled to the factory, where Vaughn used the Cerebration Mentor to destroy some of the Cybermen before being killed. With UNIT's aid, the Doctor managed to destroy the transmitter. The Cybermen made a last-ditch effort by bringing their ship closer to drop a devastating bomb, but the anti-missile battery destroyed the bomb and the Russian rocket destroyed the Cybermen ship.

Watkins helped the Doctor fix the visual stabiliser and the time travellers left Earth.

CONTINUITY

International Electromatics is part of Cybus Industries in a parallel universe where its CEO, John Lumic, created the Cybermen

on Earth. These Cybermen occasionally slip into the prime universe (e.g. **Doomsday**) to cause trouble.

The Cyber-Planner makes a return appearance (relatively speaking) and is revealed to have an organic component (it is susceptible to the Cerebration Mentor).

Isobel Watkins gets a plum job as a result of her photographs of the Cybermen. Since no one seems to know what a Cyberman is in 1986 (or why they look different), it's probable that the UN arranged for a job as compensation for the photographic suppression.

UNIT was established after the events in **The Web of Fear**. While it is organized under the United Nations, the Brigadier must still coordinate with the British Minister of Defence. UNIT's temporary British HQ is the converted Hercules aircraft.

The Cybermen formed an alliance with Tobias Vaughn five years ago. Vaughn used their technology to create International Electromatics. He is also a partially-converted Cyberman that is allowed to keep his own brain intact. While Vaughn enjoys the benefits of his new body, he has no desire to become a full Cyberman.

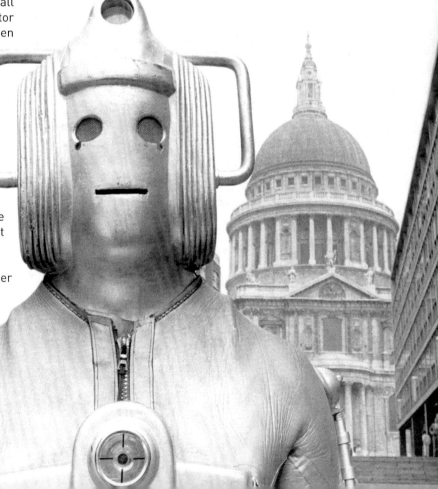

⊘ RUNNING THE ADVENTURE

When the Doctor arrives on Earth, he immediately looks for Professor Travers. Instead, he discovers Isobel Watkins and meets her uncle Professor Watkins. They end up filling the same role as Travers and Anne, to the point of using the same residence (with the original inhabitants conveniently away in America for the duration). The lesson here is that there are times in a *Doctor Who: Adventures in Time and Space* campaign when you might find it necessary to replace a character that you'd intended to use for an adventure but is now unavailable. Don't sweat it; a simple re-skinning of names and backgrounds and you can slot in new characters to replace them.

Similarly, the hypnotic attack that the Cybermen use to aid their invasion ensures that, once the invasion is dealt with, the evidence can be covered up. With Vaughn dead, the Earth authorities have little to go on for the future; by the time Mondas arrives their information from studying the Cybermen comes too late (it's significant that Antarctica was attacked first; useful information from UNIT is thousands of miles away). Thus, don't worry that a particular enemy is locked into a certain time for its first attack. You can always roll back the clock, providing that you give a plausible explanation for covering the tracks of the earlier appearance.

HOW CAN THIS ADVENTURE TAKE PLACE BEFORE 1986?

Unless we presume that the Doctor has made subtle changes to the time stream since his first regeneration, there seems to be a paradox here. The Cybermen in this story come to Earth at least a decade early (depending on when one dates this adventure) and are obviously more advanced than the ones that arrive with Mondas. Has history been changed?

The answer, of course, is not necessarily. With the world unconscious, UNIT could clean up the mess before anyone was the wiser and the United Nations would likely comply with removing evidence and maintaining the secret out of fear of a panic. In addition, the failed Cybermen invasion would pour new resources into UNIT and similar organisations. Both Torchwood and Van Statten took trophies from this invasion.

These Cybermen were designed for combat; they are soldiers operating under a central plan. Perhaps the Mondas government sent them ahead to prepare the Earth before Mondas arrived, making the energy transfer easier and perhaps taking Earth as a new home. Once these Cybermen were destroyed, the Mondasian government had to go with a Plan B and hope that they were strong enough to conquer Earth on their own.

PLANET 14

The Cybermen are aware of the Doctor and Jamie (though not necessarily Zoe) from 'Planet 14'. This planet is never identified and likely refers to one of two things. It's either the 14th planet of the solar system or it's the 14th planet that the Cybermen have discovered. It's also possible that Planet 14 is Telos, but the Doctor doesn't visit for another 500 years or so (or does he?).

One argument in favour of Planet 14 being in the solar system is that Cybermen space travel seems relatively limited during the 21st century, relying on radio signals. It doesn't seem plausible that the Cybermen could be travelling far on such limited technology or perhaps, as we've suggested for *The Moonbase* and *The Wheel in Space*, their deep space vessels travel slowly.

In any case, Planet 14 offers the Gamemaster a chance to run an unseen Doctor adventure against the Cybermen using any set of companions after **The Highlanders.**

FURTHER ADVENTURES

- Not all of the Cybermen perished. Some retreated into the sewers where they remained until 1985. These Cybermen attempt to complete their mission and destroy humanity (or subjugate it) before Mondas' arrival. The characters arrive in the late 1970s or early 1980s and have to stop a Cybermen plot to start World War III.

- The Cybermen recognised the Doctor and Jamie from an incident on Planet 14. Where is this planet and what were the Cybermen doing there? The characters land on Planet 14 and discover a Cybermen base, waiting to help with the invasion. Can the characters prevent an even larger force from invading Earth?

- Someone is using the Cerebration Mentor as the perfect killing machine, forcing people to have intense emotions at the wrong time and getting themselves killed. The characters arrive as UNIT investigators are trying to discover why the principal members of a particular cause are dying from mysterious accidents.

CEREBRATION MENTOR

Professor Watkins' handheld teaching device is actually an effective weapon against the Cybermen. It instils strong emotions in its victim, causing those that aren't used to emotions (such as Cybermen) to have a painful nervous breakdown and collapse.

Traits: Acts as a major weakness against a Cyberman's mental attributes when turned on. When used on humans, it can project low-level emotions, working like the Empathy trait.
Cost: 2 Story Points

PROFESSOR WATKINS

AWARENESS	3	PRESENCE	3
COORDINATION	2	RESOLVE	4
INGENUITY	5	STRENGTH	1

SKILLS
Craft 4, Knowledge 5, Marksman 1, Science 5, Technology 5, Transport 3

TRAITS
Boffin: Watkins can create gadgets through jiggery-pokery.
Technically Adept: Watkins gets a +2 on technology rolls to repair broken gadgets or use unfamiliar devices.

TECH LEVEL: 5   STORY POINTS: 12

ISOBEL WATKINS

AWARENESS	3	PRESENCE	4
COORDINATION	3	RESOLVE	4
INGENUITY	2	STRENGTH	2

SKILLS
Athletics 2, Convince 4, Craft 3, Subterfuge 2, Technology 2

TRAITS
Attractive: Isobel gets a +2 on rolls in which her appearance would be a factor.
Charming: Isobel gets a +2 on rolls in which her charisma would be a factor.

TECH LEVEL: 5   STORY POINTS: 6

BRIGADIER ALISTAIR GORDON LETHBRIDGE-STEWART

AWARENESS	4	PRESENCE	4
COORDINATION	4	RESOLVE	4
INGENUITY	4	STRENGTH	4

SKILLS
Athletics 3, Convince 4, Fighting 3, Knowledge 3, Marksman 3, Medicine 1, Science 1, Subterfuge 2, Survival 3, Technology 1, Transport 3.

TRAITS
Brave
By the Book
Five Rounds Rapid (See *Defending the Earth: The UNIT Sourcebook*)
Friends (UNIT)
Impulsive
Indomitable
Military Rank (Brigadier)
Obligation (UNIT)
Tough
Voice of Authority
Experienced
UNIT Veteran (See *Defending the Earth: The UNIT Sourcebook*)

GADGETS: Space Time Telegraph

TECH LEVEL: 5   **STORY POINTS:** 9

TOBIAS VAUGHN

AWARENESS	3	PRESENCE	5
COORDINATION	3	RESOLVE	5
INGENUITY	5	STRENGTH	7

SKILLS
Convince 5, Craft 3, Fighting 2, Knowledge 4, Marksman 2, Technology 3

TRAITS
Adversary (Major): UNIT is closely investigating International Electromatics.
Armour (Minor Trait): Vaughn's cyborg body is protected by metallic armour, which reduces damage by 5.
Cyborg: Vaughn has had his entire body replaced except for his head and internal organs.
Hypnosis: Vaughn has the ability to hypnotise weak-willed people.
Indomitable: Vaughn is determined and gets a +4 bonus to any rolls to resist being possessed, hypnotised, or otherwise mentally controlled.
Menacing: Vaughn gets a +2 bonus on attempts to get people to do what he wants. Characters he has menaced also get a +2 to resist attempts by others to act against him.
Obsession (Major): Vaughn wants to rule the world.

TECH LEVEL: 5   **STORY POINTS:** 6

THE KROTONS

'We only know what the Krotons tell us. We don't think. We obey.'

⚙ SYNOPSIS

Gond Home Planet, Unspecified Time

The time travellers arrived on a barren planet that smelt of sulphur. They spotted a settlement nearby and, while on their way, discovered a structure that the Doctor deduced was some kind of machine. A door in the structure opened and a disoriented Gond walked out, only to be disintegrated by guns on the door. The Doctor and his companions entered the Gond city, but the locals were suspicious of the new arrivals as visitors were unheard of. Vana, a Gond who had been chosen for a particular ceremony, rushed into a similar door to the one they had seen outside the city. The Doctor told the assembled Gonds what had happened earlier, and the travellers rushed back into the wasteland to save Vana.

After a successful rescue, the group went to the Gond leader, Selris. He explained that the 'Krotons' came to the Gonds' world thousands of years ago. The Gonds attacked and the Krotons poisoned their world, killing most Gonds. The Krotons aided the survivors, giving them teaching machines and occasionally recruiting the two best students to join them in their machine, the Dynatrope. The Gonds didn't know what the Krotons looked like.

Vana's lover, Thara, led a group of youths against the Dynatrope but were stopped, first by the Doctor and then by the Krotons, who demanded obedience. They vaporised a rebel to make their point. Selris regained control and dispersed the crowd. The Doctor and Selris explored the 'underhall' beneath the Dynatrope while Zoe tried a teaching machine. By the time the Doctor returned, the Krotons had selected Zoe to join them. The Doctor then tried a teaching machine and scored high enough to be selected along with her.

Inside the Dynatrope, the Doctor and Zoe were made to sit and the Dynatrope drained their energy; only quick thinking by the Doctor allowed them to remain cognisant. They reasoned that their brainwaves were being used to power the ship and discovered a slurry pool within the control centre. As they fled, two crystalline Krotons emerged from the pool.

Fearing for his friends, Jamie tried to enter the Dynatrope and the Krotons captured him. Through Jamie, the Krotons learned about the TARDIS. One of the Krotons left the Dynatrope to destroy the TARDIS and capture Zoe and the Doctor. A growing dissent manifested amongst the Gonds over whether to obey or destroy the Krotons. The faction that wanted to fight was hampered by their lack of knowledge about weapons – the Krotons had been very selective in their education of the Gonds.

The Doctor discovered that the Krotons are mineral creatures and likely blinded by the sun. He used this information to escape the Kroton that was following them, assisted by Jamie distracting the Kroton back in the Dynatrope that was directing its fellow.

The Krotons tried to destroy the TARDIS but its Hostile Action Displacement System sent it to safety.

Zoe and the Doctor collected sulphurous rocks and returned to the city to learn that Selris had organised a group to damage the Dynatrope from beneath. The Doctor gave the rocks to Beta, a Gond scientist, with instructions for making an acid that would work against the Krotons. Selris' group managed to damage the alien structure but falling debris broke Thara's leg and killed another Gond. Jamie escaped the Dynatrope and met the Doctor as a Kroton emerged on the other side and demanded that the Gonds hand over the Doctor and Zoe.

It turned out that the Krotons need two more 'high brains' to provide energy for their ship. A rebel Gond leader who had seized power from Selris captured the Doctor and Zoe and gave them to the Krotons in exchange for the aliens leaving the planet. Selris sacrificed his life to sneak a vial of the acid to the Doctor. Zoe dumped it into the slurry, which poisoned the Krotons. Jamie and Beta destroyed the Dynatrope by pouring acid over it from above. The time travellers slipped away as the Gonds elected Thara to be their new leader.

CONTINUITY

The TARDIS' Hostile Action Displacement System (HADS) is used for the first time. Its activation implies that the Krotons are able to damage the TARDIS. The Doctor needs to set it, which is why it didn't activate during the Cybermen missile attack.

⊙ RUNNING THE ADVENTURE

This is a standard 'our gods are evil' adventure. The Krotons' Dynatrope was damaged in a space battle and two of the four Kroton crew were killed. They landed on the planet and educated the Gonds to become the higher brains they required. Once the Krotons take two appropriate Gonds, they plan to leave.

The Krotons aren't moustache-twirling villains; they are simply callous in their methods. As a crystalline race they hold organic beings in little regard (much like a human would feel about a plant, sentience notwithstanding). Thus far, they've been using 'high brains' to keep the Dynatrope powered and disposing of the 'waste' (i.e. killing the Gond). They seem to realise that killing the Gonds in front of their comrades could cause problems.

When running the Krotons, you need to emphasise that these are utterly alien beings that are incapable of thinking in human terms. They do what is necessary to get their ship up and running; no more, no less. While the Gonds see them as gods the Krotons don't play this role; they simply 'feed their stock' until two of them show enough promise to be invited inside the Dynatrope.

One way to update this adventure is to play up the crystalline aspect of the Krotons. The Dynatrope becomes a large rock that has slowly been turning into crystal as more mental energy has been absorbed over the years. The Krotons themselves and their learning machines can also have a more crystalline appearance. It's even possible that the Dynatrope is the intelligent creature, with the Krotons mere extensions of its will.

The educational and cultural stagnation of the Gonds can also be emphasized. With the best and brightest being pruned, the Gonds that remain would be of lower intellect and perhaps force the Krotons to adapt their method of harvesting high brains. The Gonds see the Krotons in an even more overtly religious way and treat their lessons as scripture. Perhaps there's a subversive element whose members have been fooling the Krotons for centuries, keeping their intellects intact until they can find a way to fight back.

It's possible that other tribes survived beyond the wastelands. Maybe a few scouts have crossed the now-safe wasteland and foster another threat to Kroton control.

WHAT REALLY HAPPENED IN THE PAST?

Selric tells the story of the Gonds attacking the Krotons and the resultant retaliation destroying most of the world, with the Krotons then suddenly deciding to care for the survivors of the race that just attacked them. The Krotons, by contrast, don't mention this war at all. By their account they simply crashed on the planet in a damaged Dynatrope and began teaching the natives how to help them leave.

So what really happened? Given that it's in the Kroton's best interest to keep as many genius-level Gonds alive, it doesn't make sense that they'd want to cull the herd that brutally unless, on average, the Gonds were too 'low brain' without the teaching machines.

What makes the most sense is that the Krotons destroyed much of the world, either due to the Dynatrope's exhausted power (the Doctor feared an explosion from the exhausted power supply – a curious notion) or simply that, by irradiating most of the world, the Krotons could 'pen in' the surviving Gonds. The war story is designed to keep them docile and grateful that the Krotons spared them from their own short-sightedness. In this sense the Krotons are farmers, fattening up their stock with intelligence before picking the best ones for slaughter.

SHAPESHIFTING KROTONS?

Given that they can dissolve into a type of slurry and reconstitute themselves through mental energy, and the fact that they modified their appendages when necessary, it's probable that the Krotons can reconfigure their bodies into different forms. Given their limited knowledge of organic life, it's likely that their current form is a rough approximation of what they see in the Gonds (similar to a child drawing an adult). They also lack the energy in this adventure to do more than sustain themselves for minutes at a time, hardly enough to start flexing their shapeshifting abilities.

FURTHER ADVENTURES

- Presuming that the Krotons can shapeshift into any type of silicate life form, a battle between the Krotons and the Rutans would be very interesting. The characters arrive at a human space colony that is about to become the latest battlefield in a war between shapeshifting races.

- So, who were the Krotons fighting thousands of years ago? What lead to them landing on the planet of the Gonds? Why did the rest of the Krotons not come looking for their missing ship – were these the only survivors of some genocidal war, or are the Krotons so long-lived that a thousand years is only a short time for them? ("Sorry I'm late, dear – I had to force-evolve a higher brain over the course of five hundred Gond generations. Is my dinner in the oven?")

- The characters arrive on a world where a group of Krotons are helping the 'primitives' create a civilisation and stabilise a series of planetary quakes. An interstellar coalition arrives to try the Krotons for war crimes but they claim to be 'evolved' and their mission one of benevolence. The characters arrive and learn that, without the Krotons' aid, the primitives are doomed to a planetary disaster. Should the characters aid the Krotons or not? And is their mission really as benevolent as it seems?

KROTONS

The Krotons are a crystalline race that has little regard for biological life. They cannot die but they dissolve into their constituent elements when exhausted, requiring a mental boost to get them reconstituted in a solid form again. This energy can be taken from human mental energy but only from a 'High Brain', the best and brightest of a humanoid species. It could take several thousand years for enough High Brains to be harvested from a local community to be of use to the Krotons.

Krotons have little concept of death and, as a mineral species, don't really understand or care for biological humanoids. They ruthlessly disintegrate the Gonds they drain (even though the evidence suggests that they'll recover) just to maintain their ruse. They also won't hesitate to kill any Gond that questions their authority.

The Krotons fly in a ship they call the Dynatrope and have a symbiotic relationship with it. Like the Krotons, the Dynatrope is also powered with mental energy and is vulnerable to sulphuric acid.

KROTON

AWARENESS	3	PRESENCE	3
COORDINATION	3	RESOLVE	5
INGENUITY	4	STRENGTH	4

SKILLS
Fighting 3, Convince 3, Knowledge 3, Marksman 3, Science 3, Technology 4, Transport 4

TRAITS
Alien Appearance: As crystalline lifeforms, Krotons may actually be mistaken for robots.
Armour (Major Trait): The Kroton's crystalline body reduces damage by 10. The mass of a Kroton makes it slower and its Coordination is reduced by 1 (already taken into account in the Attributes).
Immortal (Special): A Kroton cannot die, although it may dissolve when its energy supply is exhausted.
Impaired Senses (Major): A Kroton is effectively blind in sunlight.
Natural Weapon (Acid Gun): Krotons use acid weapons that can instantly dissolve a victim. 4/L/L.
Networked: The Krotons are connected to each other via the Dynatrope.
Special (Multiple Configurations)*: As a silicate life form, a Kroton can reconstitute itself in multiple configurations while still retaining a silicate appearance. This allows the Kroton to mimic two minor traits or one major trait at a time (so a Kroton could grow additional arms and legs, or reconfigure its body to enable mentally-powered major Flight). The Gamemaster has the final say on how a Kroton can reshape its body.

TECH LEVEL: 7   STORY POINTS: 6-8

*This trait is only alluded to in **The Krotons**, as a Kroton can dissolve and reconstitute itself from soup and the occasional arm modification. If you wish to ignore this trait, simply remove it from the stat block.

GOND

AWARENESS	2	PRESENCE	3
COORDINATION	3	RESOLVE	2
INGENUITY	1	STRENGTH	3

SKILLS
Athletics 3, Convince 2, Craft 2, Fighting 3, Knowledge 1, Medicine 2, Science 1, Survival 3

TRAITS
Enslaved: While largely unaware of it, the Gonds are effectively slaves to the Krotons.
Knowledge Gaps: The Krotons only teach the Gonds what they need to survive. They've especially restricted their knowledge of chemistry and other topics that can be used against the Krotons, as well as ensure that the history lessons remember the Krotons as saviours.

TECH LEVEL: 4   STORY POINTS: 2

CHAPTER ELEVEN:
THE SEEDS OF DEATH, THE SPACE PIRATES, THE WAR GAMES

THE SEEDS OF DEATH

'Your leader will be angry if you kill me. I'm a genius.'

⊙ SYNOPSIS

Great Britain and the moon, 21st century

The Moonbase was the central hub for the Travel Mat, or T-Mat network, which teleports people and goods all over the Earth; it has become the sole means of long-range transportation. Unfortunately, it was occupied by the Ice Warriors just as the TARDIS arrived in a rocket museum on Earth. To prevent an invasion of Earth, the commander of the base sabotaged the T-Mat before the Ice Warriors could stop him. The time travellers learned about the T-Mat and the lack of rocket progress from the curator and former rocket engineer, Eldred. They were soon joined by Commander Radnor, who explained that they'd lost communication with the Moonbase and needed Eldred's secret rocket project to send a team up and make repairs.

Eldred initially refused but after some coaxing agreed to prepare the rocket. Due to a lack of trained astronauts, the time travellers piloted it to the moon. In the meantime, Ice Warrior leader Slaar forced moon technician Fewshaw to repair the T-Mat enough to allow it to receive transmissions. T-Mat Earth Control Manager Gia Kelly took two technicians with her to the moon. The Ice Warriors only revealed themselves once she had finished her work. They then turned off the beacon that the rocket needed to make a safe landing.

Phipps, a moon technician that was hiding from the Ice Warriors, realised what had happened and provided a radio signal for the travellers to navigate by and land. The Doctor was separated from the others and

captured by the Ice Warriors. He learned that they wanted to transport 'seeds' to Earth. He discovered the hard way that the seeds were poisonous, as one almost killed him and rendered him unconscious.

Slaar orders Fewshaw to transport several seeds to different locations on Earth. The seeds emit fumes and grow fungus that absorbs oxygen, asphyxiating any humans nearby.

The planet was destabilised by the breakdown of the T-Mat, as the people feared starvation and essential supplies such as medicines couldn't be transported. Eldred suspected it was instead an alien invasion. Slaar also sent an Ice Warrior to Earth in order to take over the Weather Control station and keep the weather 'dry' before destroying the controls. The T-Mat then broke down again. The Moonbase technicians made their escape by turning up the heat, which choked the Ice Warriors. The time travellers and humans used a solar gun to destroy enough Ice Warriors so that they could escape via T-Mat.

Fewsham remained behind. He opened a channel to Earth, allowing Earth Control to discover that Slaar was using a beam to bring an invasion force to Earth and that this invasion force lacked the fuel to correct any miscalculations. Slaar realised he'd been duped and killed Fewsham. The Doctor, now back on Earth, determined that the seeds were transforming the Earth's atmosphere to more closely resemble Mars, but that the only substance needed to destroy them was water.

Jamie and Zoe went to the Weather Control station to create rain and were menaced by the Ice Warrior. The Doctor found them and he and Zoe created another heat weapon to destroy the Ice Warrior. The Doctor then fixed the weather controls. Kelly launched a satellite to broadcast a false signal to the fleet from Mars, while the Doctor returned to the moon to disable the real one.

The Doctor was captured by Slaar and the remaining Ice Warrior but had first managed to sabotage the beam. When Slaar transmitted the signal, the fleet followed the wrong one and plunged into the sun. Jamie arrived on the moon in the nick of time and he and the Doctor destroyed Slaar and his final subordinate. The Doctor and Jamie returned to Earth and slipped away with Zoe as the technicians argued over whether to maintain an emergency rocket fleet.

CONTINUITY

The Ice Warrior fleet is destroyed at the end of this adventure. The Doctor justifies its destruction by claiming that the Ice Warriors tried to destroy an entire world, leaving open the possibility that, as a race, the Ice Warriors survive. As they go on to join the Galactic Federation, perhaps a peaceful faction of the Ice Warriors seek another world on which to settle (their lack of knowledge about Earth culture in the Federation seems jarring if Earthlings are their planetary neighbours), leaving Mars open for Earth colonization. As the fleet is destroyed by a homing signal error, it is likely that the Ice Warriors solve that problem and create interstellar spacecraft.

In **The Ice Warriors** Mars was only implied as the Ice Warrior's home world (the Ice Warriors themselves only referred to it as 'the Red Planet'). Here the Doctor explicitly states that they are from Mars.

For the first time three ranks of Ice Warriors are clearly distinguished by their armour designs. The bulkier Ice Warriors from **The Ice Warriors** are clearly the rank-and-file, while Slaar's slimmer look is for higher-ranking members (Slaar is never given a rank). The Grand Marshall has a different helmet to Slaar's.

The Doctor shares the name 'Ice Warrior' with the staff of Earth Control. Obviously the name and the race are forgotten between this invasion attempt and Varga's thawing a few centuries later (possibly lost during the Dalek occupation).

Earth has completely abandoned spaceships and space exploration in favour of the T-Mat. This proves to be a short-term situation, as a spaceship is needed for the Doctor to get to the moon after the T-Mat fails. Spaceships are again in vogue by Zoe's time.

Capital punishment apparently exists for Europeans in the 21st century (in spite of its abolition in almost all European countries by 2010) although it's possible that Fewsham lied about its existence to Slaar.

The United Nations controls the world. As this adventure seems to take place after Salamander's time, it can be guessed that the World Zones Authority returned to its old name.

⊘ RUNNING THE ADVENTURE

The Seeds of Death is a cautionary tale of putting too many eggs in one basket. By exclusively relying on a centrally-controlled worldwide transportation service, Earth is ripe for conquest by a small invasion force. The Ice Warriors easily send their seeds throughout the world. The fact that they can change the Earth's weather by sabotaging one weather control station attests to this as well.

That said, the Ice Warriors also put their eggs in one basket. Their entire battle fleet is headed to Earth with so little fuel that a single calculation error sends the entire fleet spinning into the sun. While impractical, adventures designed with a single Achilles' heel make it easy for the characters to get involved and win against what would normally be impossible odds. The Ice Warriors' plan involves the T-Mat; once it's disabled their plan is on hold until it can be fixed. This gives the characters plenty of time to gather intelligence, undo the damage, and come up with a plan to defeat them.

PANIC!

One of the most intriguing elements of The Seeds of Death is how quickly human society breaks down the moment T-Mat goes offline or the seeds start killing crops. Within minutes, the world falls into chaos, with world panic threatening to destroy humanity long before the Ice Warrior invasion arrives.

Closely related to the panic is the theme of dependency. The Travel Mat has become so convenient that all other forms of transportation have been abandoned, from automobiles to rockets. This convenience also carries with it complacency; mankind has stopped exploring the stars. Once the dependency is no longer dependable, the people panic.

How can this happen so quickly? We need only look at our current society for answers. With 24-hour news services, the internet, and instant communications, it takes only seconds for a politician's gaffe or a major accident to circulate through society.

It isn't difficult to imagine that, a few decades from now, a few videos of darkened skies, vegetable-eating foam, and marching green aliens with sonic guns would panic the populace within minutes. Supermarkets would be raided, homes boarded up, and people fleeing into the wilderness where they're less likely to be attacked by large green reptile-men.

FURTHER ADVENTURES

- The characters arrive at an Ice Warrior colony on a planet outside the solar system. It soon becomes obvious that these are the survivors of the Ice Warrior battle fleet that was plunging into the sun. Who rescued them and why?

- The characters arrive on Earth when there's another problem with the T-Mat; travellers start disappearing. The travellers then reappear, but something is 'off' about them. The Chameleons are back and they are stealing people and imitating them long enough for several thousand to be captured before all of them head into the T-Mat at once and return to their mother ship.

- Not all of the seeds were destroyed by rain; a terrorist group has managed to catch a few whole and is now using them as biological weapons. This group, like Eldred, wants to return Earth to rocket technology by sabotaging the T-Mat and sending the seeds to the moon, where it will poison the air of the central hub.

DANIEL ELDRED

AWARENESS	2	PRESENCE	3
COORDINATION	2	RESOLVE	4
INGENUITY	4	STRENGTH	1

SKILLS
Craft 4, Knowledge 4, Science 3, Technology 5 (rockets), Transport 5 (rockets)

TRAITS
Eccentric (Minor): Eldred wants nothing to do with T-Mat and believes that the world should return to the older rocket technology.
Selfish (Minor Bad): Eldred puts his own needs first
Technically Adept: Eldred gets a +2 bonus on Technology rolls within their areas of expertise.

TECH LEVEL: 5   STORY POINTS: 3

GIA KELLY

AWARENESS	3	PRESENCE	4
COORDINATION	3	RESOLVE	5
INGENUITY	5	STRENGTH	3

SKILLS
Convince 3, Craft 4, Knowledge 3, Science 3, Technology 4, Transport 4

TRAITS
Attractive: Kelly gets a +2 in situations in which her appearance would be a factor.
Boffin: Kelly can use Jiggery-Pokery, especially when involving the Travel Mat.
Technically Adept: Kelly gets a +2 bonus on Technology rolls when dealing with the Travel Mat.
Voice of Authority: Kelly commands authority when she speaks. She gets a +2 to Presence and Convince rolls to get people to do what she wants.

TECH LEVEL: 5   STORY POINTS: 6

THE SPACE PIRATES

'Well, these old mining prospectors like Clancey were the first men to go out into deep space. For a time they had the place to themselves, roaming the spaceways, looking for planets, jumping each other's claims. They were a wild breed, Ian, and they learned to live without the law.'

⬡ SYNOPSIS

Fourth Sector, the Future

Earth's space beacons have been the subject of piracy, as criminals destroy them for the precious argonite that they're built from. The TARDIS landed on one of these beacons as a group of pirates led by Caven blew it apart and attached rockets to the pieces, leaving the time travellers separated from the TARDIS. The pirates avoided a trap by General Hermack of the Earth Space Corps, whose ship was not fast enough to catch them. Hermack did interrogate a local argonite prospector, Milo Clancey, about the thefts, believing that he had something to do with them. Clancey protested that he'd been a victim of the pirates as well.

Clancey boarded a piece of the beacon and rescued the time travellers, taking them aboard his ship before using a trick to outfox Hermack's vessel. He decided to head to Ta, the headquarters of the Issigri Mining Corporation, although he had fallen out with Madeleine Issigri (he used to be partners with her father before he disappeared several years ago). Caven, meanwhile, diverted the beacon segments towards Lobos, Clancey's home planet, to throw suspicion on him.

Zoe determined that the pirates were heading toward Ta. The time travellers explored the bowels of Ta and spotted pirates before they fell into a chasm. They survived the fall, and headed to Madeleine Issigri's office with Clancey. There, they discovered that Madeleine was in league with Caven, who captured them. Caven imprisoned Clancey and the time travellers in a study, where they discovered Dom Issigri, Clancey's former partner, still alive and Caven's prisoner.

Madeleine Issigri realised that Caven was planning to kill the prisoners and decided to break her alliance with him. She alerted Hermack to Caven's presence on Ta. Caven learned of this and got her to rescind the request by revealing that her father was alive and in his custody. The time travellers escaped, but Caven installed a remote control on Clancey's ship, activating it when Hermack, unswayed by Issigri's change of heart, arrived anyway. Only Clancey and Dom Issigri were aboard when it launched.

Caven had the oxygen cut on the ship to kill Clancey so that the Space Corps would blame him for the theft of argonite and he wouldn't be able to argue

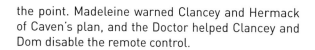

the point. Madeleine warned Clancey and Hermack of Caven's plan, and the Doctor helped Clancey and Dom disable the remote control.

Frustrated, Caven revealed that he rigged Issigri's office to explode and the blast area would destroy the pirates, Issigri, and Hermack's ship. Fortunately the Doctor disabled the detonator and a Space Corps fighter pilot destroyed Caven's ship. Dom Issigri was reunited with his daughter while Clancey offered the time travellers a ride back to their TARDIS.

CONTINUITY

Earth is now run by a single government ('Earth Government') and polices its colonies through the Space Corps. Large corporations handle most resource-retrieval operations in the colonies. Earth Government seems to be confined to the Milky Way.

New Sarum, Lobos, and Ta all appear to be in the 'fourth sector' of the galaxy (Hermack's use of 'our galaxy' implies that Earth's jurisdiction may be intergalactic). A colloquial name for the fourth sector is 'New Sarum sector', indicating that New Sarum is likely the most important planet in the fourth sector. Reja Magnum, where Hermack had his first tour of duty, is also likely in the fourth sector as Milo Clancey is considered a legend there.

There are at least three 'brush-fire' wars in different sectors under the Space Corps' jurisdiction. This is apparently enough to occupy almost all of its resources. The Space Corps has a prison planet called Nevan.

Mining prospectors were the first humans in deep space. It was a lawless time until the Space Corps established order. Apparently, there is no 'deeper space' or new expeditions must be more tightly regulated, as Milo Clancey is considered a dying breed.

Argonite is the most valuable mineral in Earth's economy. It has many useful applications and is the most expensive mineral in the galaxy. Argonite attracts copper, and argonite sensors can be disrupted in the presence of copper. There's a black market for stolen argonite on Ruta Magnum.

Space beacons are made of eight sections that are held together by electromagnetism. There are usually eighteen space beacons in the fourth sector, each millions of miles apart. All are made primarily of argonite. Newer ships, such as V ships, Beta Darts, and Minnows, are constructed of argonite. Older ships, such as the LIZ 79, are made of tillium. Tillium is not attracted to copper. The LIZ 79 uses a thermo-nuclear power source.

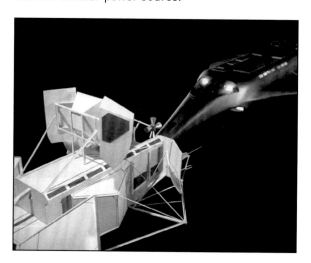

Hermack's vessel is the V41, a V ship. The pirates use a Beta Dart freighter (one of the latest models, and twice as fast as a V ship), and Clancey's ship is LIZ 79, an obsolete C class freighter in operation for over 40 years. Clancey uses 'floaters' to carry argonite ore. These are unmanned vessels that lack propulsion units. V ships contain smaller ships called minnows. All rockets need to have a feedback to Central Flight Information.

The Space Corps uses Martian missiles (either supplied by now-friendly Ice Warriors or, more likely, built at a human colony on Mars) and has mind probe technology. Mining vessels are typically unarmed.

The pirates use thermite guns. Clancey's rifle has a 'quarter blast' setting that only stuns foes. Explosives used to destroy electromagnetic locks are known as scissor charges.

Locks are generally auditory as combination locks were too easily cracked by portable computers.

RUNNING THE ADVENTURE

This adventure has two overarching themes that sometimes seem to scrape against each other. The first is space opera or, perhaps more accurately, the space western. Many Old Western American elements are present, a rough frontier, bandits, prospectors, valuable ore, hidden camps, a femme fatale, and even a cavalry, all re-filtered through the lens of space opera. While the Doctor has certainly seen his share of space adventures, this is the first that really embraces the space opera genre and does so without a single non-human alien in sight.

Conflicting with the space opera is the second theme, which is realistic space travel (which was constantly in the news during this period). Rather than swooping in and out of sectors at the speed of plot, the V41 spends most of the adventure plodding along, taking several hours to get from point A to point B, usually just after its quarry has left. It is this element that allows the Doctor and his companions to take part, as they can't rely on the cavalry to arrive in time.

While **The Space Pirates** is a good model for incorporating space opera into your adventures, it is also a cautionary tale. The Doctor and his companions are almost superfluous to the plot and it would be very easy to edit them out altogether. When running this scenario, you should be careful to ensure that the player characters are the ones who shine, rather than the supporting cast. Still, if your players are the swashbuckling type, then this is just the type of adventure for them.

COWBOYS AND PIRATES

Besides space opera, this adventure borrows heavily from both the high seas piracy and American western genres. As a result, **The Space Pirates** is a lesson in taking tropes from one genre and putting them into another. While we've covered the western tropes above, the high seas piracy tropes are vessels with valuable cargo floating in space, isolated from any aid. The pirates seize these vessels to melt them down and fence them later. They also disguise their efforts by pinning the blame on someone else (i.e. 'raising their flag'). Finally, the pirate ship is fast, allowing it to stay one step ahead of government ships.

When looking for inspiration, don't be afraid to see what other genres have to offer. **Doctor Who** has a long history of adapting adventures from other genres

and, with a few tweaks and a bit of re-skinning, you can easily mould diverse plot elements into a single cohesive adventure.

FURTHER ADVENTURES

- Milo Clancey and Dom Issigri were prospectors back when the space frontier was practically lawless. This is a great setting for space opera adventure, especially with far-flung colonies just getting their start with little support from home. When an enemy threatens one of these small outposts, the colonists only have the recently-arrived characters to rely on for protection.

- Argonite is running out. Drastic measures are taken and the Earth government begins to fracture between the needy developed worlds of the inner territory and the newly-rich but less populated and protected frontier worlds. The Earth government decides to nationalise the argonite mines and the frontier worlds respond by hiring the Judoon to protect them. The characters arrive on a luxury liner that is intercepted by a Judoon cruiser. As it turns out, there is argonite on board, but the crew denies any knowledge of smuggling. The penalty for smuggling is death; can the characters sort this out before the Judoon wipe out everyone on the ship?

- Earth prospectors discover a new source of argonite on an alien world that is seemingly uninhabited. Unfortunately this turns out not to be the case as the excavation team soon discovers a vault that contains several sleeping Cybermen. The characters arrive after some team members disappear and must convince the miners of their innocence while imploring them to heed the threat of awakened Cybermen.

MAURICE CAVEN

AWARENESS	3	PRESENCE	5
COORDINATION	3	RESOLVE	5
INGENUITY	5	STRENGTH	3

SKILLS
Athletics 3, Convince 5, Fighting 4, Marksman 4, Subterfuge 4, Survival 4, Technology 3, Transport 3

TRAITS
Adversary (Major): As a space pirate, Caven has the Space Corps coming after him.
Menacing: Caven gets a +2 bonus on attempts to get people to do what he wants. Characters he has menaced also get a +2 to resist attempts by others to act against him.

EQUIPMENT
Blast Armour (6), **Thermite Gun** 4/L/L

TECH LEVEL: 6 **STORY POINTS:** 6

SPACE PIRATE

AWARENESS	3	PRESENCE	2
COORDINATION	3	RESOLVE	2
INGENUITY	1	STRENGTH	3

SKILLS
Athletics 2, Fighting 2, Marksman 2, Subterfuge 3, Survival 2, Transport 2

TRAITS
None

EQUIPMENT
Thermite Gun 4/L/L

TECH LEVEL: 6 **STORY POINTS:** 2

MILO CLANCEY

AWARENESS	3	PRESENCE	4
COORDINATION	3	RESOLVE	4
INGENUITY	4	STRENGTH	3

SKILLS
Athletics 2, Convince 3, Fighting 2, Marksman 3, Subterfuge 3, Survival 5, Technology 4, Transport 5

TRAITS
Adversary (major): Throughout this adventure Milo is suspected of being a space pirate.
Argumentative: Milo is a free spirit and doesn't take kindly to being ordered around.
Brave: Milo gets a +2 bonus to any Resolve roll when he needs to show courage.
Charming: Milo can be quite charming in his own way and gets +2 to rolls in social situations.
Eccentric: Milo is the last of a dying breed and has many quirks.
Technically Adept: Milo gets +2 on Technology rolls to fix broken devices and using gadgets.

EQUIPMENT
Cutter Rifle: Blast Settings - Quarter (S/S/S), Half (2/5/7), Three-Quarter (3/7/10), Full (4/L/L)

TECH LEVEL: 6 **STORY POINTS:** 6

THE WAR GAMES

'You asked me to justify my actions, I am doing so. Let me show you the Ice Warriors, cruel Martian invaders, they tried to conquer the Earth too. So did the Cybermen, half creature, half machine. But worst of all were the Daleks, a pitiless race of conquerors exterminating all who came up against them. All these evils I have fought while you have done nothing but observe. True, I am guilty of interference, just as you are guilty of failing to use your great powers to help those in need!'

⊙ SYNOPSIS

War Lord's Planet, Unspecified time

The time travellers arrived in what appeared to be a European battlefield during World War I. They met a nurse, Lady Jennifer Buckingham, who drove them to the British headquarters in her ambulance after a rescue from German soldiers mounted by Lt. Jeremy Carstairs. They were taken to General Smythe, who immediately court-martials them and sentences the Doctor to execution. Unbeknownst to them Smythe was an alien with an ability to hypnotise people and a strange communications device in his office.

The Doctor's firing squad was interrupted by a sniper attack, and Lady Buckingham and Carstairs helped the time travellers escape. Smythe ordered the British forces to attack the escapees, and the Doctor tried to evade them by driving the ambulance through a strange thick mist, where they found themselves confronting a Roman legion. Fleeing back the way they came, the Doctor reasoned that must be a force-field barrier separating the different time periods. The fugitives broke into the British HQ, where the Doctor discovered a map divided into separate zones, each corresponding to a different Earth war. The time travellers left the British HQ but were captured by German soldiers who took them to their leader, Captain von Weich, who was also an alien masquerading as a human leader.

The time travellers and Lady Buckingham escaped and decided to go to a black triangle marked on the centre of the map. On the way, they find themselves in the American Civil War zone, where they discovered a travelling capsule, a SIDRAT, transporting Confederate soldiers to the battlefield. The Doctor and Zoe snuck aboard the SIDRAT as it

dematerialised, taking them to Central Control. They discovered that they were on an alien world, and that the aliens were bringing in batches of hypnotised soldiers from Earth's history and making them fight. The aliens were being plagued by the Resistance, a group of soldiers from various zones that had resisted their conditioning. Infiltrating the base, they learned that the conditioning could be reversed, and found files on the soldiers whose conditioning had failed and which of them were known to have joined the resistance. While attending a lecture on the mental conditioning programme, one of the alien leaders, the War Chief, seemed to recognise the Doctor, so he and Zoe fled.

Meanwhile, Jamie had fallen in with a band of resistance fighters. They were attacked by a force arriving in a SIDRAT, but defeated them and boarded the travel capsule to gain access to Central Control. The War Chief was waiting for them with a group of guards, and they attacked and captured the rebels as they disembarked from the SIDRAT.

The Doctor and Zoe staged a rescue, and Zoe and the resistance travelled back to the war zones to recruit an army. Jamie, Carstairs and the Doctor stole the mental processing equipment and, narrowly escaping from the War Chief, they seized a SIDRAT along with the circuits needed to control its travel. The aliens' leader, the War Lord, arrived in Central Control and sought the advice of his advisors, the Security Chief and the War Chief. The two advisors obviously had a rivalry, but the War Lord took command and sent a strike force after the Doctor, capturing him and bringing him back to Central Control.

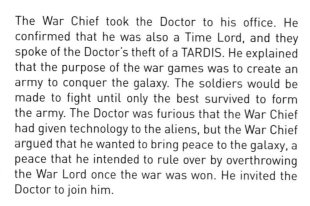

The War Chief took the Doctor to his office. He confirmed that he was also a Time Lord, and they spoke of the Doctor's theft of a TARDIS. He explained that the purpose of the war games was to create an army to conquer the galaxy. The soldiers would be made to fight until only the best survived to form the army. The Doctor was furious that the War Chief had given technology to the aliens, but the War Chief argued that he wanted to bring peace to the galaxy, a peace that he intended to rule over by overthrowing the War Lord once the war was won. He invited the Doctor to join him.

The War Lord arrived and forced the Doctor to prove his loyalty by capturing the Resistance, which he did. Still, the Security Chief wasn't convinced and got evidence that the two Time Lords were conspiring. The War Chief was arrested, but the Doctor freed the Resistance leaders and they rescued the War Chief, who killed the Security Chief in the process.

The War Chief stopped the games while the Doctor, unsure of how he could get all of the soldiers home, sent a message to Gallifrey. The War Chief tried to escape, but was killed by the War Lord, who was subsequently seized by the Resistance. The time travellers and Carstairs escaped Central Control in a SIDRAT.

The Time Lords arrived and forced the Doctor to return to Gallifrey, where they held two trials. The first was for the War Lord and his race, who were found to be guilty. The War Lord and his guards were erased from history and his planet sealed from the rest of the universe forever.

The second was for the Doctor for violating the Time Lords' policy of non-interference. After a spirited defence, the Doctor was found guilty. Jamie and Zoe were returned to their own times with only the memories of their first adventures with the Doctor. The Doctor was sentenced to exile on Earth after being forced to regenerate.

CONTINUITY

The Doctor is revealed as a Time Lord for the first time and as a renegade amongst his people, for which he is forced to stand trial. Another renegade Time Lord, known to the aliens as 'the War Chief', is responsible for granting them time technology. Gallifrey is also seen for the first time, although it is not named as such. The Time Lords have a policy of strict non-interference; they relax this policy for the Doctor after his help in **The Three Doctors**.

A cruder version of the TARDIS, a SIDRAT, is used extensively in this adventure. The Doctor seems much more proficient piloting SIDRATs than his own TARDIS.

The Time Lords return Jamie and Zoe to their own time periods, with all of their adventures with the Doctor except their first erased from memory (this means Zoe would remember Jamie, but Jamie would not remember meeting Zoe). They also 'dematerialise' the War Lord and his planet. There seems to be limits to the Time Lords' powers, however, as the removal of the War Lord's planet from the time stream does not affect the events that took place in the War Zones.

The Doctor dons disguises again in this story, first as an alien student (along with Zoe) and later as a soldier in a gas mask.

⊙ RUNNING THE ADVENTURE

At its core, **The War Games** is a mystery. While it appears that the characters are in one location, there are subtle hints that things aren't what they seem. Enigmatic leaders making strange decisions, anachronistic technology, and enveloping mists make for interesting clues. Once the characters have started noticing these things anachronistic soldiers show up, some of them not acknowledging their circumstances. Once the mystery is revealed the characters have to work against the aliens and the adventure becomes more of a standard action-adventure.

HARD CHOICES

If the players don't have the Story Points to spend for a dramatic deus ex machina ending like calling down the wrath of the Time Lords of Gallifrey, then the Gamemaster can offer to strike a deal. Give the players a hard choice – "I'll give you the extra Story Points you need... but then something awful will happen to your character". Or "You can save the planet... but at the cost of one of your companion's lives." Or "you can change history... but you'll be erased from the timeline, and no-one will ever remember your character". The player characters should always be able to pull out a victory against all the odds, but sometimes, they should pay a heavy price for that victory.

WAR CHIEF

The War Chief is the second Time Lord that the Doctor meets in his adventures, following the Monk. Like the Monk, the War Chief is a renegade Time Lord. He has chosen to throw his lot in with the War Lord and his army, as he hopes that by working clandestinely he can escape the notice of the High Council.

The War Chief is an opportunist and, once the Doctor had discovered his involvement with the War Lord, realised the potential threat to his scheme. He tried to salvage his plans by offering the Doctor an alliance. They would overthrow the War Lord and lead the army themselves. While the Doctor played along, the War Chief's betrayal was exposed and the War Lord had him executed.

While it appears that the War Chief is dead, it is entirely possible that he simply regenerated and escaped in the closest SIDRAT. Gamemasters deciding to use this possibility should give the War Chief a new appearance. Rules for randomly generating a new appearance can be found in the *Time Traveller's Companion.*

WAR CHIEF

AWARENESS	4	PRESENCE	4
COORDINATION	4	RESOLVE	5
INGENUITY	7	STRENGTH	4

SKILLS
Athletics 1, Convince 3, Craft 3, Fighting 2, Knowledge 5, Marksman 1, Medicine 1, Science 3, Subterfuge 5, Survival 4, Technology 6, Transport 3

TRAITS
Boffin: The War Chief can create gadgets through the fine art of 'jiggery-pokery'.
Charming: The War Chief gets a +2 bonus on Charm rolls.
Epicurean Tastes: The War Chief gets a +2 bonus when judging the quality of a luxury item or to impress others with their impeccable taste.
Feel the Turn of the Universe: The War Chief has an innate ability to sense when something is amiss or temporally not right. He senses something wrong with an Awareness or Ingenuity roll with a +2 bonus – the more successful, the more likely he is to know what is wrong and how to start to fix it.
Indomitable: The War Chief gets a +4 bonus on rolls to resist being mentally controlled.
Quick Reflexes: The War Chief always goes first in the Action Round phase.
Selfish: The War Chief is always looking out for himself and willing to shift allegiances as it suits him.
Technically Adept: The War Chief gains a +2 bonus to any Technology roll to fix a broken or faulty device, and to use complex gadgets or equipment. The bonus also applies to any gadget-creating jiggery-pokery.

Time Lord: The War Chief is from Gallifrey and managed to keep his affiliation with the War Lords secret from other Time Lords.
Time Traveller: The War Chief is not only familiar with the Tech Level of Gallifrey, but also of most other time periods.
Voice of Authority: The War Chief gets a +2 bonus to Presence and Convince rolls to get others to trust him.
Vortex: The Vortex trait adds +2 to any roll that involves piloting a time travel or vortex manipulating device. The War Chief primarily uses this trait to steer his own TARDIS as well as SIDRATs.
Wanted Renegade: The War Chief is wanted by the Time Lords. He gains 6 story points if the Time Lords appear in the adventure.

TECH LEVEL: 10 STORY POINTS: 8

DID THE WAR GAMES TAKE PLACE AT ALL?

At the conclusion of the War Lord's trial, the Time Lords sentence him to dematerialisation 'as if [he] never existed.' While this could simply mean disintegration and perhaps a hypnotic suggestion to the War Lord's race to forget him, it could also mean that the Time Lords rewrote the timeline so that the War Lord never menaced Earth. In this case the events are completely erased from history. Soldiers that died in the war games return to life, and anyone the Doctor encountered before wouldn't remember him.

SIDRAT

A SIDRAT is a rudimentary time travel capsule created by the War Chief for the use of the War Lord's race. It looks like a green box on the outside with a door that slides forward. It is quite primitive compared to a TARDIS and although it is bigger on the inside than the outside, it is not nearly as vast as a TARDIS interior. The exterior of a SIDRAT actually looks like the exterior of the "default" TARDIS exterior.

SIDRATs are piloted remotely from a central control room and have only minor interior controls (door, atmosphere, etc.) of their own, which can be overridden. They are dimensionally transcendental in a limited, finite fashion, but their interior dimensions can be changed at whim within those parameters by the remote operator. This dimensional flexibility, along with remote capability, comes at a price, however, speeding up the already shortened lifespan of the individual units.

ALIEN COMMANDER

AWARENESS	3	PRESENCE	4
COORDINATION	3	RESOLVE	5
INGENUITY	4	STRENGTH	3

SKILLS
Athletics 2, Convince 4, Fighting 2, Knowledge 3, Marksman 4, Subterfuge 4, Technology 3

TRAITS
Menacing: An Alien Commander's words carry weight. They get a +2 bonus to get people to do what they want and a +2 to resist attempts by others to act against them.
Military Rank: An Alien Commander of a particular army has the highest rank of that army.
Voice of Authority: Alien Commanders get a +2 on Presence and Convince rolls to get others to follow their orders.

EQUIPMENT: Hypnotic Spectacles, era-appropriate sidearm

TECH LEVEL: 7   **STORY POINTS: 6**

TIME LORD COUNCILLOR

AWARENESS	4	PRESENCE	5
COORDINATION	3	RESOLVE	6
INGENUITY	9	STRENGTH	2

SKILLS
Convince 5, Knowledge 5, Medicine 3, Science 3, Technology 3, Transport 3

TRAITS
By the Book: Time Lord Councillors are notoriously bound by the Laws of Gallifrey.
Feel the Turn of the Universe: Time Lord Councillors can sense when something is wrong.
Time Lord
Time Lord, Experienced: All Time Lord Councillors have regenerated at least once.
Time Traveller (All TLs): Time Lord Councillors have at least a passing familiarity with all TLs.
Voice of Authority: Time Lord Councillors always have the final word and gain a +2 bonus on Presence and Convince rolls.
Vortex

STORY POINTS: 10

Traits: Bigger on the Inside (Special), Force Field (Major), Transmit, Vortex, Restriction (Lack of Interior Controls, Limited Lifespan*)

*Every use of a SIDRAT to travel through the vortex requires a permanent expenditure of 1 Story Point. When all of these are gone, the TTC stops functioning.
Cost: 6 Story Points

FURTHER ADVENTURES

- Perhaps the War Chief didn't die, but simply regenerated (if the War Lord was erased from history, then he may not have died at all). He still has ambitions for a peaceful galaxy under his rule. The characters could come across multiple War Chief schemes in this regard, although he's probably adopted a new sobriquet.

- The Resistance members crossed time zones and some of the older members may have picked up newer equipment, especially if the Time Lords were a bit sloppy (and, again, history wasn't erased). A Roman soldier bringing back a rifle or machine gun could wreak havoc with history.

- It's also possible that the Time Lords were a bit sloppy with where they dropped off the soldiers. In addition to unexplained deaths (for those that died in the games), a Resistance member or even a soldier that accidentally wandered across zones may end up being sent home at the wrong time, creating all sorts of complications.

THE WAR LORD

AWARENESS	4	PRESENCE	6
COORDINATION	3	RESOLVE	5
INGENUITY	5	STRENGTH	3

SKILLS
Athletics 2, Convince 5, Fighting 3, Knowledge 3, Marksman 4, Subterfuge 4, Technology 3

TRAITS
Menacing: The War Lord gets a +2 bonus to get people to do what he wants and a +2 to resist attempts by others to act against them.
Military Rank: The War Lord is the ranking officer of his people.
Voice of Authority: The War Lord gets a +2 on Presence and Convince rolls to get others to follow his orders.

TECH LEVEL: 7   STORY POINTS: 10

LADY JENNIFER BUCKINGHAM

AWARENESS	3	PRESENCE	4
COORDINATION	3	RESOLVE	4
INGENUITY	2	STRENGTH	2

SKILLS
Athletics 3, Convince 3, Marksman 2, Medicine 4, Transport 3

TRAITS
Brave: Lady Jennifer gets a +2 on Resolve rolls that require courage.
Charming: Lady Jennifer is sociable and gets a +2 on rolls where charm would apply.
Empathic: Lady Jennifer gets a +2 bonus on rolls to empathise or 'read' another person.
Healer: Lady Jennifer gets a +2 bonus on Medicine rolls when trying to reduce Injury levels.

TECH LEVEL: 4   STORY POINTS: 6

INDEX

DOCTOR WHO

ADVENTURES IN TIME AND SPACE BBC

CB71104 $34.99

DEFENDING THE EARTH: THE UNIT SOURCEBOOK

Front and centre, soldier! You're part of UNIT now, the Unified Intelligence Taskforce. We are the Earth's best defence against the myriad alien forces who would try to subjugate and conquer our planet. It's not an easy job, and even those recruited for their scientific knowledge can find themselves on the front lines of combat against almost unstoppable foes. We will protect humanity from extraterrestrial terrors or die trying.

Defending the Earth is a 160 page full colour sourcebook for the Doctor Who: Adventures in Time and Space roleplaying game. Within, you'll will find:

* The history of UNIT
* Rules for creating UNIT characters, including new Traits and Areas of Expertise
* Expanded firearms and combat rules, including mass combat and skirmish rules
* Details on major UNIT personnel, including the legendary Brigadier Lethbridge-Stewart
* Two new adventures

and more...

THE TIME TRAVELLER'S COMPANION

Time flies when you're having fun, but flying through time can present a whole host of problems. Whether accidentally creating paradoxes, upsetting the course of history or trying to Put Things Right, you're going to need to know your way around the Vortex. You need a guide...a companion.

This 240 page hard cover supplement for Doctor Who: Adventures in Time and Space gives more information on Time Lords, temporal mechanics and time machines, including:

* Gallifreyan culture, history and law
* New options for creating and playing Time Lord characters
* More on the physics of Time, temporal phenomena and Time Travel
* Detailed information on the TARDIS, and rules for creating your own
* Secrets of the Time Lords...

CB71103 $39.99